This absorbing account of the Russian
women revolutionaries who were active during the reign of
Tsar Alexander II (1855-81), redresses a view of history
which has consistently denied the importance of women's
role in political events. Cathy Porter describes Russian
women's gradual emergence from traditional family
seclusion, and shows how, in their search for work and
education, many became convinced of the need for wider
political action and joined the first Russian revolutionary
parties.

The book centres on the lives of the most prominent of
these women activists – those who successfully organized the
assassination of the Tsar in 1881, when many of these
remarkable women were executed, or condemned to life exile
or imprisonment. Her vivid account of these heroic 'lost
women' of the nineteenth century tells us much about
women's contribution to the past.

Cathy Porter, twenty-eight, is a graduate in Russian and
Czech from London University, and is now doing her
doctorate in Russian radical journalism.

V I R A G O is a feminist publishing imprint:

'It is only when women start to organize in large numbers that we become a political force, and begin to move towards the possibility of a truly democratic society in which every human being can be brave, responsible, thinking and diligent in the struggle to live at once freely and unselfishly.

Sheila Rowbotham, *Women, Resistance and Revolution*

FATHERS AND DAUGHTERS

Russian Women in Revolution

CATHY PORTER

VIRAGO
in association with
QUARTET BOOKS LONDON

First published by VIRAGO Limited 1976
in association with Quartet Books Limited
27 Goodge Street, London W1P 1FD

Copyright © 1976 by Cathy Porter
ISBN 0 704 32802 X

Computer typeset by Input Typesetting Ltd
4 Valentine Place, London SE1.
Printed in Great Britain by
The Anchor Press Ltd, and bound by
Wm Brendon & Son Ltd, both of Tiptree, Essex

For my mother,
because she didn't live to read it

Foreword		1
Author's Note		3
A Brief Chronology of major Reigns and Events		4
I	The Upper Stories	6
II	Into Society	39
III	Aristocrats and Nihilists	69
IV	Into Exile	116
V	To the People	175
VI	Utopia Abandoned	210
VII	Terror	246
A Selective Glossary of Names		285
Select Bibliography		296
Index		301

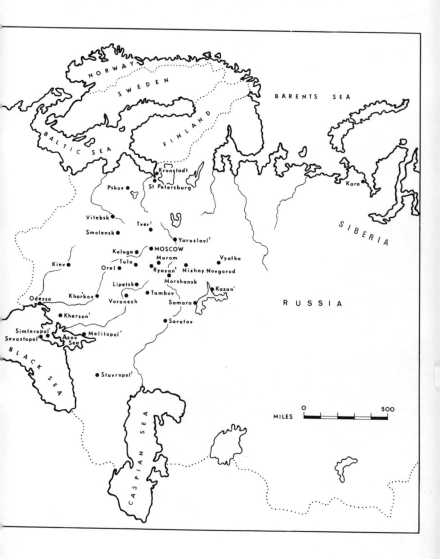

NORWAY

SWEDEN

BALTIC SEA

FINLAND

BARENTS SEA

Kronstadt

Pskov ●   ● St Petersburg

Kara

SIBERIA

Vitebsk ●   ● Tver'

Smolensk ●

● Yaroslavl'

Kaluga ● ● MOSCOW

Murom

Vyatka ●

Kiev ●

Tula ●

Orel ●   Ryazan' Nizhny Novgorod

Lipetsk ●   Morshansk

Kharkov ●   ● Tambov

Kazan' ●

Odessa ●

Voronezh

Samara ●

RUSSIA

● Kherson'

Saratov ●

Simferopol'

Azov

Sevastopol' ●   ● Melitopol'

Sea

BLACK SEA

● Stavropol'

CASPIAN SEA

MILES 0 ———————— 500

FOREWORD

'I don't think the job of historian fits a man for psychological analysis. In our work we have to deal with simple feelings to which we give generic names such as Ambition and Interest. And yet if I had an iota of self-knowledge, now would be the time to use it.'

The alienated historian has never been so eloquently exposed as in the disintegrating hero of Sartre's *Nausea*. Ambition and self-interest are the dubious privileges of the self-absorbed, and become the driving forces of a version of history that effectively removes the writer from his writing and alienates the individual from his society. Roquentin's existential Nausea is a confession of lost identity.

Now, under the pressure of accumulated experience, the Women's Movement is able to review the history of women with new insight and to reach some conclusions as to how woman's personality has evolved and continues to evolve. To admit women into the historical analysis is to introduce a more authentic psychological analysis of political events, and tentatively to trace the historical evolution of personal power relationships. If the story lacks the symmetry of historical omniscience it is not only because the historical process itself

1

will not allow it but because male historians have consistently deleted women from the record. The historical bias will ultimately be redressed; it must now be exposed and an alternative version offered.

C. P.
London, November 1975

2

AUTHOR'S NOTE

Translation from the Russian: there are two acceptable forms of transliteration from the Russian, the Matthews (English) system, and the International System. I have tried simply to make my transliteration of names, places, and journals comprehensible and pronounceable, often using a mixture of these two systems. In the bibliography I have kept to the Matthews system, so what in the text may be transliterated as '-sky', for example, will appear in the bibliography as '-skii'. 'Ë' is pronounced as 'yo', and the apostrophe (as in oblast', Yaroslav') denotes a softening of the last consonant. All characters are called by the most commonly used forms of their names, so that Alexandr and Sofia, for example, are rendered in the anglicized forms Alexander and Sofya. The terrorist 'Narodnaya Volya' Party is often translated as The People's Will Party, but since Volya means both 'will' and 'freedom' I have preferred not to translate the term. The 'Zemlya i Volya' Party I have translated consistently as Land and Liberty.

A BRIEF CHRONOLOGY OF MAJOR REIGNS AND EVENTS

1682-1725	Peter the Great
1762-96	Katherine the Great
1796-1801	Paul I
1801-25	Alexander I
1825	Decembrist uprising
1825-55	Nicholas I
1853-5	Crimean War
1855-81	Alexander II
1861	Official emancipation of the serfs; peasant riots; student demonstrations
1862-3	Beginnings of Land and Liberty Party
1864	Administrative and judicial reforms
1869	Student uprisings in St Petersburg and Moscow
1870	Russian section of the First International in Geneva. First strikes in St Petersburg
1870-73	Chaikovsky group starts propaganda work in factories and villages
1877-8	Russo–Turkish war in Balkans; populists' 'colonies' in Don area
1877	Trial of 50

1877-8	Trial of 193
1878	Vera Zasulich's attempt on life of Trepov
1878-9	Outbreak of strikes in St Petersburg
1879	Soloviev's attempt on Tsar's life crystallizes conflicting tendencies within Land and Liberty Party
17 June 1879	Lipetsk meeting; formation of Executive Committee of new terrorist party
24 June 1879	Voronezh meeting; Land and Liberty Party's adoption of terrorist policy
August 1879	Formation of Narodnaya Volya 'People's Will' Party
1 March 1881	Assassination of Alexander II by Narodnaya Volya Party
3 April 1881	Public hanging of six leading terrorists

Note: The Selective Glossary of Names at the end should be referred to for fuller details of many of the activists of this period to whom, for reasons of space, I have been able to refer only cursorily in the course of this book.

CHAPTER 1
THE UPPER STORIES

For many Russians, any mention of the women who have figured in their revolutionary history seems to induce archetypal memories of matriarchies and domestic disharmony. '*Ah, Amazonki!*' they will say, and the topic will be dropped. They have obviously forgotten the part those Amazons played in their early history – an historical bias which has continued to obscure the important part women played in the revolution of Russian society.

This book focuses on the reign of Alexander II, from 1855 to 1881, a period of unprecedented political stress and intellectual unrest in Russia. The women's movement in Russia cannot be neatly slotted into the period, 1850-70, allotted it by Soviet historians and early Bolsheviks alike in their anxiety to define it as a bourgeois minority interest separated from the larger revolutionary movement. It must be examined as a movement in which the first murmurs of the early feminists were rapidly shouted down by the more explicitly political demands of the first women revolutionaries. It is a movement that has been largely ignored by Western historians, who prefer to exclude women

6

altogether from the revolutionary movement, in which they are seen as either peripheral or merely confused and infantile participants, or as loyal wives sharing persecution and exile with their husbands. This view is relevant really only to the early nineteenth century, when some women began tentatively to reject the stultifying security of conventional family life, retaining only an unlimited but confused capacity for self-sacrifice and religious devotion – an urge still sanctified to some extent by centuries of dependency and religious conditioning. This kind of self-sacrifice may have entered the pages of literature but has not yet entered the pages of conventional history.

Freedom, *volya,* meant to the Russian of the nineteenth century almost exclusively the emancipation of the serfs, an issue that subsumed all others in the course of the century. *Emantsipatsia,* the emancipation of women, was not a concept that was readily assimilated into Russian vocabulary or culture. The female half of the population was actually unassimilated rather than emancipated, and it was in a sense as 'outsiders' – like the uprooted aristocracy, the dislocated peasantry and the radical intelligentsia – that they began to form a dynamic section of the population, independent of 'official' Russia.

Russian women's emergence into society and their search for personal and political identity was agonizingly slow. I hope to show how by the nineteenth century women were being gradually but only partially assimilated into the mainstream of Russian political life, so that when we come to read Alexandra Kollontai's accounts of her conflicts with the Bolshevik Party we shall have some understanding of the prejudices that excluded women from total participation in Soviet society.

Alexandra Kollontai's memory too has been virtually censored from the Soviet history books. Her famous disputes with Lenin and her proposals – as the only woman member of the first Bolshevik government – for the radical transformation of the family guarantee her at best an unslandered anonymity in her own country. In the West she has unfortunately been somewhat indiscriminately adopted as a heroine by those in the Women's Movement who believe that articulating social and sexual conflicts are tantamount to resolving them. We may be tempted to ignore the emendations in her *Autobiography of a Sexually Emancipated Woman* which transform it so movingly from one woman's struggle into a mass women's movement brought about by the revolt of the working classes. For it was only as a spokeswoman for this newly reformed society that she felt justified in revealing herself so openly. Without a thorough study of the social conditions of the nineteenth century that produced such a woman we in the West may be encouraged by her example to indulge in sterile self-analysis.

It was on the Amazon River, now the Don, in southern Russia that the matriarchal communities of the Near and Middle East banded together in about 1000 BC, after repeated attacks by neighbouring patriarchal tribes. It was here that they became known as Amazons, the name given to them by the neighbouring Armenians, to whom it meant 'Moon Women', since they worshipped a moon mother-goddess. By the fifth century the Amazons had been decisively defeated by the Greeks and assimilated into Greek society, where they were confined to the home and excluded from any activity in public life. The Amazons left their influence in the Don area well into the nineteenth century, but the entire episode of matriarchal dominance has been effectively censored from the collective Russian memory.

Among tribes in southern Russia, a free exchange of sexual partners was considered quite natural until the nineteenth century. But among most pagan slavic peoples marriage was no sexual springtime of mutual selection, symbolizing the marriage between earth and heaven, with mother earth as the primary pagan deity and heaven with its home in the ancestral lares of every dwelling. In fact, marriage was rather a matter of rape and abduction. The women of some pagan slavic tribes hunted and fought with the men, and in Czechoslovakia the legendary Lyubusha tried to establish a matriarchal society. But for most tribes, the distances separating small families scattered over the uncultivated land mass made it difficult for marriage to occur naturally, and most slavic peoples opted for incestual marriages between brother and sister, with the brother protecting his sister against marauding 'suitors' from other tribes.

By the first and second centuries, arranged marriages had introduced some order into this chaotic state of affairs. Now the Russian word for bride, *nevesta*, 'the unknown one', suggested strangers being thrown into each others' arms, while *zhena*, 'wife', cognate of Sanskrit *dzhan*, 'to bear', leaves no doubt as to her function. Any objections she might have to the whole idea were irrelevant; the future wife was *suzhennaya*, – 'intended by fate'. In Russian, men marry and women are given in marriage.

The early history of Russia presents a tableau of semi-mythical princes leading innumerable small tribes scattered over a great land mass, whose ethnic and cultural diversity lacked any real unifying force, and who all subscribed to various animistic and pantheistic religions. There are only six women saints in the Russian pantheon, the chief of whom, St Olga, is embellished by a wealth of oral poetry and folk song. Most women saints emerge as pallid figures sheltering behind the great mythical heroes canonized by legend, but Olga is generally regarded as the prototype of the great Russian woman. It was in 957 that she made her famous visit to Constantinople, where she embraced Eastern Christianity. Her motives for doing so are probably best forgotten; most likely it was a ruse to interfere with the Turkish Emperor's intentions to marry her. It was left to her son, Vladimir I, to decisively repudiate heathenism and to officially establish the Greek Orthodox religion in Russia in

9

about 987. Neither Vladimir nor his mother, despite their posthumous canonization, provided any very inspiring example of charity, chastity or humility. Vladimir was probably 'converted' by four of his five wives who were Christians, and he kept on his huge harem of eight hundred women until his death. His conversion seems not to have interfered with his habit of grabbing any woman who took his fancy and killing her husband. But despite these somewhat unorthodox interpretations of Christian values, it was only in the tenth century, when Russia was forcibly Christianized, brotherly love was imposed by the sword and animistic idols were demolished, that a semblance of national unity allows us to examine some of the social conditions of this vast heterogeneous territory whose trade and cultural centre was Kiev.

The official head of the Church was the Metropolitan, under whom were the bishops, served by the clergy. Even after the Church had decreed that marriages should be officially registered, a fairly free exchange of sexual partners continued and even 'official' marriages were easily annulled. In the countryside church marriages were by-passed until well into the eighteenth century. The clergy were thus able to supplement their meagre income by levying taxes on unmarried mothers, women living in sin and widows. At first widows, especially those with children, enjoyed almost equal status with men and had full control over their late husbands' property. But by the end of the eleventh century land, property, daughters and widows were inherited by the sons. The loosely knit principalities around Kiev were collapsing and power was consolidated in the hands of the grand dukes.

The nuclear family was now not merely a religious imposition but a political necessity. The laws governing family property acquired a constitutional basis, and in the face of this consolidation the smaller clans protected their independence by a strict recognition of paternal authority. Women were taken under the wing of the Church and

10

allotted severely restricted roles. Wives, confined to the fetid atmosphere of the 'upper stories' – the Byzantine *terem* – and isolated from all contact with outsiders, were to be fattened up; ideas of thinness and evil are linguistically related in Russian, and no woman under five *poods*[1] could possibly be considered as a wife. Women were to emerge, with covered heads, only to attend church, which they entered by a back door and where they stood at the left invisible to the rest of the congregation. They were to perform cleansing rituals during menstruation and were to be strictly segregated from all men during pregnancy.

By the twelfth century most of the trade and cultural centres in Russia were being wracked by fratricidal wars, and a series of particularly vicious feuds was destroying the wealth and prestige of Kiev. There was little to unite the other cultural outposts of the country, and no common interest in preserving trade, which might have produced some sense of national unity. People started to drift to the small communities around Moscow and White Russia. When in 1235 the Tartars began their first onslaughts on Russia, they confidently confronted a country in a state of virtual disintegration, and by 1241 the Tartar yoke rested squarely on Russian shoulders. The invaders' only intention was to extort as much as they could in taxes, not to interfere with time-honoured Russian customs, but in fact they faced a population whose only traditional virtues were embodied in the family structure. The local population grudgingly paid their crippling taxes to the invaders and subsidized the transport and maintenance of the khans.

The Asiatic storms that swept over the Russian steppes brought in their wake a great wave of syphilis, and the 'unclean spirit' became for the Russians some mysterious power exerted by the Mongols in collaboration with Russian women. Women fought superstition with the only weapons they had – charms, spells and potions. There are many stories in this period of women turning men into animals, but

11

Russia managed to escape the witch hunts that were already sweeping the rest of Europe – witchcraft was a traditionally male province, and women were at worst no more than a professional threat. The Mongols' open physical hatred for women did, however, encourage the brutal Byzantine Russian attitude to women; and misogyny in these barbarous times was untempered by any courtly deference, for Russian women, unlike those of Europe, had no chivalrous defendants. The Bible was frequently and selectively invoked, backed up by Hellenic wisdom. Solomon, Euripides, Pythagoras, Socrates and Diogenes all had something to say on the subject of women's spite, cunning, garrulousness and sheer devilry. Twelfth and thirteenth-century Russia was as patriarchal as China or Japan; the Russians were not opposing the civilized patrician values the rest of Europe had encountered in their Roman invaders, but a kind of barbarism that was easily assimilated into primitive Russian society. The Asiatic invasion combined with the Byzantine ceremony of the Church to pave the way for the semi-oriental absolutism of the future tsars of Russia.

By the mid-fourteenth century, the Mongol empire had begun to collapse, but by the time the Tartars were decisively defeated by the Russians in 1480 they had made a profound impact on Russian society. The grand dukes imposed a kind of servitude on the lesser landholders that resembled the Mongols' despotic treatment of their Russian servants. Society was more distinctly divided between the free – the landowners – and the slaves.

Ironically, it was the 'free' women who remained cloistered in their upper stories, while the peasant women, although still condemned to childbearing and heavy labour on the land, played an increasingly important part in the events of the village. Although excluded from the Church, which they usually attended for the first and last time at their marriage, they were revered for their apocryphal embellishments of biblical stories, their ability to speak in tongues and their knowledge of herb lore. Women were now respected rather than feared for the 'special powers' that they had used, apparently successfully, against the Mongols. They were regarded as guardians of national custom, giving expression to traditional feelings in the critical moments of birth and death, harvest-time and seasonal changes. It was women who knew, and often invented, the songs in which the rituals of funerals, weddings, christenings and the departure of soldiers were solemnized.

St Fevronia is clearly a part-mythical product of peasant imagination. She was said to have lived in the fourteenth century, a woodcutter's daughter from Murom. She was able to talk to animals and plants, and when the prince of Murom was on his deathbed he called for her to cure him, promising to marry her if she succeeded. As soon as she had cured him the prince was persuaded by his courtiers to break his promise, whereupon he immediately relapsed. She cured him again, and they married. Forced off the throne, the prince returned with her to the woods of Murom, but they were soon summoned back to the court and together they ruled 'wisely' until their deaths, which occurred within a day of each other. Such charming legends show the peasants' desire for fundamental social and sexual equality, and counteracted the landowners' persistent exclusion of women from all spheres of life. The stories also provided a semi-religious opiate for a peasantry that was gradually drifting into a state of serfdom, and served to make more palatable the austere precepts imposed by Christian morality.

From the thirteenth to the fifteenth centuries there was a multiplication of small appanages,[2] over which the princes and the grand dukes exercised full control. These were similar to the extended autonomous family, and had virtually no contact with each other. Moscow was now emerging as the major commercial and cultural centre. It was in a strategic position for the defence of the important neighbouring principalities of Vladimir and Suzdal', and had been a major centre of migration since the disintegration of Kiev in the eleventh century. The Moscow princes were unbound by any blood ties with the Kiev dynasty, and now embarked on bold measures of expropriation and expansion. By reinforcing the close joint-family system, they were able to withstand the steadily increasing power of the Church and the constant inflow of newcomers who threatened to loosen old patriarchal bonds. Family and property were still bequeathed to next of kin, but a strange new hierarchy was emerging, based rather precariously on genealogical standing, a hierarchy ruling all aspects of conduct and rights to land. The princes in their homes enforced an elaborate, somewhat Byzantine code of etiquette.

If the family was regarded as a microcosm of society, without distinct social or national obligations, sixteenth-century Moscow with its established centralized Church was a microcosm of the embryonic Russian nation. The Church remained as omnipotent moral arbiter and sole agent of literacy among an almost totally illiterate population. One of the many moralistic tracts produced by the Church in the mid-sixteenth century was the *Domostroy,* a word that cannot be translated but which suggests the disciplined, structured family. Unlike the domestic manuals that appeared in the twelfth and thirteenth centuries in western Europe, the *Domostroy* is totally lacking in humanity or imagination. The assumption was that if living 'on earth' – that is, not in a monastery – excluded one from a state of sanctity, then the monastic spirit must be introduced into the home. The father, as an agent (or weapon) of imperial and ultimately religious authority, was a sort of domestic bishop exercising full control over his household – the same word *chado* applies in Russian to servants, children and wives. He had his own apostolic mission to perform in the home, where he acted as both saviour and teacher.

Now that the Tartars had left and the unclean spirit had been exorcized, women could be granted some modest

14

function within the family and that was, through devoted and efficient performance of domestic duties, to inspire their children and servants with an example of humility and 'virtue', But this 'virtue' was valid in terms not of God or the State, but solely of their representative, the husband. The conditions imposed on women could produce only the most sickly specimens of this 'virtue'. The 'clever' wife was considered unsuitable as a mother and her children were given over at birth to a wet-nurse. All women were to be denied any intimacy with their children, and strictly forbidden to play with them. Any indulgence in dancing or games would condemn them to the eternal flames of hell, and sex was forbidden between husband and wife on Wednesdays and Fridays, as well as on all the countless religious holidays. The wife was to keep herself in her quarters and avoid all contact with visitors; she would prepare food and drink for feasts and then withdraw to her room. Servants were to keep their masters informed of any deviation from these rules, which might be dealt with 'in a way that is reasonable but painful, terrible yet beneficial'. To prove that beating was regarded as an act of love there are panegyrics in the *Domostroy* to the rod and the whip, which in any well-ordered home should hang over the bed. There is also a section entitled 'Praise to Women' that somehow omits to mention any feminine virtue besides that of obedience.

The wealthier the household, the more secluded its women. Isolated from all contact with outsiders, even relatives, surrounded by servants and spies, lacking any sort of comfort, many women in desperation would seduce their servants, only to find themselves blackmailed. If sick, they were rarely allowed to see a doctor, and then only when all windows had been closed and the pulse carefully covered with a cloth. The only concession to this featureless life was the elaborate process of Russian bathday, which for women took on all the significance of a religious holiday. The bath was for the Russian woman what the dance was to her European contemporary.

In western Europe the 'art of love' had been elevated to an ideal, enslaving women in all the domestic comforts that enabled them to develop physically. In Russia, most girls were married at thirteen and sometimes as young as eight years of age. Boys would marry at seven and it was common for fathers to live with their sons' young brides until the girl had reached puberty. Divorce usually entailed public scandals and accusations of criminal proportions, and women found that the most pragmatic way of attacking their husbands was to encourage their sons to do so. This was the sordid reality behind the pious precepts of the *Domostroy*.

Ivan the Terrible's reign, from 1533 to 1584, intensified the double morality of the *Domostroy* with that Tsar's peculiar combination of piety and depravity. He was the first ruler to espouse the cause of political absolutism, which he attempted to justify by enhancing Moscow's prestige as the 'third Rome'. His own personal bodyguard, the *oprichnina,* brought the landowners under the rule of a complex hierarchy of officials directly controlled by the State. The princes and landowners lost virtually all political power and the throne was surrounded by a vacuum, a vacuum from which the Tsar could escape only by the most bizarre means. All women, high and low-born, were victims of indiscriminate rape, and failure to enjoy imperial rape involved a number of imaginatively sadistic punishments. When the Tsar passed through a village he often demanded that all the women should stand naked along the road as he passed, and any woman refusing to do so would be hacked to pieces. On discovering that one of his wives was not a virgin he immediately had her dragged to the river by horses and drowned. More conventionally, non-virgins were sent back to their parents, prohibited from remarrying and usually put in a convent. When a rumour reached the Tsar's ears that women in Moscow were amused by his sexual practices he

16

threatened to have all the women of the city killed, but he was dissuaded by his courtiers and agreed instead merely to order several hundred of them to the Kremlin, where they were to parade naked, in deep snow, before their families and the assembled court. Some of them were then beaten to death for good measure. Men's bestiality and homosexuality in the reign of Ivan the Terrible was usually blamed on women's charms and spells, and one solution to an increasingly 'disobedient' subversive female population was to exile those convicted of minor crimes to Siberia – a sensible move, since they could then marry convicts there and help to populate this barren area. Men who murdered their wives were naturally dealt with leniently. And yet, for all the hideous cruelties of Ivan's reign, the conventional rituals of Orthodox piety were still more strictly enforced. Ivan himself even toyed with the idea of asking for the hand of England's Elizabeth I, a move inspired by fear rather than respect for the Virgin Queen, since he suggested they offer one another mutual asylum.

Foreign visitors to Russia in the seventeenth century discovered to their horror that obscene anecdotes provided virtually the only subject of conversation among Russian men, and reports of sexual life in Russia scandalized civilized European society. Women of the lower classes drank in public, and passers-by could often enjoy the spectacle of a public orgy on the streets. Brothels were forbidden, but mixed bath-houses served the same purpose, and it was quite common to see naked women rushing out on to the streets and inciting people to take baths. The poorer aristocrats often publicly pimped for their wives for the sake of a few rubles, or merely sold them off to the highest bidder. Peasant girls could be bought for next to nothing, and soldiers often returned with girls they had bought in the distant provinces of Russia. There are stories of women dressed as men running off to join bandit gangs; and various sects of Dissenters – who generally respected their women as teachers and priestesses – provided

17

asylum for women truants. Infanticide and marital murder were becoming so common that the Church was eventually forced to intervene with a few cautious reforms. The Orthodox marriage service in the late seventeenth century extracted from men the promise that they would not beat their wives, and that daughters should receive some of their inheritance. Women were allowed to eat with the men, and could even occasionally take part in social gatherings. In 1702 it was officially decreed that a woman should be allowed to marry the man of her choice, although of course most families continued to break the law, and their daughters' spirits, until well into the nineteenth century.

When Peter the Great came to the throne in 1682 he embarked on a furious programme of reform, and the new greatly extended life of his court made unprecedented demands on the women of the upper classes. The new capital, St Petersburg, with its transformed social life, openly rejected all the old Muscovite traditions, and the seclusion of upper-class women ended with the regime of the new court, which flourished in the German quarters of the city: this was where the Tsar spent most of his time as a young man, in a never-ending series of monstrous festivities whose excessive ritual and grotesquely enacted fantasy horrified the citizens.

Peter had had no formal education when he came to power;[3] his manners were those of the Dutch seamen and the members of the small European communities, formerly isolated by the local population for fear of 'heresies'. Having outraged the citizens of the new capital, he went on to outrage the Synod by giving his permission to marriage with foreign women. At the age of sixteen he abandoned his first wife and took up with an ill-assorted company united by a common passion for drinking and the company of foreign courtesans. But like Ivan the Terrible, Peter managed to combine his debauchery with a fiercely defended piety, and the precepts of Orthodox faith were imposed with even more stringent legislation. The Tsar's private society, the Most

18

Drunken Assembly of Fools, was an elaborate send-up of revered Church ritual; there were obscene mock-weddings and masquerades in honour of Venus and Bacchus.

Soloviëv, the famous nineteenth-century historian, notes that no other country could compete with Russia's sexually perverse habits; nowhere else were double standards of morality so blatantly perverse. Among the upper classes promiscuity was considered as a sign of civilization, and boys of six and seven were being provided with peasant mistresses for experience. Mistresses and wives were subjected to savage and humiliating punishments for small infidelities, and Peter himself had forced his first wife into a convent when her presence became embarrassing to him. The woman who was eventually to become his wife and lifelong companion had to overcome few of the cultural obstacles besetting most women in the capital: Katherine was a Livonian peasant girl, ignorant and coarse but inquisitive and spontaneous, a real trooper's wife. Whenever he was separated from her, Peter wrote her voluminous letters in which obscenity is interspersed with a genuine tenderness.

The impact of Peter's own social life on women of the St Petersburg aristocracy in the late seventeenth century was immediate and traumatic (those further from the court were to remain in their upper stories until the middle of the nineteenth century). Women of the aristocracy were now expected to leave the deadening security of the *terem* and play an active part in the hectic social life of the new capital. Men and women alike could instantly lose favour with the Tsar for failing to keep up with his prodigious drinking and sexual appetites, and courtiers who begged that their wives be excused from these compulsory drinking bouts could be summarily dismissed from favour. Neither pregnancy nor illness could excuse women from these social gatherings, for which they were totally unprepared.

Many contemporary moralists talked about the repulsively coarse conduct of the women in the capital during Peter's

19

reign, but many others were amazed to find them attractive and sensitive; in the opinion of one visiting French aristocrat, 'Russian women fall little short of the Germans and even the French in the refinement of their conduct.' The fact is that the domestic virtues embodied in the *Domostroy* had simply not prepared women or men for the taxing moral problems posed by their new and unfamiliar social roles. Women were suddenly expected to be 'entertaining' – and yet most women, even those of the upper aristocracy, remained illiterate and ignorant until the nineteenth century. They were expected to look after themselves at the Tsar's gargantuan gatherings without the traditional support from their husbands; for the men who surrounded the Tsar, dazzled by the seductive opportunities presented by his reign, were blinded by their reliance on an entirely new kind of woman, a kind of woman who could not in fact be found to exist. This situation posed moral and metaphysical questions which they left their wives to answer. There was much talk among the men of 'principled immorality', justified somewhat precariously by a nodding acquaintance with 'free thought'. Women were to be granted more 'freedom', and many were then cruelly labelled as 'coquettes' when they succumbed to their husbands' demands that they take lovers. A few women found that they could at last form close friendships with men, but most discovered that any intellectual curiosity made them automatically suspect among the men whose company and support they so badly needed. Women's natural exuberance, now partly recognized, was thwarted, and idle vigour was deflected into gloomy and romantic daydreams; they sought narcissistic consolation in the romantic heroines of literature, playing out the roles of the melodramatic victim or the blatant coquette.

Of course Peter's orgies had a purpose beyond that of merely satisfying the Tsar's extravagant social inclinations. They were a way of assembling all the socially prominent families, and providing the Tsar with an opportunity of seeking out favourites and spying on courtiers in the more

20

intimate company of their wives and mistresses. We read about rooms especially set aside for groaning, collapsing women at these feasts. But not all the women floundered in this sea of debauchery. Now they were able to see at close quarters the ludicrous social behaviour of husbands whose social role they had until now so unhesitatingly accepted. Among the men, those who could not boast of their conquests were socially shunned; among the women, dandies and foppish poses became the butt of biting humour, and the sex war crept into the salons. The more intellectually aware women, branded as 'coquettes' and unable to explore ideas in the affectionate company of friends, would withdraw into mystical speculation. Large numbers of women were converted to Catholicism at this time, a faith that enabled them to revel in renunciation and return to the passive worship of a male figure more exalted than the now debased image of the husband. A few literate women kept diaries, and a very few began anonymously to contribute to journals. But contemporary journalism provided little scope for the speculative metaphysical problems that concerned these women. For the questions they were asking themselves were profound ones. Many women had been married off as young as thirteen, the only response expected from them being that they were 'not antagonistic' to their parents' choice of suitor. And when, after a few years of subservience to a man to whom she was merely 'not antagonistic', a woman saw her husband flaunting the very behaviour she had been taught to regard as sinful, she was forced to re-evaluate her significance in the man's world of the court.

By the early eighteenth century many landowners began to abandon the supervision of their estates for the social life of the court, unencumbered by their wives, who suddenly found themselves in sole charge of the estates. Many pined for their husbands and for the discipline and the social life they forfeited by their absence. They were totally unprepared to manage the home without the direct commands of their husbands, and loneliness, boredom and the vague realization of a new independence turned compliant wives into monsters. The extreme cruelty inflicted by these abandoned women on their serfs is legendary. Taken up with these domestic affairs, women had generally little time to spend with their children, whose upbringing was left to grandmothers and nannies. These absentee fathers acquired for their children a new dignity now that they were not degraded by the everyday affairs of the home. Daughters were encouraged to wait passively for signs of their father's distant approval, and mothers were able to punish and make demands through his distant authority. Under women's new management of the estates serfs became considered as part of the extended family, and it was common for serfs rather than land to be offered as dowry.

When the Tsar was away from the capital social gatherings were more moderate, and in quiet family gatherings in the capital and the provinces the question of women's education began to be raised. Few girls were actually taught to read, but they were now encouraged to appreciate music and art, to respect the moral precepts of Christianity and the traditional old Russian values. Provincial girls were taken round their estates and taught to appreciate the beauties of nature — of the land, that is, that they would eventually inherit. In this way they could be gradually reconciled to the idea of an impending marriage. A few girls were sent to convents, ostensibly to be educated but actually as a matter of convenience, since the nuns could act as go-betweens and invoke the fear of God to induce the girls to comply with their parents' choice. At most convents they were actually taught little but heraldry and religion. Some were rather more utilitarian, catering for girls of the bourgeoisie and the poorer aristocracy, who were taught accounting, cooking and sewing, and exhorted to engage in philanthropic work.

Mme de Maintenon's famous school for girls at Saint-Cyr

aroused some interest among the more enlightened members of the Russian aristocracy. This school had been established in the 1620s and was still flourishing. It was run on the lines of the extended family, the girls being divided into groups of eight, with a 'mother' in charge of each group. They lived austerely, with simple food and few comforts, and a genuinely communal spirit was introduced into the school, with everyone being responsible for the housekeeping. The girls were taught to speak plainly and to discuss openly their feelings about men and marriage in general; any coquetry in these matters was severely frowned on. The teaching, mostly of economics and social history, was informal and conducted mainly in the form of debate between students and teachers. But even to the Russians who were sympathetic to the ideas of eighteenth-century Europe, 'enlightenment' was a concept that was applicable only to boys. 'Education' for girls was to serve only to enhance their chances of marriage, and the intellectual training provided at Saint-Cyr was hardly relevant to the economics of the Russian marriage market. The first impetus towards any real education for girls came from the many foreigners who were arriving in large numbers in the capital in the reign of Peter the Great.

One of the earliest moves towards some kind of education for women came in 1749, when a group of Frenchmen opened a *pension* for girls and boys of the wealthy nobility. Anxious parents did not need to fear, however, for the sexes were rigidly segregated and there was no danger of the girls receiving anything like the education provided for the boys: they were to be trained in a bare modicum of female skills – sewing, heraldry and dancing – and all teaching was to be in French. They would associate with the boys only at dancing classes and at the dinner table.

In the cities, where there were more social opportunities for arranging suitable marriages, girls still tended to pick up their accomplishments as and where they could. But in the provinces marriage was an issue of considerably more

23

tension, and over the next few years schools for girls began to be opened in the provincial cities providing instruction in dancing and deportment, to enable their students to compete for husbands with the more socially accomplished girls of the capital. The girls of the capital, meanwhile, particularly the wealthier ones whose parents could afford to be more selective about husbands, were beginning to chafe at the restrictions these meagre skills imposed on their lives. It was again a couple of Frenchmen who in 1757 opened a school in the capital that aimed to give girls some sort of intellectual training. All teaching was in French, the language girls used exclusively at home anyway. History and geography were taught as well as the mandatory dancing and music, and a course in 'morality', whatever that may have meant, was provided. The price paid for the extremely superficial teaching at this school was excessively high, although subsequent competition from similar schools later forced down the fees somewhat. Most families were naturally anxious to give their sons priority in education, and since the annual income from an estate of average wealth could be spent on providing girls with little more than a familiarity with the map of Europe and the ability to read French newspapers, the whole thing was seen as a rather unnecessary luxury. Boys' education was expensive enough, with the eldest son often being sent to school for one year, to be replaced the following year by the younger son. Girls were to be granted the luxury of education only if there was any excess from their dowry, and since most girls were considered marriageable by the age of fourteen there was little time for dormant minds to be awakened and for girls to be trained as responsible and independent women. Most enlightened fathers still contented themselves with educating their daughters themselves, by means of rational conversations in which they could inspire them with 'proper ideas'.

There were of course always exceptional women who managed to overcome all these inherited obstacles. Princess

24

Dashkova, who later exerted such a strong intellectual influence over Katherine the Great, was encouraged to make use of her father's extensive library, where she absorbed the ideas of Voltaire, Boileau and Montesquieu. Princess Golovina, another of Katherine's close associates, was already reading the works of the great French *philosophes* at the age of fourteen and, like Princess Dashkova, rarely left the house to play any part in the social life of the capital. Yet for all their erudition, these two women, like most Russian girls and like Katherine herself, barely knew their own language.

When Katherine the Great came to power in 1762, she firmly announced her intention of producing a 'new species of human being'; the 'new woman' was to be an educated, fully integrated member of Russian society. And even though Katherine's own much-vaunted learning was insouciant and superficial, her intellectual appetite was avid. She wanted to inspire girls with the enthusiasm and confidence to develop their intellectual interests at their leisure, in the company of educated men — although she has little to say about the 'new man' who was suddenly expected to be receptive to a new, intellectually curious breed of women. It was presumably Rousseau whom she was able to bring to her aid in asserting that girls' education should concentrate primarily on the development of the personality rather than on the distillation of knowledge; and she could exploit her somewhat inflated reputation for scholarship to justify this nebulous notion. Girls were, in effect, to be given the kind of moral and practical training that would turn them into good wives and mothers, and then they could while away the long years of marriage by profitably indulging their tastes for reading. Katherine's most serious concern, however, was that young girls should no longer be exposed to the mercenary machinations of the marriage market, and she proposed that they should be removed as early as possible from the corrupting social life of the capital, and allowed to develop

25

more freely in a secluded environment. Her Utopian feminist dreams corresponded to the needs of the women in the capital, who still longed for domestic comfort and security, with the woman at home and the man in his place. For vague yearnings for independence had elevated women's consciousness to the point where they could, in the comfort of their homes, imagine themselves somehow uncorrupted by the real world.

Katherine's dreams for the enclosed institutional environment were realized in the famous Smolny Institute for Girls, which opened in 1765 in the Voskresensky Convent. To get some idea of Katherine's educational principles we should look at the school itself, rather than try to decipher her own hazy pronouncements on the subject. A year after her accession, Katherine had written to the Department of Education in Moscow: 'Is it necessary,' she asked 'to teach girls what has been laid down for boys?' The answer was predictably ingratiating and inconclusive: 'We are all obligated to women. But we men are so vain of our superiority in strength and power, so proud, so obstinate and unjust, that in providing instruction and enlightening minds, we obstruct the very sex to which we are so obligated.' The following year Katherine's General Statute on Education for Both Sexes came out. Girls were to be taught the 'arts of life and citizenship', housekeeping and accountancy. They must learn to be courteous, just and happy: 'Sing and laugh,' she admonished girls, 'be always cheerful and contented.' The Smolny Institute was to be filled with charming contented girls; its vague and exalted aspirations were not to be tempered by any of the more practical concerns of St Cyr that had so impressed Katherine. The Empress was to be the great imperial mother presiding over her own little matriarchy and personally subsidizing deserving girls of the lower aristocracy and the merchant classes.

Shadows of the old Voskresensky Convent still hung around the school; when a girl entered it she was there until her course had finished. Girls were taken at the age of five and usually stayed until they were eighteen. Most families naturally feared that their daughters would return home as pampered capricious strangers, but contemporary witnesses found the girls naive and unpretentious, and the awesome, ever-present influence of the Empress ensured that their behaviour was always scrupulously discreet. An educational inspector testified later, however, that he had been horrified by the teaching standards, which were indeed rudimentary. Katherine had read her *Emile* selectively. 'It follows that one should not *educate* children, but rather give them the desire and love of knowledge,' she said. But in fact she regarded girls' *entrée* into society as something to be learnt like anything else, and the week at Smolny revolved round the parties with eligible young men, at which even the youngest were expected to act as 'hostesses'. Soon the more socially successful of them were taken to society balls, which took them very far from the 'enclosed institution' that Katherine had first envisaged.

Such teaching as there was at Smolny concentrated on arithmetic, Russian and foreign languages, history, heraldry, architecture, music, singing and drama. The girls were encouraged to produce concerts and plays, which gave them some creative outlet, but at all such occasions they were closely watched by their teachers, and their social accomplishments carefully noted. At these events it rapidly became obvious that girls of the poorer classes were being outshone by their more privileged classmates, and soon the school was officially divided into two departments; now, while little girls of the aristocracy played hostess to admiring young men, the poorer girls studied accountancy and housekeeping in a separate part of the building. The girls were all fairly indifferent to any disciplined work, and the general apathy of the teachers gave little stimulus to develop their 'desire and love of knowledge', as Katherine had put it. Some of the older girls from the aristocracy were allowed to teach the younger classes while girls from the other department were expected to supervise the cooking and keep the accounts. Naturally the two departments produced girls with rather different expectations of marriage. Katherine's intention was that girls should go straight from the school into marriage. She took personal responsibility for their engagements, and those who left to get married bore with them her blessing in the form of a little crown. Probably Smolny's only real educational achievement was that it taught girls, most of them brought up in entirely French-speaking homes, to read and write their own language for the first time and to get to know something about Russian literature. But most of them, like Katherine, acquired only a clumsy and inaccurate command of spoken and written Russian.

Smolny remained virtually unchanged until Katherine's death in 1796, and was one of the few institutions to escape the increasingly reactionary measures of the later part of her reign. During her lifetime, 850 girls completed the course, 440 from the aristocracy, 410 from the merchantry and the poorer classes.

Katherine was always openly contemptuous of serious analytical study; 'dangerous ideas' were the inevitable result of 'free throught', via 'introspection', and she must have been well aware that women, once granted some measure of intellectual independence, would be particularly susceptible to the more 'dangerous ideas' of the Enlightenment. Women should be encouraged to study, she wrote (anonymously), but their minds should not be clouded by 'useless knowledge, which would not enlighten them but plunge them into a nocturnal gloom'. The educated woman should be able to engage in rational discussions with her husband without arguing, and she should exert a pacifying influence over men in conversations. She would thus be better prepared to educate her children and run the home. This was answered by a timid article in a Moscow journal, expressing the hope that women would soon be educated on the same lines as men. In 1773 the Professor of Law at Moscow University proposed that civilizations could be judged by the status of their women; Russian society had transcended its past, when women's 'precious gifts were buried in poverty and oblivion'.

During Katherine's reign, indeed until the late nineteenth century, women's education was an issue unrelated to any other. The advances in this field were not symptomatic of general educational reforms, and women were never actually integrated in the new officially 'enlightened' society ushered in by the Empress. Katherine had little sympathy for the 'popular schools' that began to open up throughout the country, and which catered to the more materialistic, less socially ambitious girls of the provinces around Moscow and the capital. The actual percentage of girls in these schools was low. In the years 1771-96 a total of 164,135 boys and 12,595 girls emerged from the 'popular schools': the boys with a superficial grounding in the conventional 'male' subjects; the girls, with their traditional lightweight 'feminine' accomplishments, now qualified as governesses and private teachers. While the men from these schools could enter the lower ranks of the bureaucracy, the girls could only begin to compete with the *fräuleins* and *mesdemoiselles* for teaching jobs.

It was not necessary to propose any concrete measures for the advancement of women in Russian society in order to ingratiate oneself with the Empress. The enervated, physically incapacitated woman of the upper stories was to emerge from Smolny to embellish the social life of the capital. 'Women are taught that beauty is their sceptre, and that the mind shapes itself to the body, and, roaming around its gilt cage, seeks only to adorn its prison,' wrote Mary Wollstonecraft some twenty years later in her impassioned *Vindication of the Rights of Women*. Many girls who had been beating their wings against their gilded prison at Smolny

29

emerged, initiated, into the complex ritual of the St Petersburg mating season. In December, carriages would slowly start arriving in the capital, many having travelled as far as 9,000 *versts* (about 5,000 miles). By January the 'season' would be in full swing, with the city teeming with carriages and nubile young women in carefully chosen 'coming out' costumes. It was a tense period for everyone; each woman had her place in an inflexible social hierarchy. All eyes would turn first to the 'famous beauties' – 'beauty' for the marriage speculator inevitably being synonymous with wealth. Then came the wives of high officials, who could be relied on for some serious flirtation, and after them the 'frauleins' and the 'mesdemoiselles'. The provincial girl in search of a husband came right at the bottom. Many of the more socially prominent families had a sort of permanent 'season', and kept open house throughout the year for families of comparable standing, but some refused to take the whole thing too seriously and, spending a minimum on gowns, would take their daughters to a 'season' just for the holiday.

Most provincial families, however, were intimidated from entering their daughters in the marriage-race by the fiercely competitive atmosphere in the capital. They preferred the more relaxed gatherings at their estates, which lacked the social tensions and pretensions of the capital and allowed girls to emerge from puberty at their own pace. At these gatherings men and women would stage little plays together and play cards. Peasants would be brought in to entertain the company with songs and dances, and the evening might end with a firework display. Even in the capital it was gradually becoming easier for young men and women to meet in a more leisurely fashion. Masked balls were popular, and they introduced a rather audaciously democratic spirit into the whole incestuous and stultifying procedure; for, once the urge to capitalize on a pretty face or an aristocratic pose had been removed, people became more accessible to each other. Love

30

matches now became increasingly acceptable with the more liberal aristocratic families.

Many men who set out for the capital in search of a wife in the mid-eighteenth century were unsure of the kind of woman they were going to meet there. No longer were they looking merely for wealth and elegance, but for the elusive 'new woman' they had heard so much about – who actually initiated conversations and asked questions. Prince Andrei Bolotov, a high government official whose fascinating memoirs were discovered only in the nineteenth century, arrived in Moscow in 1763. He was an enlightened young man, eager to find an intelligent and sensitive wife. He met there a couple of sisters who entranced him with their spontaneous and intelligent discussions of literature and philosophy. 'I could hardly believe,' he writes, 'that I was discussing *literature* with a woman!' Nor could he believe that the sisters talked to him as they would to any intelligent visitor, and had no patience with his amorous insinuations. They gently mocked him for his 'sentimentalism' and he left, deeply hurt, convinced that the girls had merely exploited their charm and intelligence to wound his pride. Bolotov renounced the company of 'coquettes' and returned to his estate where he became enamoured of a little girl of twelve who, despite her delightful innocent charm, dismayed him with her unsophisticated response to his proposal. She had, not surprisingly, not the least idea of how she felt about Bolotov, or whether she wanted to marry at all, and seems to have lived her entire married life in a kind of apathetic trance.

Prince Dolgorukov took his time looking for a bride. In his memoirs he describes a hundred and fifty women he met in the course of this arduous search; all of them, he candidly admits, 'I more or less fell in love with.' But his memoirs are more than mere amorous confessions, they record the search for the 'new woman'. And for all his admiration of the women he meets, they all emerge, in his descriptions of them, as exhibits, briefly dazzling a selected audience with their

31

accomplishments, and then returning to their place. His first love was a witty fourteen-year-old little charmer, with a talent for writing that was to remain with her all her life. Then there was the accomplished woman of thirty, a Smolny product; after her came a young orphan, an introspective and widely read girl living with relatives who had forced her out into society in order to marry her off.

Although both these men were looking for more than mere 'accomplishments' in their women friends, they were still unable to accept any notion of a feminine intelligence. It was Karamzin, the deservedly popular novelist of the period, who was to express most succinctly the search for the 'new woman', a friend who inspired love and confidence by her 'inner qualities' of mind and heart, for *La Nouvelle Héloïse* and its description of the *amitié amoureuse* made a great impact on the new 'Sentimentalist' movement in Russian literature. The heroine in Karamzin's lachrymose novel *Poor Liza* is portrayed with respect and tenderness, but her 'inner qualities' are embodied solely in her 'sweetness'; she is a 'muse of enlightenment', and no mundane psychological interpretations of her character are ever allowed to mar her exalted image.

Karamzin's novels made a deep impression on Russian salon society. He discarded the lugubrious Russian literary style and moralistic plots for a lightness and simplicity that ensured him a wide readership among men and women alike. His effect was generally a healthy and democratic one, for he opposed natural feelings to patriarchal severity and mere crude debauchery, even though this opposition brought disillusion, lamentation, tears and premature death. For Karamzin, tears were the measure of a noble heart. To be sure, the modern reader would find his works self-centredly masculine; the *amitié amoureuse* may enhance the life of the hero, but it places impossible demands on the innocence and 'sweetness' of the heroine. However, Karamzin introduced a more self-critical attitude into the salons. Men and women

32

now felt able to discuss their more intimate problems among sympathetic friends, and this new *amitié amoureuse* forced them to take more seriously the consequences of passion. The dismal fates of Karamzin's heroines taught women to come to terms with arranged marriages in which companionship should predominate over passion.

Paul I came to the throne in 1796, and in the five gruelling years of his reign subjected Russian society to a heavy dose of Prussic acid; for almost every institution, including the school system, was Prussianized. As all educational statutes of the period refer to students only in the masculine gender, it is safe to assume that the educational changes of his reign had little to do with girls' education. Boys' schools were now rigidly divided into three separate grades; girls' education was left entirely in the hands of the Tsar's wife, Marya Fëdorovna, who continued Katherine's system of personal patronage but lacked any of the imagination and ambition of the great Empress. Unlike Katherine, she limited herself to the strictly practical demands of Russian society. Smolny's ambitious aim had been to develop girls intellectually, socially and domestically. Marya Fëdorovna denounced any ideas about the 'new species of person' as 'futile and dangerous', epithets conventionally used to express fear of subversive ideas. But Smolny had of course catered only to a very small select group, and most of the wealthier girls continued to receive their education privately at home or in foreign *pensions*. The impoverished nobility and the rising merchant classes could rarely afford to educate their daughters at all, and it was with these classes that Marya Fëdorovna was concerned. In the 'institutes' that the Empress envisaged for her *protegées* there was to be a strong spirit of the convent. Girls were to enter the schools at the age of nine and to stay there for the next six years. Visits home were discouraged, and those whose parents were considered to exert a harmful influence were immured for the duration of

33

the course. Over these 'institutes' the Empress was to preside as a sort of Mother Superior.

The first 'Mariinsky Institute' was opened in the capital in 1797, subsidized by the Empress, who covered the fees of the less wealthy girls. Education was a gift bestowed by a bountiful ruler on her less fortunate subjects, and a group of philanthropic ladies attached to the court was not slow in setting up the Women's Patriotic Association, which subsidized similar institutes in Kazan', Poltava and Khar'kov. Dancing and etiquette were still considered essential training for these future wives and mothers, but a smattering of French and Russian language and literature was also thrown in. Orphans of soldiers were encouraged to enter, and their fees were to be subsidized; these less socially advantaged girls were to learn needlework and crafts, to prepare them to earn their living as sempstresses and craftswomen. Midwifery, although now accepted as a medical discipline rather then some occult feminine craft, was still considered the province of the lower classes. In 1785 Katherine had opened the first midwives' school in the capital, and under Marya Fëdorovna several more were opened.

The Empress was an uninspired woman, ignorant of such educational pioneers as Pestalozzi. She rejected the extravagant sociability that had crept into Smolny, and there were no visits to the opera or ballet, no drama groups or balls. She was anxious only that her institutes should provide a harmonious environment in which girls could grow up gracefully. There were occasional dances at the school but any relatives or friends bold enough to attend these elaborately formal occasions were separated from the girls by a wooden barrier. Inevitably the more elegant of the girls somehow found their way to the more distinguished balls in the capital, and some of them were presented at court, with Marya's blessing. She busied herself with arranging marriages for her pupils, and with finding jobs as governesses and teachers for the 'failures'. The Khar'kov Institute even laid down specific conditions under which a girl could leave to get married, carefully screening all suitors before they were accepted.

But the more elect girls, like Marya's own daughter Alexandra, continued to go to Smolny. Later, in 1836, Alexandra was to admonish girls at Smolny; 'whatever situation you may find yourself in, make people aware not of your mind, not of your talents, but of your modesty, your discretion and your womanly virtues. Do not try to dazzle, but fulfil your duties strictly and conscientiously, and then you will have God's blessing.' These modest ambitions were to be the model for the institutes, and although many teachers at the new schools enthusiastically tried to rouse the girls from their intellectual apathy, 'learning' and 'knowledge' were still too deeply rooted in most girls' minds as male provinces, separated somehow from the ideas they were now hearing so passionately debated in the salons. The teachers quickly became disillusioned, teaching became perfunctory and guarded, and girls' educational standards advanced very little.

Paul's successor Alexander I, who reigned from 1801 to 1825, spoke movingly on the need for improvement of women's lot. He distinguished himself by these emotional pronouncements on the necessity for reform, but his liberal views were an eclectic and inconsistent ragbag of enlightened European thought, and he lacked the personality and authority to carry out the reforms he advocated. He derived from Condorcet his notions about sexual equality, and announced that women's education should be improved. After Paul's death, however, he left Marya Fëdorovna with the independent administration of the 'Mariinsky Institutes', and by the end of his reign there were still only twelve of them, plus six for the daughters of men in the Army and the Navy. Popular schools flourished, thanks to local private patronage, but it was in the predominantly Jewish towns of

35

Odessa, Mogilev, Vitebsk and Dorpat that girls in the *Tochterschule* could expect the best education. For all of Alexander's 'liberalism' this was a particularly anti-Semitic period in Russian history, and the isolated Jewish communities were especially anxious to provide sons and daughters alike with the education denied them in the official school system. In Vitebsk there were twenty such *Tochterschule*, in Mogilev thirteen and in Novgorod three.

Girls' education advanced little more during the reign of Nicholas I. He came to power in 1825, determined to consolidate the autocracy and to pander no longer to his liberal intelligentsia. The popular schools were seen as exerting a dangerously democratic influence on the official school system. Nicholas chose as his education minister the incomparable Uvarov. 'Political religion has its dogmas,' said Uvarov, 'eternal, like those of Christianity. Why touch them when, fortunately for us, they have been preserved by a powerful hand?' This remark expressed the educational values which, with the blessing of the Church, embodied in microcosm those of the Russian state in the early nineteenth century. Boys' schools, now named *gimnazia,* were open to sons of the nobility and the higher ranks of the bureaucracy. The course was of seven years, during which period boys were accommodated in monastic hostels, strictly separated from the dangerously free-thinking effects of society and women. 'Our noble young men, the flower of our intelligentsia, must be educated separately,' said Uvarov — separately, that is, from boys of the lower orders and from women. In 1845 fees were raised in a deliberate attempt to exclude boys from the poorer classes; a secret government decree of the period shows that Uvarov was merely looking for a 'plausible excuse' to exclude boys for whom education was only a 'superfluous luxury, removing them from their natural position in society, without benefit to them or to the State'. These less wealthy boys tended to 'lack any real ability, but boast of their capacities and achievements, and generally become restless citizens, especially when they cannot find an outlet for their overexcited ambitions'. Uvarov had little to say on the subject of women's education, but his remarks applied only too blatantly to the underprivileged female half of the population.

There was no reform in the syllabus at these *gimnazia,* and if by any chance 'free thought' should creep in through the locked doors of this prison-like system, then young minds must simply be filled with more wholesome material, such as classical languages. 'Free thought' was of course defined with the kind of circular reasoning peculiar to government thinking of the time. The study of geography and modern history, for example, was considered 'dangerous', liable to give rise to 'useless reasoning'. 'The less people know, the more easily they are governed,' said Uvarov, and he could not have put it more succinctly. Corporal punishment was administered mercilessly, and the 'incorrigible' were given a 'wolf's ticket', which excluded them from further education, debarred them from the services and disenfranchized them, effectively depriving them of all basic rights. Stricter discipline was introduced into the institutes and great emphasis was placed on physical training.

Mercifully there were a few exceptions. As a young man in the 1830s, Alexander Herzen, the first great Russian philosopher, had briefly taught at a girls' *pension* run by French Catholic priests. Tanya Passek, daughter of one of his literary colleagues, was one of the pupils, and subsequently a lifelong friend. For her, as for her friends there, Herzen's teaching was a revelation. She had spent her early years at a Moscow Institute, where she recalled volumes of incomprehensible hieroglyphics, the coldness and severity of the teachers and the constant fear of punishment: having to wear a dunce's cap, or being led on a string around the building. At the age of twelve she had begged her parents to move her to another school, and she had entered the *pension,* where the teaching was haphazard but rather more humane.

Herzen encouraged her to read and write, and had even shown her secretly the more politically 'dangerous' poems of Pushkin. The two years in which she knew Herzen encouraged her to embark on a writing career. At the age of fourteen however she was considered ready to enter society, and after an informal examination by her father was taken away from school. Herzen encouraged her to write her own moving account of her paltry education.

Girls in the early nineteenth century picked up intellectual interests as and where they could. Mothers who had been encouraged to raise their children in the humanitarian values of the Enlightenment now found these values to be officially 'dangerous'. They were appalled by their sons' barbarous initiation into Russian society, and began to lose their former enthusiasm to improve the educational opportunities for girls. If education was to enhance their moral authority in the home, they realized that this authority would be undermined, rather than enhanced, by the primitive school system that was separating them from their sons.

NOTES

1. That is, about fifteen stone.
2. 'Appanage' is the conventional translation for the Russian *udel,* the small independent principalities that flourished from the tenth to the fifteenth centuries.
3. As an adolescent, bored and frustrated with the life of the court, Peter had taken to roaming round the streets, where he had picked up a variety of friends and skills.

CHAPTER II
INTO SOCIETY

'The idea of martyrdom has a sanctity
instilled in childhood by the traditions of Christianity, and
reinforced by the struggle for the rights of the oppressed.' [1]
When Vera Figner said this she was recording not only her
own evolution as a major political activist, but the history of
women's consciousness in nineteenth-century Russia. A
lifetime's involvement in the revolutionary movement allows
Vera Figner to speak authoritatively about her experiences,
and I shall make good use of her fascinating autobiography.

In the early nineteenth century, Russian women rebelling
against the oppressive security of family life clung only to a
vague but unlimited capacity for self-sacrifice, a capacity
instilled into every woman by her long encultured dependency. The women who struggled now to abandon this
security found an independence that was frightening and
dangerous. The conventional marriage of the *Domostroy* had
at least provided a woman with the consoling illusion of
sacrificing herself to an omnipotent husband. But Peter the
Great's reign had shattered this illusion; how could a woman
sacrifice what she had never had, an independent identity?
Throughout the nineteenth century, when women began

painfully to discover their abilities and limitations, this urge to self-effacement was directed at the Church. Wifely obligations could be fulfilled in a spirit of mystical ecstasy, for girls then as now know that their greatest moral triumph may be assured by their deepest resignation and humiliation. But though this urge remained, its object was gradually shifted from the husband as supreme moral arbiter to the State that had so defined him.

For many girls, 'entering into society' began to take on new meaning, for they were experiencing the intimate conflict between devotion to one man and an active identification with their social and intellectual *milieu;* they were suffering from the first painful pangs of class-consciousness. The cloistered atmosphere of the ladies' parlours was transformed into the circles and discussion groups which women no longer passively attended, but over which they now actually presided. They were not merely enhancing and extending the life of the city intelligentsia; they were able to mediate between the liberal 'repentant noblemen' and the *déclassé* intellectuals to form a new and powerful intelligentsia.

The more radical of these 'circles', however, the secret political societies that began to flourish in the early nineteenth century, could not afford to admit the critical and self-questioning presence of women, and the Decembrist uprising in 1825 called forth all women's powers of self-sacrifice. The uprising was organized by a group of young officers who had taken part in the various conspiratorial groups that were finally consolidated into the Northern and the Southern Societies. They planned to stage a military revolt that would prevent the Senate taking the Oath of Allegiance to Nicholas I, and to force from them a manifesto granting a constituent assembly. Their political ideas were hazily based on a passionate desire for the abolition of serfdom followed by some sort of redistribution of the land; the actual revolt depended entirely on the officers' ability to sway their men at the moment of insurrection. The

Decembrist uprising was a fiasco, and the government dealt swiftly and savagely with its prominent organizers, while turning a pragmatically blind eye to the three thousand or so soldiers who had responded to the appeal to revolt. The Decembrist officers were sentenced to life exile in Siberia.

The women who followed them there combined a sense of exalted wifely devotion and political duty. These were the daughters of the post-Napoleonic generation, and for them self-sacrifice was not merely a patriotic duty but a right, a right to a kind of vicarious independence. It was their duty to ensure that their husbands were not consigned to public oblivion, and by their decision to accompany them during some twenty years of exile they forced them to be recognized still as important members of the political movement. The evolution of these women's social consciousness during their years of exile made them inspiring figures for later women activists. Vera Figner in *The Wives of the Decembrists* pays tribute to their example.[2] Few of the women had known anything of their husbands' political activities, but after the uprising it was with a feeling of awe, rather than resentment, that they confronted the men who had suddenly become strangers to them. 'It had never entered their heads that people who were so close to them could plot the overthrow of the government and discuss the killing of the Tsar,' wrote Vera Figner, and even the most politically uninitiated women could find inspiration in those who rejected a privileged aristocratic life-style for the miseries of self-imposed exile. For men, the Decembrists' wives were wives *par excellence:* 'Women have given some beauty to our story,' wrote Prince Viazemsky, one of the officers not arrested.

Fonvizin, the most prominent of the Decembrists, was the only one to tell his young wife Natalya of his activities and political programme. Natalya Fonvizina came from a provincial conservative family, deeply rooted in patriarchal values. She had received almost no education or parental guidance, and as a young girl veered wildly between

41

impulsive acts of defiance and private mystical ecstasies. Pushkin, who met her briefly, may have used her as the model for Tatiana, the deeply reflective, essentially Russian heroine of his famous poem *Evgenii Onegin*. In her late teens she had run away from home to a convent. Dragged back by her parents, she had been immediately disposed of in marriage to her forty-year-old cousin, General Fonvizin. He was an authoritative but humane husband, who shared his young wife's moral fervour. Natalya gradually overcame her fears of the encroachments that this enforced marriage would make on her private mystical world, and grew to respect her husband's moral certainties. Towards his political interests, however, which took him into the world of ugly social reality, she felt a deep coldness. But when she heard of his arrest she did not hesitate; her place was with him, rather than with her two young sons in the capital. 'How sweet the thought that I shall share your fate fully,' she wrote to him while he awaited exile in prison. 'This will enhance my whole existence.' In Siberia Natalya bore her husband a child who died shortly after birth, but she adapted to her new life with an almost religious ecstasy which she imparted to her women friends there.

Princess Marya Volkhonskaya was the daughter of a hero of the Napoleonic Wars. She was by all accounts an extremely attractive woman, well educated, with a lively interest in literary and historical matters. She was devoted to her husband, from afar – twenty years older than she, his political activities and work left him with little time to talk to her. If consideration had prompted him to spare her the details of the uprising, however, he need not have feared for her delicate nerves. She was twenty when she heard of his arrest and had just suffered a particularly difficult childbirth, but she went straight to the prison and, falling at her husband's knees, kissed his chains and swore to follow him.

Politics also deprived Alexandra Muraviëva of her

husband's company. Although she had little understanding of the issues involved in the uprising she determined to follow him. Rather than subject her two young children to the ravages of the Siberian climate, she decided to leave them behind, a loss from which she never fully recovered. She bore a daughter shortly afterwards in Siberia, but soon died of tuberculosis. Baron Rosen's young wife had won his heart with her modesty and charm. It was only in exile that he began to appreciate her seriously as a competent and widely read woman. Exile was for both of them a period of intense reading and discussion.

These were some of the women who, far from the degradingly competitive social life of the capital, were able to discard a life of inconsequential submission for a life of activity and comradeship. Soon after their arrival in Siberia they set up their own little community near the prison, which they visited daily in the hope of a chance meeting with their husbands. For the first time in their lives they cooked and washed for themselves and the prisoners. All their property was shared, and they soon set up a hospital and library in the prison. They attended to their husbands' mail, and the Siberian outpost was gradually transformed into a little cultural centre where events from the outside world and articles in the newspapers became relevant and passionately discussed topics. One of the older women, Marya Ental'tseva, who had, according to Vera Figner, 'read everything that had been written in Russian', suggested forming a discussion group among the women.

This discussion group brought them into correspondence with several of their friends in the capital, where women were becoming increasingly involved in philanthropic activities. In St Petersburg, Agafoklei Sukharova and a group of aristocratic women friends were able to use their social status to put a word in the ear of some of the more liberal high government officials. By organizing concerts and poetry

43

readings they were able to raise funds for their Society of Women's Care for Prisoners and for the St Petersburg Patriotic Society.

The Decembrists and their wives were to draw women's attention from the confines of their conventional social obligations. The mazurka had become a wearying treadmill, and young girls still condemned to the tedious round of balls and extravagant social events were now making their boredom very obvious. They were to be seen talking animatedly amongst themselves, making little effort to exhibit their social accomplishments. Kireevesky, a progressive journalist of the period, saw this somewhat disconcertingly detached behaviour not merely as the arrogant romantic pose of fashionable disillusionment, but as the 'sickness of the thinking soul'. For although women did not enter the passionate discussions raging in intellectual circles around the German idealistic philosophers Schelling and Fichte, they made their presence felt in these circles, both in Moscow and in the capital. Most gatherings in St Petersburg were still pervaded by the match-making mentality, and girls were fearful of speaking at such occasions. Most of them spoke French anyway, and could barely express themselves in Russian, let alone in the barbarous neologisms that bad translations of German philosophy had imported into the language. Loneliness still forced them into the consolingly familiar embrace of Christianity, whose precepts they were struggling to reconcile with the ideas of romantic German philosophy. Women's feelings of isolation and disillusionment, their hatred of society and their dreams of solitude were poured out in voluminous letters and journals.

High society in the capital at this period tended to meet in salons reminiscent of those of eighteenth-century France. Princess Gagarina's salon was attended by intellectuals of the aristocracy and the higher ranks of the bureaucracy. Her evenings were extravagant events lasting late into the night. But it was in Moscow that girls were able to lose some of their social inhibitions in heated intellectual discussions that excluded none but the most timorous. Princess Elagina kept open house for a group of radical journalists, students and officials. Here women could hear radical writers like Herzen and Granovsky discussing ideas of philosophy and arguing for the need for reforms in Russia. A less socially dazzling figure than Princess Elagina was Marya Ofrosimova, whose warmth and enthusiasm drew many of the less prominent intellectuals to her salon.

The distance that sanctity had conferred on the Tsar was rapidly turning to his alienation – from an increasingly autonomous bourgeois bureaucracy, from a simmering *déclassé* intelligentsia and from an aristocracy that was extending its oligarchic powers. The new 'thick journals', in which rigorous literary analysis provided a covert context for political criticism, were the forum for an endless series of articles, letters and reviews dealing with the position of women in Russian society.

In the 1830s writers like Belinsky, Bakunin, Herzen and Ogarev, all consumed by the desire for philosophical certainties, were tentatively exploring the ideas of socialism within a framework of romantic culture. Their new friendships with women fostered the religious and sentimental aspects of this romanticism. Herzen's quasi-religious desire for inner peace prompted him to mediate between the more extreme philosophies of his friends. On the one hand there was Belinsky, with his defence, based on the Hegelian dialectic, of the Russian state and the enlightened despotism of Nicholas I. On the other there was Bakunin, whose radical interpretation of the theories of Fourier, Saint-Simon and Owen were to lead him to a more doctrinaire violence.

It is interesting to compare the two men's attitudes to women. Bakunin encouraged his four sisters to join him in his exploration of these ideas. The children of liberal, pro-Decembrist aristocrats, they had been encouraged to discuss political and philosophical matters with their father;

45

they taunted him ceaselessly for his outmoded liberalism. But while Mikhail was reading and debating furiously with his friends on social and political issues, his sisters were more inclined to the introspective contemplation of German philosophical theories. From these they derived their exalted romantic notions about marriage – the marriage of 'twin souls' and of 'perfect harmony'. Belinsky, who met his friend's sisters, was enchanted by the 'atmosphere of moral harmony' they created in the Bakunin home.

Varvara Bakunina, the eldest girl, had accepted the Hegelian notion that only through marriage could a person be one with God; and marriage with a man who did not share this quasi-religious faith would bring about her 'fall'. Instead of rejecting marriage outright, she was in fact demanding a kind of marital equality that was both premature and idealistic. Inevitably, her fears were justified, and after a few years of marriage she felt she had 'fallen'; the relationship failed to live up to her expectations of love and understanding, without which she did not feel able to bring up her child. But although in marrying at all she had been the 'pure victim of her parents' will', she was also able to blame herself for submitting to their authority. She left her husband and young child, determined to support herself as a writer.

Varvara Bakunina was a passionate, solitary person. But Belinsky, for all his awe of this woman who 'enhanced the temple of his spirit', in a letter to her brother still regretted that such a profoundly sensitive girl should deny her femininity and beauty. He was disconcerted that she should express herself so assertively without seeking her brother's confirmation. Apparently, in the middle of a conversation about music, Varvara had demanded of Belinsky with sudden vehemence that she should *know* what was being discussed, rather than just *feel* it. Mikhail showed his sisters Belinsky's letter; Belinsky, the great radical thinker, who must himself have frequently demanded to *know* what was being discussed, was yet shaken that a woman should have made this demand. Alexandra, the second sister, felt urged to write to him: 'I was so saddened by your letter ... Only feeling enlightened by knowledge can reconcile us with life, and give us peace and harmony. But can a woman really talk from the depths of her heart with a man who has no faith in her most sacred aspirations? He merely draws a line around her and threatens terrible punishment on anyone who dares go beyond this line.' Sadly, even these gently pertinent criticisms were thought to be too audacious, and Alexandra never sent the letter. Sadly too, while Belinsky's own commitment to the social and intellectual life of the city quickly enabled him to transcend these crude prejudices, Alexandra and her younger sister stayed at home with their unsent letters, trapped by romantic introspection and dreams of lost opportunities. It was women like these who were the first victims of men's growing awareness of what was now being widely discussed in Russia as the 'women's question'.

Herzen once wrote, 'Human development is a form of chronological unfairness, since latecomers are able to profit by the labours of their predecessors without paying the same price.' Belinsky, Shelgunov, Mikhailov and other leading radical writers of the day all wrestled for a definition of women's historical contribution to Russian society. And while they wrestled women waited, like victims of Herzen's 'chronological unfairness', to be defined. Ideas were acquired by the men of Russia's new intelligentsia with all the strength of physical passion, possessing mind and body, justifying everything. For them, mind took over the function of feeling; for them, it was axiomatic that pain could be eradicated, and they gravely underestimated the difficulties they would face in transforming deeply encultured sexual roles. If the primary sources of human misery were embodied in the official concepts of 'law' and 'morality', they argued, it followed that the two great urges towards sex and personal gain must simply be abolished, and Russian society would move smoothly from a metaphysical to a positivist stage in its

47

intellectual development. The articles that appeared on the 'women's question' hardly did justice to these grand assumptions, however. Even the great minds of Belinsky and Dobrolyubov were unable to cope with a problem that touched them so very deeply and to which they could not apply any of the hastily assimilated absolutes of German philosophy. The 'emancipated woman' was still a stranger to Russian society, an object of disgust and ridicule.

In 1835 Belinsky wrote an article for the progressive journal *Teleskop,* in which he aired some of the views that had so offended the Bakunin sisters. 'Women should love the arts,' he said, 'but love them for pleasure, not in order to be an artist. No, never can a woman be an artist if she is to be a wife and mother. A woman writer without talent is a pathetic sight; without talent she is merely ludicrous and repulsive. A woman writer is an *emancipated* woman.' We must have patience with Belinsky; to most matters he applied a rigorous and sensitive mind, and he can have met few intelligent women who could have removed the sneer from the word 'emancipated'. At that time his views were deeply rooted in his own religious interpretation of Hegel, and only later were they transformed to a more political interpretation of the dialectic, based on the State as supreme authority. This change was accompanied by the inevitable transformation of his views on women.

George Sand was immensely popular among Russian women at that time. A woman of her enormous intellectual and moral authority would have been a total anomaly in Russian society, and articles about her life and works, thinly disguised as 'literary criticism', began to appear in all the journals. In 1838 the conservative journal *Moskovsky Nablyudatel'* ('Moscow Observer') published an article by the arch-reactionary Bulgarin who dismisses this great writer as a woman who 'invites people to a "natural" state, and considers that social institutions, especially marriage, are the chief cause of human misery.' A few years later Belinsky was to emerge as the defender of George Sand and the 'emancipated woman'; in the radical journal he now edited *Otechestvennye Zapiski* ('Notes from the Fatherland') he acclaimed her as a genius, 'to be rated above all others in modern European literature ... What humanity breathes from every page! Woman and her relation to society, an issue so based on traditions, prejudice and male egotism – this is what inspires the poetic imagination of George Sand!' No longer is a woman writer merely a 'pathetic sight', and if her genius makes her an 'emancipated woman' this status earns her respect rather than ridicule. A year later Belinsky was writing, 'If in all matters woman stands lower on the ladder of moral development, it is not because of her nature but the defects of men's brute material force, the semi-barbaric, somewhat oriental structure of society, and the sickly arcadian education given to women.' Belinsky's views on women had clearly moved far from his original concept of woman as the 'mother of our children, raised in our esteem by the sacred fulfilment of her sacred obligations ...' But even this inspiring radical thinker is unable to provide any more positive definition of women's character and role, and Shashkov, writing some forty years later, observed quite correctly that 'if the teacher thus regarded women, one can imagine what confusion reigned in the heads of his pupils! Even if he changed his views later on, he was never in the contemporary sense of the word an emancipationist.' [3]

But as journalists, Belinsky and his radical friends could encourage women to send them poetry and stories for publication or comment. Belinsky was particularly interested in the stories of a young woman called Elena Gan', who ventured to send him some of her poetry for publication in 'Notes from the Fatherland'. There was something about her work that he found touchingly forlorn, and although he criticized it for its provincial *naiveté* and lack of intellectual or social content, he encouraged her to give fuller reign to her passions and to take George Sand as her inspiration. This encouragement was unintentionally cruel, for Elena Gan' was writing precisely in order to keep alive natural passions, which were rapidly becoming stifled by provincial boredom. At the age of sixteen she had been married off to a 'good catch', a dull German officer. She had started writing to escape the company of her lazy cynical husband and a slow but sure death on their isolated provincial estate. However, writing, under the pseudonym of 'Zinaida R–va', for a distant and critical audience was little consolation for a wasted life, and at the age of twenty-eight she died, lonely and frustrated. Shortly before her death she had written her best story, 'A Useless Gift', in which the heroine exclaims, 'Men, how great are your advantages! A little patience, hard work and will-power and you can achieve anything. Whereas women, equal to you in talent, and superior in emotions, wither away in the desert, in anonymity, far from the world and from that great inspiration, the means to education, which her heart longs for.'

Women like Elena Gan' were isolated talents, isolated by their crippling educational deprivation. For in the 1830s and 1840s in Russia the talk was still of 'sexual equality' rather than 'equal rights'; men and women were concerned with the more immediate problem of sexual roles, and women's character and abilities were still defined in isolation from the broader social structure. It was not until news reached Russia about the growing women's movement in Europe and America that people woke up to the intimate connection between family and State, and to the idea that women's equality was bound up with drastic social reforms that would enable the whole nebulous 'women's question' to be discussed in terms of women's social and personal evolution. In the spring of 1850 there had been a women's conference in Ohio, followed by innumerable meetings culminating in October in a major conference in Massachusetts, where women demanded preparatory courses for advanced university education, equal pay in industry and legal equality. Such demands were a revelation for Russian women, and actually forced government attention towards the need for women's educational reforms.

When Alexander II came to the throne in 1855, Russia was tense with unexploded myths. The patriotism that had fortified soldiers and civilians alike throughout the Crimean War was shattered after the Sevastopol' catastrophe of 1854. The myth of the eternally slumbering peasantry was progressively discredited by thousands of violent peasant uprisings. The abolition of serfdom overshadowed every political and social issue in the course of the century, and Alexander proposed to buy out the landed gentry in a vast financial operation that would give him some reputation for liberalism among a simmering intelligentsia and an increasingly autonomous bourgeoisie. This operation, the official emancipation of the serfs, was finally carried out in 1861.

The Russian family, aristocratic, bourgeois and peasant, whose structure had rested on roles that had remained basically unchanged since the twelfth century, was also waking from its deep sleep. Dobrolyubov and Chernyshevsky, the leading radical spirits of the day, recorded the surge of excitement among the new radical intelligentsia of the 1860s. In 1857, at the age of twenty-one, Dobrolyubov wrote in his diary: 'The voice of one's blood ties is becoming scarcely audible. It is being drowned out by more general interests ... If intellectual and moral interests converge, respect and love for one's kin weaken and eventually disappear.'[4] The old paterfamilias, deprived of all authority over his family of serfs and children, was now regarded by his offspring as an emasculated victim of the old order, an object not so much of hatred as of pity and embarrassment. His wife, disillusioned by her husband's loss of moral authority and embittered by idleness, began to identify with her rebellious children. Economics, education, the family, social and personal morality, religion, politics and philosophy – all were now subjected to women's scrutiny. The filial love of Dobrolyubov and his contemporaries was transferred to the oppressed – to the peasantry and to women. But these men were carried away by a boundless confidence in the ability of the intellect to transform deeply rooted attitudes. 'To understand the peasantry, one has only to understand oneself,' wrote Chernyshevsky in his diary. And through prolonged introspection, women too could be understood; it was then a simple matter for any intelligent man to grant women their moral and social independence. Chernyshevsky, with all the naive optimism that characterized the 'men of the sixties', formulated his theories on women's emancipation.

He advocated that the 'stick be temporarily tipped in the other direction' – that is, that women should be granted a 'temporary ascendancy'. 'Every honest man should, in my opinion, put his wife higher than himself. This "temporary ascendancy" is necessary for the "woman of the future",' he wrote in his diary. But Chernyshevsky had the misfortune to fall in love; and he fell in love, in the most catastrophically self-destructive sense, with a woman who was the very antithesis of the 'woman of the future'. Chernyshevsky, the 'instinctive rationalist', betrayed his hopelessly entangled emotions by professing to 'respect' a woman he simultaneously refers to as a 'fallen woman'.

His fiancée's album was embellished with tender sentiments from previous lovers. Chernyshevsky's entry was no mere lyrical effusion, it was a humourless statement of faith, a formula for marital happiness:

Woman must be the equal of man.
Hitherto this has not been the case.
Woman has always been a slave.
A woman must be the equal of her husband.
Hitherto a wife has simply been her husband's servant, placed only a little higher than other servants.

All relations between man and woman, husband and wife, have therefore always been repulsive.

Chernyshevsky begged his wife not to deny her own inclinations and to give herself to any man she found attractive. He was obviously a good catch for this capricious young woman, who could escape her parents through a respectable marriage and then enjoy the social life of the capital, unencumbered by any emotional bonds to this man whom she found so alien. 'When I ask for your advice, I expect to receive a command,' he wrote to her, and she was only too happy to follow his advice. Once married she all but abandoned her husband, whom she found tedious and pedantic and whose writing and ideas she never found remotely interesting.

Nobody who has read Chernyshevsky's works on literature and philosophy will find it easy to isolate his pathetically inadequate theories on love from the main body of his work. But this brilliant 'self-taught man' derived much of his moral authority over the 'men of the sixties' from his ability to expose the gulf between reason and emotion. In 1861, when Chernyshevsky was sentenced to imprisonment for his 'dangerous views', his wife was only too glad to be rid of him and continued her amorous adventures, barely reading the passionate letters that he sent her. It was in prison that he wrote his great novel *What is to be Done?* which contained both the blueprint for the 'rational marriage' and Chernyshevsky's own disconcertingly candid confession of confusion.

Nikolai Shelgunov was older than Chernyshevsky, but shared his passionate search for the ideals on which the new Russia was to be founded. Women's emancipation was going to be a slow process, accompanied by the gradual transformation of Russian society. But like Chernyshevsky, he too had to face the immediate and painful problems of marriage, and he too grossly overestimated his own role in imposing on his wife the conditions for an equal partnership. His views on women were known: 'Most women are incapable of distinguishing good from bad; everything happens to them unconsciously; illuminating ideas are not distinguished from mere stupidity, noble feelings from baseness, love from revenge, malice and treachery from constancy, frivolity from vanity.' His wife was an intelligent woman, only too ready to separate this definition of her sex from any judgement of her; after all, it hardly made sense to attempt to establish an 'equal partnership' with such a ragbag of human vices. Nor was it easy for her to accept that her husband's insistence that she 'enjoy herself with another' if she wished was prompted only by the generosity of his love for her. 'Equality,' he told her, 'comes not from the mere promptings of the heart . . . You want a husband to submit to his wife, convinced that she knows his best interests, but I will submit to you only as to someone who learns to know herself through love.' Both Chernyshevsky and Shelgunov were making a slogan out of sexual freedom before they had actually experienced it; both, in their ignorance, were inflicting on their wives the cruel standards of the 'instinctive rationalist'.

Shelgunov could only blame himself for the painful consequences of his demands. Neither Dobrolyubov nor Mikhailov sought openly to practise what they preached, although both of them did preach very persuasively about women's equality in the leading radical journals. Mikhailov had become involved with Shelgunov in producing the illegal pamphlet *To the Younger Generation,* whose rousing democratic slogans caused such a stir among the radical intelligentsia when it came out in 1859. Meanwhile the Shelgunovs had settled in a small flat in Samara where, like Vera and Lopukhov, the hero and heroine of *What is to be Done?* they occupied separate rooms, meeting only in the 'neutral' sitting room. Mikhailov had met Lydia Shelgunova in the capital in 1853, and was soon sending her passionate

54

love poems. A few years later after they married she left Shelgunov for Mikhailov, and when both men were arrested for their pamphlet she moved to Switzerland. There she fell in with the exiled revolutionary Sërno-Solovevich, whose political attitudes were romantic and idealistic. His attitude to women was ambivalent; he was notoriously uxorious. Lydia Shelgunova emerges as a gullible victim of radical rhetorical poses, which were inevitably demolished by the opponents of women's emancipation. The reactionary journal *Epokha* could take women like Lydia Shelgunova to justify its assertion that women's emancipation was merely the search for 'free love' or the new 'rationalist' alternative to prostitution.

Herzen had good reason to be impatient with these young men's public display of their marital difficulties and of their thunderous pronouncements on attitudes so suddenly assumed, so impetuously experienced. His gradual reconciliation with his wife Natalya led to a deep and lifelong friendship. She was the illegitimate daughter of a peasant and had been adopted by the estate owners. Troubled by her feelings of obligation to her benefactors, she had become withdrawn and deeply religious at an early age. Although at their wedding a toast was drunk 'to friendship', there was little real friendship between them. Herzen, with his penetrating and analytical mind, threatened his wife's private religious preoccupations. After ten years of marriage Natalya left with a young poet with whom she lived for a few years, and when she and Herzen met again some years later, it was, as she put it, 'as old comrades, hardened in battle'. As comrades, then, they started again a marriage that was to last until their deaths.

Women had to learn to transcend the dubious freedom of 'free love'. Stepniak-Kravchinsky, a revolutionary of the 1870s, spoke warmly of the women who managed to overcome the constraints of their new sexual 'freedom':

55

With us, the emancipation of women was not confined to the petty right of 'free love', which is nothing more than the right of always selecting her master. It was soon understood that the important thing was to have liberty itself, leaving the question of love to individual will, and as there is no liberty without economic independence, the struggle changed its aspect, and became one of acquiring free access to superior institutions and the professions followed by educated men. The struggle was long and arduous, for our barbarous and medieval family life stood in its way. It was maintained very bravely by our women, and had the same passionate character as most of our recent social struggles. The women finally vanquished. The government itself was forced to recognize it.[5]

Support for women gaining access to these institutions and professions took time to develop. Official sympathy went out earlier and more easily to the girls who had volunteered as nurses in the Crimean War; their efficiency and devotion in the midst of appalling conditions and scandalously inadequate medical provisions had impressed Russians and Turks alike. In 1857 the politically neutral and inappropriately named journal *Morskoi Vestnik* ('Naval Herald') carried an article 'Questions of Life' by Nikolai Pirogov. He had been a surgeon during the war and was now rector of Kiev University. His brand of 'official liberalism' was very acceptable to the new tsar, and his views carried much weight in government circles. The nurses he had met during the War had convinced him of the need for women's education, but despite its reasonable tone, the article never went beyond the most hazy definition of what form this education should take. The family, he argued, had no right in deciding the future of Russia's children; all children should be given the advantage of some moral and scientific training. 'At present, women's education tends to turn them into dolls. It dresses her up and puts her on a stage, on display for idlers.

Women's place in society, her education – this is what needs change.' So women should be educated, certainly, but not in such a way as to make them fear for their 'destiny'. If they are granted the intellectual independence to see through the cracks in their education, they will only try to succeed in the world on their own, and then they will certainly fall after the first step. Rather let them be proud of their ignorance. After all, 'not everyone is a doctor, not everyone must look at society's sores'. A free will, an understanding of art and a clear idea of her aims will equip a woman to educate her children properly.

> If women pedants understand emancipation to mean education, they are right. But if they want the emancipation of women's social role, they do not know what is good for them. Education will give women an even greater liberty than men ... Women's role is to unite and enhance society . .. Women are men's cradle, the very cornerstone of society ... The nation's women should not be trained as soldiers, bureaucrats and ministers of state; nor should they be patronized, as at present, as empty-headed dolls. They should be challenged academically, as intelligent human beings ...

I have not misrepresented the article by condensing it; the argument was circular and soothing enough to appeal to government liberals and the more muddle-headed of the liberal intelligentsia. It was generally considered an important and enlightened article.

Even the radical journal *Sovremmenik* ('The Contemporary'), one of whose declared aims was the emancipation of women, supported the view that as 'intelligent human beings' educated women would make better wives and mothers. In response to Pirogov's article it brought out a piece entitled 'Women's Grievance'. Women, announced the article, were not naturally equipped to compete professionally with men; equal educational opportunities were of less

57

importance than family education – whatever this was supposed to mean. The tone of the article was naive and sentimental, clearly intended to ingratiate its women readers. But not all women were so easily ingratiated; many were beginning to contribute articles themselves, anonymously for the most part, or under andronyms. In the late 1850s there were innumerable articles in all the journals on the futility and degradation of women's lives. Women writers quoted Fourier, Lassalle and Condorcet; they declared war on Proudhon, and began to write openly, urging their sisters to stop lamenting their wasted talents and put them to some use.

'Women's Grievance' inspired one Ekaterina Burnasheva to reply in an angry article for *Vestnik Vospitania* ('Educational Herald'). It is we women who are largely to blame for this kind of article, she says in effect. We have forgotten the little we have been taught and merely await our intellectual deliverance from those who oppress us. Many women found this kind of positive criticism more supportive than anguished condolence or exalted definitions. Ekaterina Burnasheva received many letters of encouragement, but there were some angry responses too. A Mrs Kh–va felt moved to write for the same journal a series of 'Letters to Russian Women'. She feared the new *'femme savante'*, whose intellect would be to the detriment of her soul and who threatened to destroy the harmony of the feminine character. Mrs Kh–va felt that women's special gift was their ability to influence people and events indirectly, by the subtle exercise of their moral authority.

The first woman to play a really important part in the world of contemporary journalism was Marya Shigaeva. In 1850, at the age of nineteen, she had married Vernadsky the eminent professor of law at Moscow University. She was a widely read woman, whose husband encouraged her interest in politics and economics. In 1856, when the couple moved to the capital, they started up a journal together: *Ekonomichesky Ukazatel'* ('The Economic Index'). Marya

58

combined her journalistic activities with the care of her young son whom she was determined to educate herself. She brought out a series of articles whose moderate and lucid style does justice to their passionate conviction. The first of these, 'The Freedom of Choice in Labour', stresses that if women are truly accepted as the equals of men there can be no fear that independent work will tempt them to jettison their families along with their petty domestic preoccupations. She wasted no time on pleading for women's innate intellectual capacities, pointing out that since in the more advanced civilizations physical strength plays a lesser role in the work force, the choices opened up to women are greatly increased and it becomes more difficult to restrict women to any one particular kind of job. Marx's *Wage, Labour and Capital,* written nine years earlier, had not yet come out in Russian, but it is not too facile to suggest that she may have absorbed some of its ideas on the extension of the labour force. Her next article was more trenchant. There is only one possible way for women to gain their independence, she says – by being economically self-supporting. She had nothing but contempt for women's bourgeois inhibitions against working. 'Our cooks, our nannies and maids are much more independent than their mistresses. The prestige of a bourgeois home is nothing but a fetter, inducing this terrible squeamish attitude to work.' Only through independent work will women be able to identify their oppression with that of the working classes. 'Why not be a flowergirl or a sempstress?' she asks. 'Is this so debasing?' In her last article, 'Women's Destiny', she attacks the conventionally frivolous attitude to marriage as something heaven-ordained and inescapable. 'Mesdames! Stop being infants! Try to stand on your own feet, live by your wits, work with your hands, learn, think, work like men.' Sadly she died shortly after writing these articles, at the age of twenty-nine. It would have been interesting to see how she developed as a writer, and how she dealt with her critics.

In 1858 *The Contemporary* began to receive Mikhailov's 'Paris Letters'. He had little time for the arrogant and self-enclosed Paris intelligentsia but was greatly impressed by the women he met, still battling against attitudes rooted in Proudhon and Michelet. He describes his contacts with various women's groups and clubs, and then goes on to refer acidly to Michelet's pamphlet of 1845, *De la Femme,* and to Proudhon's *De l'Amour*. He turned instead to the more sympathetic views of Mill, and in 1859 was inspired to write an article dedicated to Lydia Shelgunova; the epigraph, ironically, was *Coupez le Câble*. It was written as a series of questions: How does society depend on sexual equality? What obstructs its ideas and practice? If the family is regarded as a nucleus of society, how should one reconstruct family life in a way that will positively reflect the progressive transformation of society? He points to the increase of marital breakdown in Russia, and to the sexual degeneracy of French society — depressing but inevitable signs of the collapse of the conventional family. But these observations do not prompt him to suggest any alternative structure; the message is obviously contained in the epigraph.

In 1859 a new journal appeared on the market, a 'journal of science, literature and art for young girls'. It was called *Rassvet* ('Dawn') and described in exalted tones the resplendent dawn of a new generation of Russian women. 'The genius of transformation reigns again over the Russian land', ran its mellifluous opening lines.

At the dawn of a new day, a genius flies over the sleeping Russian woman and awakens her, showing her the path she must follow in order to become a citizen and prepare for her new task — to educate the new generation. And when all around her have already woken, she is bewildered, and does not understand when people say that a woman must become a citizen. 'My destiny is to become a mother, wife and housekeeper in my husband's home,' she says. 'And a citizen of your country,' adds

60

contemporary society. And this means that a woman must delve into contemporary ideas, sympathize with them, and even participate in the movement towards social progress.

Dawn leaves the nature of this participation unstated, with no reference to the part she has played in actually creating these nebulous 'new ideas'. She is merely to 'sympathize' with them, and this does not necessarily involve any break with her traditional Christian values. By asserting her legal rights and her authority in the home, she could gradually establish herself as a 'citizen' in bourgeois Russian society. Not particularly enlightened material certainly, but more encouraging than the articles that deluged the reactionary journals, with their minute analyses of the contradictions and obstacles in the way of women's legal and educational equality.

As for girls' education, during the reign of Alexander II this 'developed along normal lines, descending further and further in the social scale, so as to reach successively into the four great classes into which Russia was traditionally divided ...';[6] and, the author might have added, so as to ensure that these four great classes remained in their places. Girls of the upper aristocracy were educated privately or at Smolny and the exclusive French *pensions,* which would familiarize them with the niceties of aristocratic social life. Girls of the bourgeoisie and the merchant classes were instructed in the Mariinsky Institutes in needlework, crafts, and rudimentary arithmetic, Russian and French, skills that would enable them at best to run their husbands' homes with the minimum of servants, at worst to support themselves as governesses and private teachers. The popular schools had waned during the reign of Nicholas I, and only a tiny proportion of the fourth great class, the peasantry (representing some eighty per cent of the population), received any education.

In 1855 there were 51,632 girls attending schools of one sort or another in Moscow and St Petersburg, and a

61

government commission tentatively suggested the establishment of girls' schools on the lines of the boys' *gimnazia*. Three years later, in one of the first of his educational reforms, Alexander II was to carry through some of the proposals of this commission. But the official school system, the new model youth army introduced by Nicholas I, provided no great incentive for girls to emulate their brothers. Even Count Kapnist, later director of boys' schools in Moscow, was to describe them as 'based on principles hostile to the advancement of knowledge ... by almost criminal methods producing a kind of bacteriological station for the inoculation of schoolboys with officially approved doctrines ...' Alexander proposed that girls' institutes and *pensions* be brought into line with the boys' *gimnazia* (graduation from which automatically entitled a student to a university place), and the *Realschulen* (which provided more utilitarian instruction for boys of the lower classes, who were then eligible to continue at higher technical institutions). There was no suggestion that improved schools could prepare girls for the university, and they were to suffer the double disadvantage of being under the direct control of the Ministry of Education, while relying as before entirely on private donations for their existence.

As a result, 131 girls' schools were opened in the major cities, 37 of the *gimnazium* type and 94 *progimnazia* catering for girls of the lower classes. The course in the girls' *gimnazium* was of seven years, an extra eighth year enabling a girl to qualify as a governess. Educational standards were certainly improved, and girls were able to emerge from these schools with the prestige of official approval in the form of a little gold medal. The course in the *progimnazia* was of three years, after which a girl was qualified to teach in primary schools. In 1859 the government took stock of its inconsistent and partial commitment to women's education, and the Ministry of Education was made financially responsible for girls' schools, officially 'open to girls of all classes and religions'. In fact most girls' parents were still unable to meet the high fees, while the wealthier girls continued to be educated privately at home. The girls who did finish the course at these new schools found that their little gold medal opened up few new opportunities to them. Most schools and families still preferred men teachers, however unqualified they might be.

Pressure began to grow on the government to prepare women for university education. As early as 1853, the major universities had been canvassed on the advisability of admitting women as students. St Petersburg was unequivocally for their admission. A university commission was set up, and the results of their investigations were embodied in a long letter sent to the Ministry of Education. 'There is no evidence that women are any less capable of accepting ideas than men,' said the letter. 'In fact in view of the benefits their admission would bring society, their fees should be subsidized.' But they had to attend courses regularly, like the men, and be subject to the same examination system. Kiev, Khar'kov and Kazan' Universities responded equally favourably, demanding in addition that women should be allowed free access to the professions and government service. The response from Moscow, the most academically prestigious of the universities, was predictably negative and of twenty-five professors only two voted for their admission; their presence 'would have a pernicious effect on the studies of the young men'. Derpt University went even further: the admission of women was 'incompatible with the present structure of the University and with the successful achievement of its scientific goals'. There was a special note added from the head of the Educational Department: 'The female sex, by its construction and by its intellectual and spiritual capabilities, is not suited to study anatomy, nor understand the consistent and strict principles of jurisprudence, nor philological concepts, and if there are any exceptions to these principles they should not serve as a basis

63

for general government measures.' It is hard to guess the purpose of this government questionnaire; clearly they had no intention of admitting women to the universities. Such a move would have been premature anyway, since women were simply not equipped to compete academically with men; the demands of Kiev, Khar'kov and Kazan' were obviously more a statement of faith than a realistic proposal. Three years later the results of the questionnaire were publicized; women's admission to the universities would have to be delayed because of student disorders.

At the beginning of the academic year of 1858 at the St Petersburg Law Faculty the students were waiting for their lecturer, Kavelin. Suddenly the rector, Pletnev, walked in leading by the hand a young girl who was deposited at the back of the hall and from that day on regularly attended lectures. Kavelin continued his lecture as if nothing unusual had happened, but for the students this was a quite extraordinary event.[7] Pletnev, with his notoriously cavalier attitudes, was apparently encouraging a woman to attend as a student. The girl was Natalya Korsini, and she had been petitioning tirelessly and privately for the right to attend. She was soon followed by her friends Antonina Blyummer, Marya Bogdanova, Nadezhda Suslova and Marya Bokova. The following year many of the oppressive measures introduced by Nicholas I were lifted. Men no longer had to wear uniforms in the schools and universities, the right of assembly was brought back, students were allowed to travel abroad, and chairs of European and constitutional law were re-established. The law of 1855, which had empowered academic authorities to vet opinions expressed by teachers and students, was annulled, and university lectures were now to be opened to the public. Thanks to Natalya Korsini and her friends, the 'public' now officially included women, who were allowed to attend as 'outsiders', which meant that they could not write essays or take any of the qualifying examinations.

Natalya Korsini and the hundreds of women who now so eagerly attended these lectures tended to sit together, and the men automatically gave them the best seats. Men and women were by now so accustomed to talking to each other outside the lecture hall that women's presence at the universities no longer caused any sensation. Gone were the days when students spent all their time after lectures drinking and picking up prostitutes on the Nevsky Prospect. Chernyshevsky was much impressed by the generally civilizing effects of women's presence at the university, and after his first lecture to a mixed audience was heard to say, 'What charming women! In my day, students kept company only with prostitutes.' Young men and women tended now to stay behind long after the lectures discussing issues raised and points that had not been understood. But as unregistered 'outsiders' there was little incentive for girls to specialize in any one subject, and most of them attended the lectures of only the more interesting and sympathetic of the professors. Kavelin himself was no great emancipationist: 'It is hard to imagine how an intelligent man like Petr Osipovich [Kavelin] could come out with such retrograde views on the women's question,' remarks Pantaleev, somewhat harshly. 'The only explanation must be that he comes from a peasant *milieu* in which women are regarded as mere tools for work.' But however ambivalent Kavelin's views on women's education, he never dreamed of patronizing them, or in any way altering the course. Reason forced him to support their admission as registered students. Several other professors made known their views about women's right to register. The lectures of the liberal law professor Spasovich were always well attended by women, as were those of the materialist historian Stasyulevich and the Ukrainian nationalist historian Kostomarov.

1861, the 'year of the great reforms', was actually more generally regarded as the year of the great student and peasant revolts. In February of that year the progressive inspector of St Petersburg Girls' Schools, Konstantin Ushinsky, read a speech to a large group of schoolgirls and women students. It was now the duty of the intelligentsia, he told them, to expiate the crime of serfdom by carrying their knowledge, their talents and their labour to the people. On the Russian woman this new epoch of emancipation imposed a special duty — 'to realize your ambitions, and fight for your rights for higher education. Make this the goal of your life, inspire your sisters with this ambition, and fight for it until the doors of the universities, academies and higher schools are flung open to you as hospitably as they are to men.'[8]

For the women who had been in contact with the progressive student circles in their three years at the universities, Ushinsky's advice was already redundant, and they were already interpreting his words in such a way as to jeopardize their rather precarious position in the university. That spring Mikhailov's pamphlet *To the Younger Generation* had been secretly circulated among the students at St Petersburg. 'We do not need either a Tsar, an Emperor, the myth of some lord, or the purple which cloaks hereditary incompetence. We want at our head a simple human being, a man of the land who understands the life of the people, and who is chosen by the people . . .' Mikhailov's eloquent appeal for a constituent assembly helped to inspire the riots of that year which threatened the stability of the university itself. A young student in the capital describes one of the demonstrations that spilled out from the university into the streets of St Petersburg: 'A sight like it had never been seen. In the streets girls who were just beginning to go to the University joined in, together with a number of young men of different professions who knew us or merely sympathized with us.'[9] The Universities of Kiev, Kazan' and Khar'kov too were all beset by student revolts that encouraged dissident workers to down tools in support. During the course of these upheavals one woman in St Petersburg was arrested, falsely as it turned out. The universities were temporarily closed, and when they were reopened her arrest served as the pretext for barring women and other 'outsiders' from lectures.

For three years women had attended lectures eagerly and regularly. But there was little incentive for them to continue studying. They had not established any sort of intellectual framework within which to discuss the ideas to which they had been exposed, and they relied almost entirely on the men to interpret what was being taught to them. Men, meanwhile, had come to rely on women's presence at lectures. Mikhailovsky's article 'Women in the Universities' appeared in *The Contemporary* shortly after women were banned; it is both a debt of gratitude to these first Russian women students and a confession of disillusionment and alienation. 'We men are reproached for our indecisiveness, our lack of firm character. But until women are our equals, we shall be incapable of creating any real social progress, and shall be depriving society of its necessary strength ... We believe in the abilities and the great future of Russian women.'

Since women had for the first time been officially recognized as representing some sort of potentially political force, it was the task of the intelligentsia to arrive at some definition of the 'political woman', like Rousseau's abstract notion of the 'political man'; 'whoever dares undertake to establish a people's institution must feel himself capable of changing, as it were, *human nature* itself, of *transforming* each individual who, in isolation, is a complete but solitary whole, into a part of something greater than himself from which he derives his life and being ...'

Like Marx himself, it took Russian radicals many years to move from these philosophical abstractions about the victims of oppression and the agents of change into more politically sophisticated distinctions between economic and social structures. Although ultimately for Marx the economic factor is always predominant in history, the decisions of individual men and women, their intellectual and moral codes, all the minute workings of the superstructure inform the basic

67

economic infrastructure. The men of the 1860s in Russia had thought that the old ideologies would disappear, and that people would be guided by the pure reasoning of the Enlightenment. Trotsky, who described the 1860s in Russia as 'our short-lived eighteenth century', helpfully corrects our tendency to apply our more leisurely Western time scale to Russian history, in which, at all periods of intense social change, there was a 'mythology of division, which managed to concentrate centuries of Western European social and cultural development into years, and years into days'. [10] The 'men of the sixties' had gravely underestimated the power of the autocracy to alienate them from their society; they had overestimated their role in granting women their newly enlightened consciousness.

NOTES

1. Figner, Vera, *Work Completed,* Complete Works, vol. 2, p.25.
2. Figner, Vera, *'Zheny Dekabristov' ('The Wives of the Decembrists'), Work Completed,* Complete Works, vol. 5, pp.369ff.
3. Shashkov, S.S., *Ocherk istorii russkoi zhenschiny* (Brief History of the Russian Woman), p.221.
4. Dobrolyubov, *Collected Works,* vol. 5, p.187.
5. Kravchinsky, S., *Underground Russia,* p.9.
6. *Reports on Education in Russia,* p.164.
7. L. F. Pantaleev, a student at the time, records the general amazement in *Iz vospominanii proshlogo,* (Memories of the Past), vol. 1, p.137.
8. Tyrkova, A. V., *A. P. Filosofova i eë vremya* (A. P. Filosofova and her Times), p.170.
9. Ventura, Franco, *Roots of Revolution,* p.227.
10. As E. Lampert puts it in *Sons Against Fathers,* p.4.

CHAPTER III
ARISTOCRATS AND
NIHILISTS

By the late 1850s in the journals and in the 'circles' the great radical thinkers were all airing their theories on the 'women's question'. But for the thousands of girls now abandoning the deadening tedium of the provinces to breathe the fresh air of the capital, the 'women's question' was not merely a theoretical one: it was a question of life and death, of being self-supporting.

The emancipation of the serfs had reduced most of the less wealthy landowners to relative poverty, and for their daughters and sometimes their wives this came as a signal for their own emancipation, a welcome inspiration to leave the now-precarious security of husbands and fathers and find work in the capital. Many girls, particularly those of the wealthier peasantry, left their husbands without a word, and the personal columns in all the newspapers were filled with touching appeals for 'lost wives'. Passportless and therefore 'illegal', [1] these 'lost wives' had a hard time in the cities. For the patriarchal Russian legal system ensured that girls remained safely in their parents' homes until removed by a carefully selected suitor. Unmarried, they could not get the passport necessary for any travel within Russia or abroad,

69

and most married women's passports remained in their husbands' care. By the mid-1850s, however, girls from more liberal families had begun to fight for their right to marry the man of their choice: and the romantic love marriage was being replaced by the marriage of convenience, with an enlightened man who undertook to deliver the girl from her parents and provide her with her passport to independence. The new, so-called 'fictitious marriage' became extremely common in the 1860s. Men and women now sought an intimate and affectionate relationship in which they could give each other moral and intellectual support; for most of them this kind of friendship excluded any sexual relationship or the raising of children. Many couples agreed to part company immediately after the ceremony; some got hopelessly entangled in the conflict between passion and independence; but many 'fictitious marriages' were transformed into deep and lasting sexual relationships. This abrupt rejection of both the traditional Orthodox marriage and the still-fashionable notions of 'twin souls' and 'elective affinities' was unaccompanied by lengthy theoretical analyses of the 'new marriage': men and women were too actively involved in these new experimental partnerships to feel the need to publicize them. Only the reactionary journals aired scandalized views on the matter, with a stock of predictably scurrilous anecdotes. Apparently a new species of virago had been born, proposing marriage armed with a shotgun and then fleeing after the marriage to the capital, where she gave herself up to the delights of 'free love'.

But these women had more important things to contend with than slanderous anecdotes. For if previously marriage had excluded any sort of social or political involvement, now their desire to learn, to support themselves and to be socially active citizens must, temporarily at least, exclude sexual commitments. In the memoirs of the men and women of the period we find a reticence about the more intimate details of their lives that frustrates one's desire to resolve the

70

political personal equation of the 1860s. Publicly, at any rate, any displays of affection between men and women were denounced as 'coquetry' or 'chivalry', and 'falling in love' came to be regarded as a terrible misfortune, especially reserved for women.

As women were vastly outnumbered by men in the cities this defensive attitude was not unreasonable. In 1860, of a population of 494,000 in the capital, only 176,000 were women and the majority of the men were under thirty and unmarried. But the girls who started to flock into the capital in the 1860s came to find not a husband but a job. Petr Kropotkin, a student at the time, recalls how eager he and his friends were to help these new arrivals to establish themselves financially and intellectually. 'The young man who would not move his hand to serve a lady with a cup of tea would freely give to the girl who came to study in Moscow or St Petersburg the only lesson he had, which brought him his daily bread, simply saying to her, "it's easier for a man to find work than it is for a woman. There's no attempt at chivalry in my offer, it's simply a matter of equality." ' [2] But for women who had broken with the tedious conventions of provincial life nothing was simple in the feverish atmosphere of the capital. Many had nervous breakdowns and were forced to return to the familiar authority of parents and husbands. There was a sudden sharp increase in the number of nuns and prostitutes.

The more sophisticated girls of the capital could however now enjoy their new independence without the inevitable and traumatic break with their families. It became acceptable for young girls, even those of the aristocracy, to pay visits and walk around the city unchaperoned. They began to dress with greater simplicity and taste. Since the reign of Peter the Great aristocratic Russian women had been morbidly clothes-conscious, frantically vying with each other for imported clothes and trying to compete with their terrifyingly stylish rivals in France and England. They indulged their

71

'gallomania' in an extraordinarily vulgar display of baubles and trinkets. Now girls were abandoning all jewellery; the simple black dress, the white collar and cuffs and the plain leather belt all denoted the life of the spirit, rather than of the body. In progressive circles, any girl heard talking French would automatically be branded as a 'coquette', and men were not slow to chide any vestiges of 'outmoded conduct' in their women friends. 'How is it you are not ashamed to talk this nonsense and wear that chignon of false hair?' Kropotkin[3] and his friends would demand of some unrepentant 'coquette'.

'Revolution is simplification' – this was the slogan of the youthful 1860s. But for girls naturally inclined to poetry and music 'simplification' was no simple matter. They would wander around in an uncomprehending trance, obeying the call of the time to pursue utilitarian, scientific studies, and to abandon the art and culture of their devalued decadent past. Naturally playful girls, persuaded that any display of their sexuality was not merely sinful but reactionary, lowered expressive eyes in company or hid them behind the rather ludicrous blue-tinted spectacles that were just coming into fashion. And for these new puritans long hair was another sexual provocation, a foolish remnant of Old Russia that must be abolished. Even Chernyshevsky and Mikhailov descended to denunciate long hair in these terms. So flowing hair was roughly cropped, and only when the 'new look' inevitably became accepted as fashionable did people realize that overt sexuality can be indefinitely redefined, never destroyed. These changes in dress and appearance were a high price for women to pay in order to be accepted as equals in the company of men, but soon even respectable married women of the aristocracy, who 'changed their feathers with every new season',[4] began gallantly and elegantly to display their solidarity with their more truly emancipated sisters. The 'nihilist look' was now in fashion. For 'nihilist' was a term that had crept into reactionary vocabulary to describe those who, in the words of the conservative journalist Katkov, 'no longer believed in anything'. The term was, according to Saltykov Schedrin, 'deprived of all meaning, less suitable than any other for describing the younger generation'. Most young girls in the capital, for all their consuming desire for knowledge and equality, were now foisted with this image.

Of course, among radical men, these girls were raised to a kind of perpetual snowline of chastity. The life of the court, the aristocracy and the bourgeoisie however was an Augean stable of illicit and generally blatant intrigues. Among officials of the emerging bureaucracy, marriage had become little better than a cattle market. It was common practice for the wife of an ambitious official to leave her husband to live with his superior, thereby manipulating his promotion.

'On what is the present family, the bourgeois family, based?' asks Marx. [5] 'On capital, on private gain. In its completely developed form this family exists only in the bourgeoisie, but this state of things finds its complement in the practical absence of the family amongst the proletariat, and in public prostitution.' 'Family life' was of course the fortress of the industrialized bourgeoisie. For the young radicals, despite their 'nihilistic' talk of fundamental changes in the marriage structure, probably the most viable form of marriage remained a liberal-bourgeois version of the traditional Russian family, with the husband as breadwinner taking a virtual monopoly on new ideas and the wife still confined to the bearing and raising of children, activities now raised to the status of 'female labour'. For the emancipated serfs who formed the new industrial proletariat there was virtually no family life in the cities. After the Emancipation the peasants had started drifting to the cities to find work in the factories, returning to their villages at harvest-time. Wives and children were generally left behind to work the land, and gradually the cohesive extended family life of the villages was disrupted. The peasant women who did leave their villages in search of work usually returned or resorted to prostitution.

73

Even as prostitutes they faced some professional competition, for in 1868 over one per cent of the female population of St Petersburg, some two thousand women, were prostitutes.[6] For many women, the occupation of wet nurse was slightly less demeaning than prostitution, and women who had abandoned their babies in the villages could sell their milk rather than their bodies.

The 'superfluous man' of the previous decade was less restricted than his female counterpart. While rejecting many of the privileges of his class, the wealthier could often resort to a legal inheritance, while the less wealthy generally had the resources to support himself adequately. He could always afford to compromise with his political beliefs to become absorbed in the professional bourgeosie. The 'superfluous woman', in abandoning the more doubtful privileges of her sex, had chosen a path she would have to cling to if she was to survive. In the 1860s women began to play an active part in Russia's industrial workforce.

In England women had been active in industry since the turn of the century, when the introduction of steam power had considerably reduced the physical demands made on workers, and Pitt's cry 'Take the children!' sums up the whole savagely utilitarian ethos of early industrialized Britain. Russia's retarded industrial development and the primitive living conditions in Russian cities make any comparison between the two countries difficult. By the 1860s, of 30,000 factory workers in the capital, 3,500 were women, 280 of them under the age of sixteen. Most of them worked in the cotton, textile and tobacco factories, where they could expect little more than half the men's pay for the same work. Appalling working conditions put an intolerable strain on the health of these novices and most women would work intermittently, between bouts of illness. But only chronic chest and lung diseases and typhoid could induce a woman to abandon a job for which she had had to compete so hard, for of the 100,000 women who found jobs of one sort or another, there were 120,000 unemployed. Factory owners made no secret of their aversion to employing women – 'you can shout and curse at the men workers' was one employer's justification.

Women's living and working conditions, if not their pay, were the same as the men's. Like the men they would live in filthy rooms, often four to one bed, in squalid areas far from the city centre. As there was virtually no public transport in the capital, workers often spent three or four hours of the day walking to and from work, along streets that were little more than mud tracks. In the cotton factories men and women worked in suffocatingly high temperatures, cleaning, separating and sorting the threads and piling them up. Part of the process involved standing barefoot in water, and most women inevitably succumbed to chest infections. Conditions were a little better in the textile factories, where women were welcomed for their 'agility'; and in the tobacco factories too, nimble fingers were put to work in the 'smoke' department, sorting out the twigs and rolling the cigarettes.

Among soldiers' families and the up and coming merchantry there was a growing need for servants, and some 4,500 girls got jobs as cooks, cleaners and menials. But most women were employed in the exclusively 'female' trades: about 1,000 were milliners, some 640 were laundresses and 85 were corset-makers; 700 women worked with men as tailors, 600 as bootmakers, 200 as hatmakers, 60 as glovemakers, 34 as binders and 30 as confectioners.

Many girls were tempted by the security of working as apprentices. They could live and work on the premises and get a small monthly wage of three to eight rubles (very roughly three to eight pounds). Their parents were obliged to sign a contract with the employer under which their daughter would serve for five years, in which period food, clothes and shoes would be provided. In fact, most apprentices learnt nothing, and while employers talked of stagnation and foreign competition the girls would be landed with the

75

unskilled jobs, leaving the more demanding work to the women who had arrived before them. They were usually just taught to operate the sewing machine, which had been introduced into some factories as early as 1834, and which was already a formidable mechanical rival, doing six hundred stitches a minute to the women's twenty-three.

Karnovich's survey[7] revealed that most women described themselves as 'without occupation', since they never knew from one day to the next what job they would be doing. The great majority of women workers, some 92,000 of them, were homeworkers, miserably underpaid and without security. Most of them sewed gloves and hats and would take home work while looking for jobs in the factories. For factory jobs would at least give them a little security. As it was, they could be sacked without reason, and then, if lucky, taken back – with a reduction in pay. It was homeworkers who did most of the more skilled sewing jobs. Corset-making, an intricate and time-consuming job, was mostly done at home and a woman could expect to get about seventy kopecks (a little less than a pound) for three days' constant work on a corset. For weeks of work on an elegant ball gown a woman would get about three rubles. However, doctors' warnings were beginning to put the corset out of fashion, while foreign competition and generally simplified fashions meant less demand for elaborate gowns.

Prejudiced employers and economic stagnation combined to make the life of the woman worker a hard one. Employers often refused work to women who were badly dressed and therefore most obviously in need of work; but the better-educated woman also tended to be distrusted by employers, and was often content with the lowest-paid jobs. The threadbare woman of the bankrupt gentry was often refused work as a governess for her shabby dress, and as a factory worker for her genteel bearing.

In western Europe there were a few women running lace or millinery businesses, but in St Petersburg there were 220 women factory-owners, all of them carrying on their fathers' or husbands' businesses. The fashion industry was almost entirely in male hands; these women ran factories producing candles, tobacco, bottles, rifles, skins and spurs. Twenty-one women managed wine and spirit factories, eighteen ran large women's clothing stores and several were in the shipbuilding business. The combined capital of these enterprises was ten million rubles.

For a few girls, these successful women capitalists helped to sustain the myth of St Petersburg as the Promised Land for women. Despite reports in the press of large-scale women's unemployment, prostitution and suicide, girls continued to flock to this Promised Land. If a woman was confused and unhappy at home, in St Petersburg she would be understood, her confusions cleared up. For did not the progressive journals still insist that with a little determination and a few sacrifices any girl could gain her emancipation? Poverty, of course, was the first prerequisite to emancipation, and most girls, arriving in the capital without money, tended to take cheap rooms in the suburbs. The young students with whom they came into contact now tended to share rooms, pooling their resources for food, clothes and rent. 'Everyone aimed at a communal style of living in those days' recalls Vladimir Stasov, a student of the time. 'It seemed to everyone the most just, most natural and simple ... "Comradeship" and "equality" were on everybody's lips.'[8] It was only after the appearance in 1863 of Chernyshevsky's great novel *What is to be Done?* with its idealized picture of the 'commune' that young people began rather self-consciously to refer to their shared quarters as 'communes'.

Industrialization was leaving in its wake a great mound of human debris: the shattered elements of the uprooted peasantry; the *Lumpenproletariat,* without compensation of security; the *déclassé* intelligentsia, alienated from official institutions; and women, cut adrift from their inherited place

77

in society. It was from these elements that the new heterogeneous intelligentsia was formed. Aware of the power man could exert over his environment, and of the human labour power that had put Russia on the road to industrial progress, they sought now to confine this power, and in the face of the ever-growing concentration of economic and political control they looked back to a world undefiled by the intrustion of the modern capitalist state − to the village *obschina* and the *artel'*, autonomous social units of the countryside and the city. The peasants spontaneously established themselves in the cities in communal groups, generally a miserably impoverished version of the traditionally communal life of the village. And for young radicals the peasant collective was one model for their own increasingly communal life-style.

In a period in which family and political upheavals were so intimately connected, no relationship could be expected to rest on the frail shoulders of two bewildered young individuals searching desperately for the blueprint for the ideal 'new marriage'. All the old concepts of God and the Truth and the immutability of family and State were dissolving, and it was natural for young men and women to start living together in intimate communal groups, which could confer their own standards of normality and encourage people to experience together all the difficulties of establishing trust and honesty between the sexes. Chernyshevsky's message − 'cure society and there will be no sickness' − although naïve, was one that inspired confidence that somehow the commune would extend its values to the 'New Russia' of the sixties.

For many young people living in poverty and confusion, *What is to be Done?* came as a consolation, and primarily as an exhortation to enjoy life. For it told young people that even in a sick society it was possible to enjoy life; it appealed to instincts too long suppressed by the harsh utilitarianism of the time. 'Rise up out of your hovel my friends!' he urges his readers. 'Rise up, it's not so difficult. Go into the bright free world. It's splendid to live there, but the road is deceptively easy.' Ten years before Chernyshevsky had been pondering in his diary whether a man had the right to link his fate with that of a woman and subject her to his sufferings. Now he announced that only by living communally could men and women resolve their most intimate personal and political problems. A large number of girls, aristocratic, bourgeois and peasant, on arrival in the cities moved into a mixed house or flat. There was of course no stereotyped 'commune'. Some were little more than a squalid overcrowded room, sharing resources as a matter of economic necessity. Some had the space and opportunity to introduce into their lives some of the spirit of the phalanstery, and even started up small collectives. Any of the young people living in these communes would have made material for a novel, and Chernyshevsky's characters merely record the experiences of his close friends in the capital. Vera, Pëtr and Kirsanov will reveal their true identities in the next chapter.

Vera, the heroine of the novel, is the victim of a cynical and dictatorial family and is easily persuaded by a young medical student named Pëtr that if he coaches her for medical courses at the university she will then be able to leave home. The plan is obviously unrealistic, and when they eventually decide to marry it is ostensibly to satisfy Vera's parents, a 'fictitious marriage' of friendship and convenience. They move into a small flat, occupying separate rooms and communicating only in the 'neutral room'. While Vera pursues her studies, Pëtr abandons his to get a teaching job that will support them both. Just as Pëtr's feelings for Vera verge dangerously on passion, a friend of his, Kirsanov, who is also Vera's professor, moves in with them. Kirsanov and Vera fall in love, and Pëtr volunteers, with a minimum of dramatics, to move out. Meanwhile Vera has established in the flat a sewing collective for needy girls, a venture that is soon financially self-supporting. She and Kirsanov live harmoniously together and it is only with the news of Pëtr's suicide, which he justifies to Vera in a letter of rationalized despair, that the harsh truth begins to impinge on this picture of domestic harmony. For these 'rational egoists', with all their asceticism and their hasty rejection of love's tyranny, are still romantic, inconsistent and vulnerable. News of Pëtr's suicide is brought to Vera by Pëtr's closest friend Rakhmetov, who was to become for many young radicals the stereotype of the 'new man', the ideal of self-made manhood. Rakhmetov is totally ascetic, fanatically pursuing a goal of intellectual and physical perfection, and committed to a life of total celibacy. But of course one does not have to be Christ to be a Christian, and it was Rakhmetov's very implausibility, the novel's lack of structure and conclusion, that made it not so much a Bible as a confession. For the characters are as likeably fallible as the author himself or any of his friends. Vera's spacious airy collective was a blatantly idealized version of the small collective enterprises that flourished within several communes. Collectives were rarely self-supporting, and peasant girls anxious to train as milliners and seamstresses were not so easily converted to collective principles. There were few collectives in which girls actually sang as they worked, and then went off skating or to the opera.

Probably the best known commune of the period was that organized by the prominent radical journalist Alexander Sleptsov, whose prolific literary activity virtually subsidized the venture. For some time he had been giving lectures to women on literature and history, teaching them binding and trying to raise money to establish a women binders' collective. After reading *What is to be Done?* he decided to open up his house on Znamenskaya Street as a commune. His plan was gradually to introduce some of the ideas of the phalanstery. But for him, like Chernyshevsky and unlike Fourier, the commune was not to be an end in itself but was to help its members to become aware of their wider social

80

obligations. Sleptsov's importance as a radical journalist was sadly undervalued by his companions; his 'aesopian'[9] literary style, adopted to evade the censor, unfortunately often concealed the power of his more radical articles. The inhabitants of the commune constantly berated him for his 'bourgeois' life-style. Although the commune was generally regarded as a failure, it did manage to create an atmosphere in which people could freely air their views, even if these views ostensibly revolved around petty domestic squabbles. Like most such ménages of the period, the inhabitants quickly divided into two hostile groups, the 'nihilists' and the 'aristocrats'. Sleptsov, for all his emphasis on 'harmony', which he had absorbed from Fourier, and on women's essential role in preserving this harmony, became the butt of both factions.

About eight people lived in Sleptsov's commune, each with a comfortable room of his or her own. There was Masha Kopteva, a 'salon democrat', a pampered aristocratic young girl who had just left her Moscow *pension* and was looking for somewhere to live. She was accompanied by her friend Elisaveta Tsenina, who boasted of having run away from home and proclaimed herself a 'nihilist'. Then there was a distant relative of Sleptsov's, a liberal lawyer called Yazykov, who took little interest in communal life and lived there merely for convenience. Appolon Golovachev, a liberal landowner recently arrived from Tver' and at a loose end in the capital, also used the commune as somewhere to stay.

The only people who genuinely hoped for some kind of communal activity were Alexandra Markelova and Ekaterina Makulova. Alexandra had met Sleptsov at one of his binding classes. She was the daughter of a factory worker and Sleptsov had urged her to write stories and support herself as a proofreader. She had just borne an illegitimate child who had died, and Sleptsov was moved by her fortitude to write one of his most touching stories, 'The Nurseling'. Ekaterina Makulova was a 'ferocious nihilist', a rather unbalanced

81

young girl from a poor family who for reasons best known to herself chose to take the title of Princess. In political arguments she was not averse to fighting literally with tooth and nail. She and her friends had nothing but contempt for Sleptsov's well-groomed appearance and 'respectable' life-style. He was also frequently accused of womanizing. The charge was hardly fair. Sleptsov, although he consistently denied in his articles any distinction between the 'women's question' and the emancipation of the proletariat, had managed to make himself the victim of thousands of women throughout Russia, for whom he became a marriage guidance counsellor, a good Samaritan and a one-man employment agency. A friend of his, Elizaveta Vodovozova, recalls visiting him early one morning. He had clearly been up all night, dealing with a huge pile of letters from confused and isolated women asking for advice. He opened a letter at random; it was from a wealthy landowner's wife who was finding her husband's conservatism increasingly intolerable. Was it her moral duty to leave her husband and children? And if so, would Sleptsov please ensure that she would be able to find a job when she arrived in the capital? Although Sleptsov was frequently to complain of 'women's despotism, which makes them articulate every request as a demand', he was unwilling to abandon these helpless protégées. [10]

Clearly there was a need for some sort of women's employment agency in the commune, but arguments between the inhabitants soon degenerated into apathy, and predictably Sleptsov was left to organize one on his own. He was also left with all the housework to do. By 1864 the Third Department, long suspicious of Sleptsov's literary activities, was keeping watch on his house, and it was not long before he was officially warned that if he did not reform his views and life-style he would be sent into exile – 'to distant parts of the Empire' as official euphemism had it. The commune was closed. It had set its sights rather higher than most, and lacked the kind of spartan asceticism that made for genuine comradeship. But all over Moscow and St Petersburg young people were experiencing equally dramatic and painful confrontations. Everywhere there were 'nihilists', 'salon democrats' and 'liberal day school girls' arguing and living together.

In 1865, *Sovremennik* published Sleptsov's long short-story *A Hard Time,* which came as a gloomy response to *What is to be Done?* The heroine, Marya Tschetinina, breaks away from her family hoping to share with others some of the self-knowledge that has enabled her to liberate herself. But she is incapable of fulfilling her vague exalted aspirations. She had 'rejected philistinism for lofty ideals, and when frustrated in her lofty ideals she became cynical and disillusioned, rejecting any kind of petty vanity'. Sleptsov had realized painfully that communal life was only one step along the road to women's emancipation. For Gorky, his heroine's fate was typical of the struggling 'new woman' of the sixties: 'She is the type who broke herself in breaking with her family, and on her corpse the revolutionary movement broke out.'

The revolutionary movement 'broke out' gradually by way of the numerous collectives and *artels* to which women gave such a powerful impetus in the 1860s. To be sure, collectives, like cropped hair and tinted spectacles, became fashionable disguises for lazy and unscrupulous businesswomen. Shashkov even cites examples of cunning *entrepreneuses* who opened women's sweat shops under the guise of 'collectives', and of 'charitable' orphanages in which children were exploited as unpaid labourers on their 'benefactresses'' estates. But these were isolated cases. For the more important collectives we must turn to the activities of the unfortunately named 'female triumvirate', three women whose aristocratic status gained them access to liberals in the government. Nadezhda Stasova, Marya Trubnikova and Anna Filosofova attracted the attention of thousands of women in the capital looking for work and an outlet for their atrophying talents.

83

In 1832 the Stasov family were in financial trouble, and so it was decided to christen their youngest daughter Nadezhda, 'Hope'. On the whole, however, the family had little to complain of. Stasov was the Tsar's personal architect, and the family lived at Tsarskoe Selo, the 'Tsar's Village', where the Tsar himself was an occasional visitor to their home. Stasov's liberalism was typical of a man of his position – for him enlightenment stopped short at the eighteenth century and Voltaire. As educated girls were prone to 'dangerous ideas', Nadezhda and her sister Sonya received a genteel domestic education. Their three brothers entered a St Petersburg *gimnazium,* leaving their sisters to dance the mazurka and engage in irksome conversations with the local gentry. Once Nadezhda overheard her brother Volodya discussing the sisters with his father: 'Don't waste your money on them,' he advised.[11] It was with a feeling of bitter resentment that the sisters embarked on an intensive and illicit reading programme – illicit because, as Nadezhda remarked in her diary, 'immediately you pick up a newspaper you're called a bluestocking'. They read Byron, Pushkin, Heine and Dante, and, swooning away on the vapours of romanticism, Nadezhda fell in love. But the great love was never consummated; her suitor abandoned her and she fell into a deathlike trance from which only the power of hypnotism could save her. She was visited by a hypnotist with 'magnetic eyes', who laid a 'magnetized ring' on her, and soon she was demanding her own medicines – in Latin too, a language she had never learned! Her brother insists that throughout her life she commanded strange intuitive powers, but as Nadezhda now recorded briskly in her diary, 'as soon as I came to myself I realized the need for social activity'. She swore never to marry, and when in 1858 she returned home from abroad where she had been nursing her sick sister, she found that 'the charm of family life had abandoned me, and now I felt love instead for the great universal family ... This became my cause'. She decided to donate most of her fortunes to needy families in the capital, and embarked on a study of botany. She read openly now, Plato, Rousseau, Voltaire, Hugo and George Sand; 'We lived by her novels, and also by the music of Lizst' she writes in her diary. It was not long before she met Marya Trubnikova, a progressive and widely read young woman, who kept open house for a group of radical young teachers and writers.

Marya Trubnikova was the daughter of a Decembrist, Pëtr Ivashov, who was still living in exile in Siberia with his French wife when their daughter was born in 1835. When her parents died she was left in the care of her grandmother in Samara. At the age of seventeen she was already reading Plato, Michelet, Proudhon, Saint-Simon, Louis Blanc, Conte and Heine and was drawn, according to her more radical daughter,[12] to a 'vague evolutionary socialism'. She firmly rejected her first suitor. Two years later she met Konstantin Trubnikov, who was running a school for peasants on his estate, and who immediately won her heart with his quotations from Herzen. The two were married, and left the following year for the capital, where Trubnikov became editor of the liberal journal *Birzhevye Vedomosti* ('Stock Exchange News'). While helping her husband to edit and translate articles she was also extending her own education and her circle of friends, and young journalists who came to the house were soon discussing with her the ideas of Proudhon, Fourier, Lassalle and Owen. As she became gradually disillusioned by Trubnikov's cautious liberalism, he in turn found her intellectual and social independence increasingly exasperating. Most of the men who visited her however did not find her feminism threatening. 'The awareness of the possibilities of her own mind, the awareness that many men, less talented than her and less devoted to ideas, could so easily apply their ideas while she, as a woman, condemned to social inactivity, could not realize any of her dreams, gave a special passion to her femininity' wrote a friend.[13] It was inevitable that Nadezhda Stasova should

85

hear of her; their first meeting 'opened up a whole new field of activity for me', she wrote. From that time on they were inseparable friends.

Another woman to fall under the influence of Marya Trubnikova was Anna Filosofova. She was born in 1837, the daughter of Pavel Dmitriev, a wealthy spirit manufacturer from Perm with a religious mania that bordered dangerously on insanity. She was educated at home, 'under a bell-jar', as she puts it, by a mass of governesses who taught her 'French, German and curtseying'. At the age of eighteen marriage seemed the only possible escape from a life that was both frivolous and monastic, and Vladimir Filosofov came to the rescue. He was a highly placed official, but proved to be a sensitive and affectionate husband, for behind the bureaucratic exterior lurked a poet and an idealist. It was he who discouraged her frivolous tastes and persuaded her to read Hugo, Shakespeare, Rousseau and the progressive journals. In 1855 she was presented at court at Alexander II's coronation, and was caught up in the whirl of social activities that followed. But already 'social activity' was taking on a new meaning for her; beneath the polished surface of aristocratic social life political arguments about the new reign were polarizing her friends. She was slowly learning to distinguish between the 'official liberalism' of the new Tsar and the idealistic liberalism of people like her husband. It was at this time that she first met Marya Trubnikova. 'At first I didn't understand a word she said,' she admitted. 'We talked in literally different languages. But she encouraged me to read and gave me books.' Soon Anna Filosofova was giving large sums of money to needy women in the capital.

There was obviously a need to co-ordinate these donations and it was decided to hold a meeting to discuss what could be done collectively to help unemployed women and deserted wives. A common fund was to be set up to provide accommodation for deserted wives and widows and their

86

children, and five hundred rubles were raised on the spot. The meeting, which was well attended, divided sharply into two factions, the 'Germans' and the more easy-going 'Russians'. The 'Germans' saw it as their duty to investigate closely the lives of their beneficiaries, but they were outnumbered by the 'Russians'. So in 1859 the Society for Cheap Accommodation and other Benefits for the Citizens of St Petersburg was formed. A large house containing a laundry and a communal kitchen was built, and twenty-three women and children were moved in.

One day Marya Trubnikova was visiting her doctor, Tarnovsky. 'What does your wife do with herself, Doctor?' she asked him. 'Oh nothing much, goes out and enjoys herself I suppose,' was the answer. 'Ask her to come and visit me,' she said. Marya Tarnovskaya was quickly drawn into the society and opened up a school in the house.

It was as well she did, for the women had almost despaired of finding a woman teacher; they were forced to recognize that there simply were not any good women teachers around. For a large number of newly qualified women teachers began to reject jobs as governesses and direct their energies instead to the great movement for popular education of the 1860s, the Sunday School Movement.

The political activities of the early sixties represent a diversity of opinions linked by a common faith in the *narod,* the 'people', more specifically the peasantry. *Narodnichestvo,* Populism, retained, despite widely differing interpretations of the term, a common belief in the communal village structure, the *obschina,* and its collective authority, the *mir.* Alexandrov, an early populist, had said, 'We want to save the people, and yet we ourselves know nothing. We must begin by learning.' The early stages of the populist movement is best described as the 'cause of the book'; 'going to the people' meant not merely educating them but learning with and from them. Women had to fight their own 'cause of the book'.

Their struggle for education and jobs brought them into opposition with the entire educational system.

In the late 1850s, with about eighty-four per cent of the Russian population illiterate and the vast majority of children unprovided for in the official school system, liberals and radicals, men and women, began to organize Sunday schools in the major cities and their suburbs. Sunday schools had existed in France since the end of the eighteenth century and had been followed in the mid-nineteenth century by similar schools in America and England. But in Europe and America these schools were merely an extension of the church service; Sunday is a great day, they exhorted, dedicate yourself to it by fortifying yourself morally and spiritually. In Russia Sunday came to be regarded as a day when those who laboured all week could make up for the mindless routine of their daily work. Popular education in Russia was now no longer the province of the liberal philanthropist, who bought pens, paper and improving works and then sat back to wait for the peasants to come begging for education. The Sunday school teachers were people of widely differing persuasions. There were those who regarded education as a kind of gift bestowed by a benevolent autocracy on a grateful people, and there were those who hoped that mass education would instil a spirit of rebellion into a new class-conscious peasantry and proletariat. The Sunday School Movement exposed the political differences between women like Nadezhda Stasova, who saw the labouring classes as children in her great universal family, and the younger girls who, through their contact with student radical circles, now learnt to view their own frustrations in a wider political context. There were women like Elisaveta Garshina, the mother of the great writer, who wrote to the radical teacher Zavadsky describing her experiences as a teacher: 'I have children,' she said, 'and I love them more than my own life. But there is something else, even higher than one's own children. Now I am not a mother, or a wife, or a sister. I am a citizen of my country, and I should be happy above all earthly happiness if I could give my small mite to the common cause.'[14] There were women like Antonina Blyummer and her friend Natalya Korsini who together ran one of the largest Sunday schools in the capital. The two girls who a year before had entered the doors of St Petersburg University with such trepidation were now committed to working for mass education. Experience had taught them that women were not yet ready to be educated together with men, and their school was for women only.

All Sunday schools were privately supported, providing free education for children over the age of ten and for adults – workers, craftsmen and officials. The first Sunday school was opened in Poltava in 1858 by some grammar school teachers, student cadets and a group of wealthy women. The following year the first such school of major importance was opened in Kiev. Nikolai Pirogov, whose article 'Questions of Life' had demanded that women 'be challenged academically' had, as Curator of Education in Kiev, gathered around him a large number of women anxious to become 'citizens of their country'. They taught in the school that he and the progressive historian Professor Pavlov opened, rather than in a second, more radical, school opened a little later by students who hoped to impart to the workers some of the turbulent idealism of the Kiev student movement. This school established links with students in other cities, and soon there were six similar schools in Odessa and eight in Mogilev.

In April 1859 the first Sunday school was opened in the capital. Natalya Shpilevskaya was a governess who also gave free lessons to less wealthy girls. At the age of twenty-five she was already well known as a translator and critic of Swedish literature. She decided to open up her house on Sundays, and to give free classes in arithmetic, reading, writing and needlework. She was unattached to any group, and decided to take on all the teaching herself. Twenty-nine girls were soon coming regularly to her classes, and she was a devoted and adored teacher. As in all the Sunday schools, there was

89

no need for any coercion or incentives. The pupils, young and old, avidly hung on their teacher's every word and stayed long after classes were over to discuss the moral and religious fables they were now learning to interpret for themselves. She became a welcome visitor to her pupils' homes, where she brought books and journals for families to read and discuss among themselves. Groups of women in Tiflis and Chernigov were soon prompted to ask her advice on the establishment of similar schools there.

By 1860 there were already 2,500 people teaching in the Sunday schools, and it was now the social and political implications of the reading matter that teachers were discussing with their pupils. Meanwhile the government was having grave doubts about a project they had initially welcomed as a useful conduit for potentially more radical activity. Even the moderate Pirogov was branded as a 'radical' and had to resign as Kiev Curator of Education. Professor Pavlov, sacked from Kiev University for his 'subversive views', left for the capital where he was to play a leading part in what was becoming known as the Sunday School Movement. Already, one year after the opening of Natalya Shpilevskaya's school, there were twenty-six schools in the capital of which six were for women. The largest was that run by Antonina Blyummer and Natalya Korsini. It was attended chiefly by women from the Neva cotton-spinning mills and various *artel*s, and had a large library of some four thousand books. Antonina Blyummer was now working closely with Sleptsov, who a year after the collapse of his commune had organized the Samsonevskaya School for men at the Alexandrovsk factory. Together with Sërno-Solovevich, who had opened up his vast library in Tsarsko-Selsky Prospect to workers eager to read after work and women who had no opportunity to read at home, they were trying to organize radical teachers into some sort of collective. Soon weekly meetings were being held, and were reported in the collective's new journal, *Vestnik Voskresnykh*

Shkol ('Sunday School Herald'), which was edited by Antonina Blyummer. Under its new organizer, Professor Pavlov, the collective expanded and was renamed the Council for Sunday Schools. Formally, in the schools, and informally, in pupils' homes, political ideas were gradually being made accessible to men and women workers. Ideological differences with the feminist 'old guard' did not deter Pavlov from approaching Nadezhda Stasova; someone with her moral authority and social standing, he argued, was positively obligated to open a Sunday school. Nadezhda Stasova immediately applied to the Ministry of Education for a room, and before long she was holding classes for fifteen women between the ages of twelve and thirty. Antonina Blyummer taught there briefly, along with five other women, but she rapidly lost patience with Nadezhda Stasova's genteel feminist idealism. This idealism was seriously undermined when she actually began to visit the girls, mostly from small craftsmen's families, in their homes. For the first time in her life Stasova was exposed to all the horrors of working-class family life in the capital. However, the old confidence remained unshakeable; visiting one little girl suffering from tuberculosis and abandoned by her parents to a paupers' hospital, she wrote a long letter to the Tsarina begging her as a wife and mother to improve the standards in Russian hospitals. When the benevolent Empress ordained that another hospital be built, Nadezhda wrote in her diary 'Hurrah! This shows the significance of the Sunday schools, and our intimacy with different sections of the population!'

Actually, of course, it showed rather the government's policy of encouraging the Sunday School Movement — as long as it was represented by people like Nadezhda Stasova. Already by the end of 1860, intense police vigilance on most Sunday schools was beginning to make revolutionaries out of people who had merely made disrespectful references to the Tsar or indulged in armchair socialist speculations. Factory-owners already had reason to fear the consequences of an educated proletariat. By 1861 the Minister of the Interior, Valuev, reported that Sunday schools were 'spreading liberal ideas among simple people, people more than any other inclined to revolution because of their discontent with their situation.' A year later the manager of a large textile factory informed Valuev that a couple of workers from Sleptsov's school were propagating 'evil ideas' among their fellow-workers. The whole thing was becoming a source of both embarrassment and alarm to the government, and Prince Dolgorukov, head of the St Petersburg police, could not have put it better with his humiliating confession that 'the government cannot tolerate a situation whereby half the population owes its education not to the State but to itself, or to private benefactors of some particular class'.[15] He did not in fact have in mind the female half of the population, which did indeed owe its education now largely to such 'unofficial' sources.

In 1862 the Sunday School Movement was one victim of a series of repressive measures ostensibly justified by a wave of fires in the capital which was probably instigated by the police. The more radical teachers were arrested and the schools closed down 'pending their reorganization on a new basis'. Antonina Blyummer, who had met Herzen briefly abroad the previous summer, had returned as a confirmed 'subversive'. She, along with prominent teachers like Zavadsky and Merkulov, were imprisoned for 'distributing proclamations and propaganda in the Sunday schools'. The charge was misleading; they were in fact being arrested for the political nature of the discussions with their pupils. If the Sunday schools were to be 'reorganized on a new basis', it was presumably on the gently Utopian basis of most of the women's Sunday schools. For few of these were closed down; Natalya Shpilevskaya's school was allowed to continue, and in 1862 in Khar'kov a women's Sunday school was opened that continued until the end of the century with the blessing of the government. These schools could at least divert attention from the pressing demands on the government for improved women's education.

The Khar'kov school, with its genuinely collective spirit, was a model for many collective enterprises of the 1860s that were foundering in poverty and dissension. Kristina Al'chevskaya had been discussing the ideas of Fourier and Mill on popular education with a group of women friends. The circle widened to eighty women – governesses, wealthy married women and young girls fresh from school – all eager to open a school for peasant women and factory workers and their daughters. Kristina Al'chevskaya opened up her house, and small informal classes were started for about 250 women. Yuri Abranov, who visited the school, found small groups of people discussing and arguing heatedly. 'The teachers put so much soul into all they did, they were simply exulting in being surrounded by children, girls and women who were looking at them with such affectionate eyes. And what a look of tenderness they cast at their audience!'[16] The teachers, these 'sacred beings', were perhaps not quite so despotically maternal. They were concerned above all to make accessible to their pupils works of great literature rather than the cheap morality tales recounted without inspiration that were traditionally doled out to the peasants. They wanted to encourage pupils to read for themselves, rather than rely entirely on their teachers' interpretation. Some of the teachers described the encouraging results of this experiment in an article that came out in 1887, 'Dramatic Works as they are understood by the People'[17]. Pupils were presented with a couple of 'popular' reworked versions of *King Lear,* in which the original characters were replaced by peasants and a king dredged from Russian folk mythology. It was only Shakespeare's original, however, that could inspire the class to tears and furious arguments about the moral issues of the work. *Othello* was also very popular, as was *Uncle Tom's Cabin.* although few of the pupils were able to

93

discuss the related issues of slavery and serfdom. Tolstoy's popular works were much read, and the school followed closely the progress of his peasant school at Yasnaya Polyana, which inspired them to set up a student council in which matters of school policy could be discussed. A communal teashop was established, and men and women workers were encouraged to stop by after work to read newspapers in a comfortable well-decorated room and to be served tea by children in Little Russian national costume. For many enlightened educationists the school was an inspiration; for the government it posed no obvious political threat.

There were few women who had entered the Sunday School Movement with any very definite political goals, and those who did soon moved into more direct propaganda work. Teachers like Nadezhda Stasova were now determined to make women's educational reforms their first priority. But it was to be a deferred priority. Since the education received in the girls' *gimnazia* did not qualify them to compete academically with men, any demands for women's admission into the universities were obviously premature. There should be advanced women's courses to prepare women for the university, so that they would no longer have to rely on the whole paraphernalia of fictitious marriages and part-time tuition from men friends. In 1862, after the banning of women as 'outsiders' from the universities and the closure of the Sunday schools, the question of women's education was on everybody's lips. 'Everything we had done so far was merely preparatory for the advanced women's courses', wrote Nadezhda Stasova later in her diary.

Since there seemed little hope at present of achieving any reforms through increasingly reactionary government channels, Nadezhda Stasova returned to devote all her energies to the Society for Cheap Accommodation. Most of the women who had moved into the house were unable to pay the small rent that was asked, and few of them were able to find work. The whole venture was in danger of collapsing and the answer seemed to be some kind of women's employment agency in the house. It was the young Petr Lavrov, then teaching at the Military Academy and a valuable supporter of the Society, who proposed establishing the Society for Women's Labour. He read, to a large and lively meeting of women, a paper that described the life of the underpaid female proletariat, the increase in prostitution and the collapse of family life in the cities and the countryside. This paper brought to a head the simmering conflict between the 'nihilists' and the 'aristocrats'. For the younger more radical girls, women like Anna Filosofova who could afford to be generous with her fortunes, were all too reminiscent of the philanthropists of Nicholas I's Society for Housing the Poor, which enabled noblemen to make public repentance with sentimental utterances about the fate of their serfs. Nadezhda Stasova recalls two 'nihilists' at the meeting:

> ... one with a yellow scarf on her head, the other in a pink dress covered in large inkstains. Then Anna Filosofova came in, in her formal velvet dress. 'We're not going to get anything done with these people dressed up like dolls,' said the girl in the pink dress, jumping on to her chair so that everybody could see her. 'My dears,' Anna Filosofova turned to them gently and calmly, 'you know quite well that dress does not make a person.' These mild words disarmed her opponent, and the discussion continued.

Of course in the 1860s as now, dress very much did make a person, and 'nihilist' dishevelment was as contrived as 'aristocratic' elegance. 'Mild words' were more likely to infuriate than disarm. Marya Trubnikova was more sympathetic to the 'nihilists' — she had after all been described by her husband as one often enough. She always encouraged her four young daughters to dress simply, work hard and be self-sufficient. 'We have to wear our velvet gowns and our chignons because we are dealing with fools for whom dress

95

represents political "reliability",' she told the younger girls. 'But girls like you can be free in your inclinations and tastes.' She went on to speak in support of Lavrov, describing the tragic waste of women's minds and the increase in immoral earnings. The militant 'nihilists' were in a majority, however, and decided then and there to break off all contact with the Society. The Society for Women's Labour came to nothing, and Marya Trubnikova had to content herself instead with organizing a sewing collective in the house. After one year the collective had made the house self-sufficient, and three years later it was making a profit of ten thousand rubles.

Lavrov's paper had forced the Triumvirate to think more seriously about the underprivileged women in the capital, and Nadezhda Stasova decided to contact a member of the Society called Marya Alekseeva. She had been a nurse at Sevastopol' was now working at the Kalinskaya Hospital for Prostitutes. Overcoming her distaste for these 'repentant Magdalens', as she describes them, Nadezhda started to visit the hospital regularly. Prostitutes who came in for medical attention were persuaded to stay and talk to the nurses, and reading and sewing classes soon transformed the hospital into a cheerful social centre.

Nadezhda Stasova is rather reticent about her ventures into the gutters of St Petersburg, admitting that Dostoyevsky describes his Sonya better than she could ever describe these women. But the experience certainly helped to turn her attention to women workers in the city. Thousands of women were struggling to support themselves as writers and translators, and many more could easily be trained as typesetters and binders. The Sunday School Movement had exposed the terrible inadequacy of children's books; and since most members of the Society knew several foreign languages it was decided to form a collective in order to translate works for use in schools. In 1864 the first meeting of the Society of Women Translators was held at the house of Anna and Alexander Engelhardt.

Anna was born in 1838, the daughter of the famous guitarist Makarov. She had been educated at a Moscow institute and had read widely – Herzen, Dobrolyubov, Chernyshevsky, Dostoyevsky and Turgenev. Engelhardt had been a simple artillery officer when she met him, but he was a brilliant and energetic man and by the mid-1860s was professor of chemistry at St Petersburg University. They were both active in radical circles, and Anna had taken over Serno-Solovevich's bookstore and library after his arrest the previous year. She herself had been arrested shortly afterwards for 'distributing forbidden books'. After her release she started to contribute articles to the radical journals and translated, among other things, Audubon's *Wild Birds of America* and Shtein's work on bees.

The first meeting was a stormy one. Heideburger, editor of the liberal journal *Nedelya* ('The Week'), read a paper on women's emancipation without once mentioning women in the workforce. Marya Trubnikova and several others countered this by insisting on the need for a society to campaign for improved work conditions and pay for women. It was decided to set up a collective and book store for women binders, printers, translators and writers, with the clearly expressed aims of '1) producing useful literature for the younger generation, 2) providing work and moral support for women writers, and 3) satisfying their demands for higher wages.'

One of the women attending this meeting was Evgenia Konradi. She was one of the more brilliant women moving in these liberal progressive circles, but like many 'superfluous women' of her time her literary brilliance was sadly wasted. A friend once said of her. 'Her best articles weren't her written articles. Every time, she used to say "I'll write that, I'll write that!" But she never did, she spoke instead.' She did write though, and was a regular contributor to various journals.

She was born in Tula in 1838, the daughter of a

moderately wealthy landowner named Bochechkarov whose dissipated fortunes dwindled to almost nothing after the Emancipation. She was educated at home on the cheap, and at the age of fourteen the process was considered complete. She spent the next four years 'lazing around' as she put it; 'the ballast I carried from my domestic education was almost totally wasted. I could chatter away in three languages, but like all young ladies educated as I was, this apparent polyglotism concealed a basic lack of vocabulary. At the age of eighteen I was still writing ungrammatical Russian.' She awaited eagerly the emancipation of the serfs, which, as she knew, would spell the bankruptcy of her family and so provide her with the necessary incentive to establish her independence. 'The only acceptable alternative for young ladies of "our time", a suitable marriage, was simply unthinkable. There was nothing heroic or dramatic in this choice. It was all very simple.'

At the age of twenty she left for the capital, where she introduced herself into progressive Slavophil circles and got a job as a teacher at the Petrovsky Institute for Girls. Her appearance and her fluent and imaginative teaching caused an immediate sensation. 'We were struck by her beauty and youth,' wrote a former pupil. 'Some of the bolder students asked questions, for the others her teaching was like a bolt of lightning ... The past seemed cloudy, the future vague and exciting. She took us into a whole new realm of ideas ...' She talked to them of Herzen, of Garibaldi, of the Emancipation movement, she read them the latest copies of *Sovremennik* – and thus she initiated her pupils into the exciting realm of 'forbidden ideas'. It came as no surprise to them a year later when she was dismissed for alleged 'anti-religious views'. She moved to Yaroslavl', where she got a job as a governess and married the progressive journalist Dr Konradi. In 1863 they moved back to the capital, where Evgenia had dreams of establishing a shoemakers' collective. She ends a letter to a friend on the subject; 'Destroy this letter. What! a shoemakers' collective! Is this some kind of anti-government plot? God, what stupid times we live in — you're scared just to look over your own shoulder . . . ' The sharpness of her tone angered some and attracted others. She clung tenaciously to her independence, and although she supported the new collective she was determined to make her own way in the male publishing world. Besides, the new Society for Women Translators was concerned less with people like Evgenia Konradi than with women who had not yet achieved any professional success.

The collective itself was to be restricted to a hundred women who were all expected to make contributions in money or work. It was not long before the collective was inundated with articles and translations, far exceeding the resources available for publishing them. It was decided to select works on the basis of a ballot, organized by Nadezhda Stasova and Marya Trubnikova; preference was to be given to poor or inexperienced writers. There were also hundreds of women who had to be refused work as typesetters and binders. Many had been forced to abandon jobs in the publishing industry, in which their pay was less than half of the men's, and where they had to suffer lewd comments from male colleagues and editors who often deliberately jumbled their type. With the introduction of the telegraph into Russia women were now being accepted as telegraphists, for which they were scandalously underpaid and expected to work a quite disproportionate number of nights. Many of these women contacted the Society for jobs. The Society was clearly a drop in this ocean of women's unemployment and exploitation. The works produced, although undoubtedly 'useful for the younger generation', caused no great stir in the literary world.

The first books appeared in 1866: Hans Andersen's *Fairy Tales* and Betts' *A Naturalist on the Amazon River*. The *Fairy Tales* were well translated but marred by some quite inexplicable deletions by the censor — 'The Snow Queen' could apparently be construed as 'casting an unfavourable light on the Tsar'. Betts' work followed through many of the theories of Darwin and anticipated some of Wells'. *Origin of Species* had appeared in Russia the previous year and had caused a great stir. Tiresome and demoralizing confrontations with the censor were an occupational inevitability for any editor, and women writers realized that the chaotic and arbitrary Russian censorship apparatus could operate especially harshly on women; this was of course one of the reasons why so many women wrote under assumed names. The next book produced was a translation of Hermann Wagner's *Blick in die Natur,* which was less well received.

In 1868, the firm of Trubnikova, Stasova and Co. was formed, and translations of scientific and historical works continued to be produced. Marya Trubnikova's relationship with her husband was meanwhile steadily deteriorating. She had borne him seven children of whom only four, all girls, had survived. In 1869 she decided to leave him for good and go abroad, and in the same year Nadezhda Stasova was summoned abroad to nurse a sick relative. With the departure of its two leading members the collective virtually collapsed, and although still flooded with works by women writers from all over Russia, it could not produce them fast enough to make the venture financially viable. The last works produced were Louisa M. Alcott's *An Old Fashioned Girl* and *Little Women:* it is sad that these last works should have embodied such insidiously patriarchal values.

Meanwhile, the Society was attracting the attention of feminists abroad, and Jenny d'Héricourt, who had just launched into a vituperative polemic with Proudhon in her article 'La Femme Affranchie', wrote a letter to Marya Trubnikova saying 'If my aspirations have any influence on your decisions, I'd say to you: organize the emancipation movement, form committees, surround yourself with women, establish a great model institution, bring out a journal, but don't meddle in general politics. Let the exclusively male regime perish on its own. It is so powerful in Russia that once you start attacking it, it will crush you.' However Marya Trubnikova and her friends were not prepared to be crushed by the exclusively male regime. Now all their energy was to be directed at the campaign for advanced women's education, education that would give political meaning to their feminist activities. 'The rights they were fighting for,' said Kropotkin, 'the leaders as well as the masses of the women, were not the rights to higher education in itself, but much more than that: the right to be useful activists among the masses. That was the cause of their success.' [18].

It was in 1867 that Evgenia Konradi went quite independently to the First Congress of the Natural History Faculty at St Petersburg University and read her petition pressing the urgent need for advanced women's education. By now she had established her reputation as a writer with her translation of *Adam Bede* and as a journalist she was known chiefly for her long article in *Russkoe Slovo* ('Russian Word'), 'Slavery in America'. She was also writing regularly for the liberal journal *Zhensky Vestnik* ('Women's Herald'), and in a series of articles 'On Life Abroad' she had discussed women's position in Germany, the American Women's Rights Society, the Women's University in London, [19] and the Society of Women Garibaldists. In a long and searching article on George Sand's *Last Love,* she had asked whether a woman who is not prepared to 'sacrifice herself at the altar of Hymen' is permanently rejecting all family life and condemning herself to a 'grey eternal solitude'. 'You won't find many women eager for such solitude,' she concludes, 'because, say what you will, this would amount to a total atrophy of the personality.'

Evgenia Konradi was known to the faculty she was addressing not merely as a writer or the friend of Pëtr Lavrov, Nikolai Kurochkin, the caustic radical satirist, and Gleb Uspensky, the populist writer; she was also known as the wife of a university professor, and it was as a wife and mother rather than as an independent women writer that she decided to address the Congress. 'If this congress is to further the interests of all sections of society, and of science itself, it is to be hoped that it will not ignore the voice of that section of Russian society which has until now been ignored – the mothers and educators of the future generation, who at the moment are incapable of developing their children's talents.' Although she was warmly applauded, neither the Congress nor the Science Faculty of the University had the executive power to enact her proposals. Many of her more conservative friends felt that her petition was excessively categorical, while many others were saddened by her emphasis on women's wifely role. She was neither a radical nor a liberal, a true 'superfluous woman' in the feminist movement. Later with the support of her friends Kurochkin and Uspensky she became editor of the ailing liberal journal *Nedelya* ('The Week'). In general the journal spoke in politically bland tones, announcing 'We are determined to make our paper a direct reflection of society itself and its most active members. We reject both empty phrases and tendentious outbursts' (which two phrases, in the semi-'Aesopian' vocabulary of nineteenth-century Russian journalism, commonly described 'official' liberalism and revolutionary rhetoric). On the issue of women's emancipation, however, *Nedelya* spoke with the voice of its editor. Despite our families we are alone, it said; we are ignorant, all of us. Konradi's feminism exasperated many of her colleagues, and 'people who knew me as well as my janitor began spreading anecdotes about me in public'. Her difficulties on *Nedelya* and her growing alienation from the feminist movement finally forced her abroad, where she lived in poverty and isolation, supporting herself by giving lessons and writing occasional articles.

Nevertheless, she had, in 1867, opened a crack in the doors of the University, and the Triumvirate was soon besieged by women asking to subscribe to the petition. In May 1868 the petition, reworded with the help of Nadezhda

Stasova and Marya Trubnikova to include specific demands for advanced women's courses, was sent to the University. The was no mention of motherhood; women's education was not a matter simply of educating the future generation. 'We demand it for ourselves, whatever our age, whether married or not. We ask for permission for lectures within the walls of the universities, in hours free from teaching. The fees and expenses we will take on ourselves' it said. At the bottom were the signatures of four hundred women, who all agreed to be self-financing. Similar petitions were presented to the other universities. In Smolensk, Anna Shabanova had organized a women's collective on her estate, and she was able to collect sixty-eight signatures for a petition that was sent to St Petersburg University.

The Triumvirate was now deluged with letters from women all over Russia asking how long they would have to wait before being accepted at the universities. Many of the letters were semi-literate, and the question was generally posed in just these naïvely optimistic tones. Nadezhda Stasova had had no idea that so many working-class women would be drawn into the campaign. At last a university commission was appointed in the capital to consider the question, and the Minister of Education, Tolstoy himself, agreed to give an audience to Nadezhda Stasova and Anna Filosofova. The Russian women's movement was now attracting the attention of writers and politicians abroad, and on 18 December 1868 the *Dames organisatrices de l'enseignement supérieur à S. Petersbourg'* received a letter from J. S. Mill, who applauded 'these enlightened and courageous women'.

Count Tolstoy was minister of something he clearly did not believe in. 'The less people know, the more easily they are governed,' he once said. He was also a reactionary misogynist. As Procurator of the Holy Synod he had relentlessly persecuted Roman Catholics, and for all national minorities – Jews, students and women – he showed a genteel distaste. Classical languages had been his remedy for the

103

student disorders of a few years ago: 'Another six years of Latin and you'll see how young people will calm down' he had said in 1859. The two women who went to talk to him in September 1868 had little hope of any direct answer from him. 'So at last you've come!' he addressed then gallantly. 'I've been hearing from all sides about the opening of women's institutions. Even the Tsar has said: "So you're going to open women's universities are you?" But *I* don't know what's happening. What can I do for you?' When shown an augmented list of five hundred signatures to the petition, he laughed: 'But they're all sheep! You've raised all this hue and cry, and they would have followed you whatever it had been about. It's just a novelty, that's all.' The offensively meaningless banter, the offensively meaningful glances at Anna Filosofova were only too depressingly predictable, and the women left demoralized. Anna Filosofova began to seek out Tolstoy's company at select social gatherings. In her prolonged flirtation with the repulsive Minister of Education quite a few feminist principles were sacrificed. They would engage in playful private arguments about women's education, and the whole thing was turned into a rather perverse waiting game between them – a game that was to last two years. In these two years women were granted a succession of compromises and concessions.

Meanwhile a group of about fifty women were meeting regularly at Nadezhda Stasova's house to listen to informal lectures from various liberal professors, including the eminent physicist Usov, who offered to lecture regularly in algebra and geometry. Women all over the city began to invite professors and school teachers to lecture and discuss with them. Concerts and dances were organized to raise money for advanced women's courses, and touring foreign acting companies found a new cause for which they could give unpaid performances. Even the great Princess Elena Pavlovna once sent a lady-in-waiting to Nadezhda Stasova's house saying: *'Tous les rayons de ma bibliothèque sont à votre disposition.'*

But it was university professors, not great princesses, whose advice and support was needed now, and the eminent liberal professors Beketov, Mendeleev, Petrushevich, Gradovsky, Sechenov and Borodin were invited to discuss the whole issue with a large group of women. 'What we want,' said Marya Trubnikova, 'is to fill in the gaps. We're inexperienced. We turn to you.' Mendeleev the renowned chemist immediately raised the crucial problem of finance. The women had no capital, only enough to cover their fees, which they suggested should be fifty rubles a year. Mendeleev retorted that the venture would cost millions, but he eventually agreed that the professors would teach the first year unpaid. Convinced now that they would be donating their knowledge to a worthy cause, they thanked the women for asking them to join this 'great enterprise'. The results of the meeting were communicated to the university ´rector Kessler, who was generally sympathetic to the idea.

Any optimism was quickly dampened by Tolstoy's first response to the petition, which came in December. He made it clear from the start that the decision rested not with him, but with the St Petersburg Supervisor of Education.

Without going into the actual need to admit women to higher education, there can be no question of a women's university. They would not pass the examinations. There can only be preparatory courses. Any concession to women on this point would amount to lowering the standards of university lectures to mere public readings. And if women think that these lectures can be within the university itself, there is certainly no room for them there. So the chief goal must be not to open the universities to them, but to set up establishments in which they can be educated – something that is especially necessary if

105

women are to be true mothers and useful members of their families.

The tone of the response was as offensive as its specific proposal – public lectures for men and women. The women were furious at Tolstoy's mutilated version of their original petition, but Kessler immediately urged them to take whatever they could get. He was supported by the Minister of War, Milyutin, whose wife and daughter had shamed him into putting a word in Tolstoy's ear. Nadezhda Stasova called a large meeting of women whom she begged to take this chance, as there would not be another, and there was always hope for some improvement. But many women, including Evgenia Konradi, left the group in disgust. The 'restless element', as Nadezhda Stasova described them, were gradually drifting away from compromises and aristocratic pressure-group politics, sickened that their future could be settled by women like Anna Filosofova and the Milyutins, who exploited aristocratic charms to dictate official attitudes to women.

Anna Solodovnikova and a group of her 'nihilist' friends had been working with the Triumvirate for some time, but as an uncompromising radical she had little time for official reforms. She had audited at university lectures in 1859 and had been arrested, falsely as it turned out, in the demonstrations a couple of years later. She and her friends had been busy raising money for a girls' school on the lines of a boys' *gimnazium*. Several radical young teachers volunteered to teach there for nothing, and in April 1869 girls' courses were opened in the Fifth Boys' Gimnazium on the Arlachinsky Bridge. This bold venture attracted a lot of girls who were tired of regarding themselves as victims of official charity. About three hundred girls attended the 'Arlachinsky courses', which soon got quite a reputation for revolutionary politics. Women like Nadezhda Stasova complained that the courses would compromise academic standards for women, and even Marya Trubnikova lamented Anna Solodovnikova's 'petty vanity'.

Compared with the Arlachinsky courses, the public lectures were a truly squalid business. They were blatantly done on the cheap, and at first no faculty would agree to give them space. Eventually, after confronting innumerable bureaucratic obstacles, Milyutin found them a place at the Medical Faculty. The professors at least were academically respectable; Bestuzhev was to teach history, literature would be taught by Miller, anatomy by Ovsyannikov, botany by Beketov, chemistry by Mendeleev and physics by Petrushevich. Lectures were to be given four times a week. About four hundred people attended the first lecture, among them a small number of men, a disreputable crowd of police spies and men who had come to pick up an 'emancipated' woman. They sat apart, and the professors tried to ignore them as best they could. The accommodation was cramped, the atmosphere strained. For Tolstoy, however, who attended the first lecture, the arrangement apparently left nothing to be desired; *'ce que femme veut, Dieu le veut,'* he was heard to sigh with fatuous complacency. His wife and daughter were instructed to attend regularly and report back to him on the 'moral conduct' of the women. Meanwhile the number of students increased, and early in 1870 the courses were moved to the Vladimirsky High School. More professors volunteered to teach and Tolstoy was eventually forced to donate 1,400 rubles of public money for restoration of the building. This meant that fees had to go up from five to six rubles, an apparently small increase which nevertheless deterred many women from enrolling. Evgenia Konradi finally withdrew all support from the lectures.

The atmosphere at the Vladiminsky courses was one of growing excitement. Even though the courses represented an obviously mangled version of the original demands, for the first time women from widely differing backgrounds and with very different expectations were meeting and talking to each other. Nevertheless while men students, assured of their position in the universities, were united by the intellectual problems raised by their work, women, exposed for the first time to any systematic teaching, expended their energy in being punctual, keeping up and taking notes. Women who had so confidently demanded their educational rights now found that they could not so confidently demand the form these courses should take, and although the Vladimirsky courses, like the Arlachinsky courses, were supposedly run by pupils and teachers in collaboration, the professors found few points of contact with their large and diverse audience. For this reason the courses never had any of the systematic character of the men's university courses, and lectures usually consisted in little more than the reading of addresses given at the boys' *gimnazia* or universities. For the women students whose emotional welfare was so closely tied in with the attitude of their professors, this was just one more irksome and demoralizing reminder of their intellectual inadequacy. They began to find more pleasure in each others' company, and the courses gave some structure to the discussion groups and self-education circles that sprang up outside the lecture hall.

In traditional Moscow there was no group of socially influential women to fight for similar educational reforms. The university there was still adamantly hostile to the idea, and the police kept a vigilant eye open for any signs of creeping nihilism. In 1872 the well-known mathematician Professor Guerrier managed to start a series of lectures for women that were academically far superior to those in the capital. They were thwarted from the start by lack of funds and support, and there were only seventy women who could afford the high fees. After three years attendance had dwindled to almost nothing and the courses were closed. Women still preferred to go to the capital, and the continuing influx of women there was now a source of serious alarm to the government. Attendance at the Vladimirsky courses was

108

dwindling too. The conspicuous presence of police spies and the depressing lack of communication between teachers and pupils forced many girls to abandon the course altogether and to study in the more congenial atmosphere of student discussion groups. By 1873 the number of girls leaving for the radical circles had so alarmed the government that the courses were placed under the special supervision of the Third Department, but by then hundreds of girls had left Russia to study at foreign universities. Nadezhda Stasova could only deplore the effect this was having on family and national interests; she believed, firmly and indomitably, that a new era had opened up for women in Russia, and she saw this desire to study abroad as a lamentable but temporary phenomenon, a mere 'rush for immediate advancement'. In fact, these girls were to set an inspiring example to their sisters in Russia, as we shall see in the next chapter.

Most of the girls who left Russia were determined to study medicine, since the pursuits officially recognized as suitable for women certainly did not include any practical or specialized training. There were a few midwives' schools in the capital, established long ago by Marya Fëdorovna, but it was only in 1872 that medical education was brought into line with the general advances in women's education. Experiences in the Crimean War had taught the government that girls could now be trained as nurses for war, and it was the War Ministry that provided a generous annual grant of fifteen thousand rubles for a midwives' course, opened in the Medical–Surgical Faculty in 1872. Women students were allowed to practise in the military hospital – which is to say they were used as unpaid nurses to supplement inadequate nursing amenities. Meanwhile two women – Nadezhda Suslova and Varvara Rudneva – were fighting independently to qualify as doctors. Nadezhda Suslova had audited at St Petersburg medical courses in 1862, but despairing of qualifying in Russia had left to study abroad. Varvara Rudneva managed to fight her way through a series of prejudices and bureaucratic obstacles to study at Orenburg Medical Institute, where a full thirteen years later she was eventually allowed to qualify as a doctor. From 1876 to her death she devoted herself to working among Muslim women bashkirs.

The professional success of these women was an inspiration for aspiring women students and a lesson to the government, which at last recognized the need for women doctors, especially in the Muslim areas. One student at the first St Petersburg medical courses who was interested in becoming a doctor rather than a nurse or a midwife was Lydia Rodstvennaya. She had set up a small laboratory in her home where her friends would meet and conduct experiments. After attending the courses for a year she decided to donate her entire inheritance of fifty thousand rubles to the government for the establishment of women's medical courses. This was an offer the government could hardly refuse and medical courses were set up almost immediately, roughly on the same lines as those for men. But the girls, lacking any systematic medical training, found little support from the teachers, who did little to help them catch up. Accommodation was cramped, the course oversubscribed, and applicants far exceeded the number of places. Most girls were discouraged from continuing under these conditions and in the years 1878-9, of 959 women enrolled only sixty qualified as doctors. Girls who had stayed in Russia to qualify sought instead a more immediate outlet for their knowledge, and at the outbreak of the Russo-Turkish War in 1877, thirty women volunteered as nurses. Many of these girls who had volunteered in a charitable spirit became ardent supporters of the Serbians against Russian and Turkish domination, and returned to Russia after this baptism of fire with a new revolutionary consciousness. Anna Korba was one woman who in her two years as a medical student in St Petersburg quickly became dissatisfied with the courses and left for Rumania, where she worked as an agitator on the front line. She returned to Russia a committed revolutionary. I shall return to her later.

Meanwhile the Vladimirsky courses continued as erratically as before. In 1874 they were moved again, to the Ostrovsky Gimnazium. By now the government was seriously embarrassed by a venture that owed its existence entirely to private women's pressure groups and was still without official financial backing. While the issue came under government scrutiny the courses were forbidden to appeal for funds, and in 1876 the Ministry of Education issued a decree announcing the establishment of advanced women's courses in the major cities, comparable to the men's university courses. The Vladimirsky courses were to be granted an annual subsidy of a thousand rubles while these new courses were being set up. Thus finally, a full eleven years after the original petition had been presented to the St Petersburg Natural History Faculty, the first Advanced Women's Courses were opened in the capital. They received the approval of the Ministry of Education in the form of an annual three-thousand-ruble grant, and the women were expected to pay their own fees, which were high – fifty rubles. Presiding over the courses was a pedagogical council, with Nadezhda Stasova as chairwoman and the eminent historian Bestuzhev-Ryumin as director. With the support of the Ministry, Anna Filosofova organized a society to collect money to subsidize the poorer students. There were to be three departments: literature and history, physics and maths, and pure maths.

In September 1876 the courses were officially opened in the house of a wealthy well-wisher named Elisaveta Botkina. Nadezhda Stasova sat at the door and registered the women, eight hundred of them, as they came in. The first lectures caused a furore in the reactionary press. At the very first one a girl was said to have stood on a chair and 'expounded socialist principles', and the floor was strewn with the students' cigarette-ends and cucumbers. Nadezhda Stasova's

111

only complaint, however, was the headlong rush through the door and the squabbles over seats. She recalls only one girl smoking and she stopped immediately on being asked.

One lecture in particular caught the attention of conservative St Petersburg. The students were said to have behaved disgracefully, attacking and shouting at the lecturer. In fact, the lecturer had seen fit for some reason to launch into a thunderous tirade against women; the lecture, entitled 'Journalistic Knowledge', detailed rather more than the pernicious effects of radical journalism on women. Journalism, he announced, was responsible for turning playfulness into depravity, enthusiasm into caprice: 'Just look at her!' he shouted, pointing at his audience,

> ... with her man's coat and hat, her dirty skirt, her torn dress, her sallow skin, her aggressive jaw, her lacklustre eyes. Listless, tired, spiteful, contemptuous – a real daughter of Cain. Now she is alone, with the cold of the graveyard on her heart, oppressed by malice and melancholy. There is nobody to mourn or pray for her – everybody has abandoned her. The best she can hope is that when she dies of typhus or in childbirth, there will be no scandal at her funeral ... [20]

Words of encouragement indeed for women whose finances did not extend to new clothes and good food as well as the high fees; women who had been up all night reading or doing part-time jobs rather than flirting could surely be forgiven their lacklustre eyes. The lecture was interrupted by catcalls, and only by warning the women that the government could close the courses at any time was Nadezhda Stasova able to restore peace. A group of women known as the 'Jews from the Maths department' walked out. In a period of intense anti-semitism, the Jewish students obviously had most reason to take offence, but most girls' living conditions were truly abysmal. Generally they had to work as governesses or sempstresses in order to support their studies, and constant hard work took its toll in nervous breakdowns, exhaustion

112

and anaemia. They lived frequently three to one bed in damp squalid rooms, eating little more than black bread, beans and tea. Many women succumbed to typhus, bronchitis and malnutrition and had to abandon their studies, while many others, attempting to support not only themselves but their families in the provinces, had to drop study for full-time paid work.

This is what makes the articles in reactionary journals like *Grazhdanin* ('The Citizen') so particularly offensive. 'It is as if women had conspired to be not merely unattractive but repulsive,' thundered *Grazhdanin*.

All of them, in their faces and manners, betray their anxiety to show that they are not of the weaker sex, but have strong minds. And this is absolutely repellent. For immediately a girl becomes a *kursistka* and crops her hair she is consumed by the desire to show that she is not of the weaker sex but has a 'vocation', and this thought will allow of no other. She hates the men who teach her, but is not intelligent enough to criticize them, and so an intense irritation of the brain sets in. She can only put up a futile show of strength, and with no hope now of marrying or getting a job, she just shrivels up.

Any woman involved in the Advanced Courses was fair game for this kind of attack, and even Nadezhda Stasova became a victim of indiscriminate slander. Officially, too, she was now being described as 'dangerous' or at best 'muddled'. A few years later the Minister of the Interior was to regret that 'obviously these courses could not be taken seriously while their chief organizer is such a muddled individual as Nadezhda Stasova'.

The great strength of idealistic feminists like Nadezhda Stasova was in their abiding faith that all discrimination, national, cultural and sexual, would ultimately be eliminated by education, and that the attitudes against which they were battling were merely the result of male ignorance. However, the feminist triumvirate of the 1860s was now the *'salon*

113

libéral' of the 1870s, always ready to put a word in the ear of some government official. 'And yet,' said Kropotkin,

> ... the women who were the initiators of the movement never broke off contact with their younger sisters, even when these had advanced much further and begun to adopt extreme political attitudes. They pursued their goals in the higher social circles and stood apart from all political agitation, but they never forgot that the strength of their movement was in the mass of the younger women, most of them attached to the revolutionary circles. The pioneers of the women's movement were models of correct behaviour, and they forebore to break with the younger students with their typically 'nihilist' appearance, parading their democratic ways.[21]

By the 1870s the social pulse had quickened, and the breach between the 'philanthropists' and the 'nihilists' was irrevocable. But emancipated mothers were more tolerant of their extremist daughters than fathers and husbands had been a decade ago, and the integrity and solidarity of the pioneer feminists were an inspiration to the later revolutionary movement. Marya Trubnikova had often quoted the gospel to her four daughters: 'In any place and under any circumstances, you need only two or three people of good will to accomplish something useful.' All of her daughters emerged from their *gimnazium* committed revolutionaries, and she listened with both sympathy and alarm as they and their friends, the Figner sisters, propounded radical views that challenged so many of her Utopian assumptions. When two of them were arrested in 1881, however, she worked strenuously for their release, forced at last to recognize the futility of reformist pressure groups in an autocratic régime.

For 1881 was the year of Alexander II's assassination, and the reign that had seen such dramatic advances for women in Russian society had come to an end. The Advanced Women's Courses, along with hundreds of other institutions, were closed down as 'centres of revolutionary activity'. But most women activists had already abandoned their search for officially approved education; specific demands for women's education had called for a criticism of the entire state system, and eighteenth-century concepts of 'enlightenment' were now replaced by the concept of political education. For the girls who left Russia in the seventies to study abroad, education was to be specialized, utilitarian and political.

NOTES

1. A note here on 'illegal' status, and on passports in general. Passports, that is identity documents, were issued only very selectively. Anyone living without a passport outside his or her place of birth was automatically an 'illegal'. The emancipated serfs could not actually leave their villages without a passport issued at the discretion of the village authorities, a situation that was reformed properly only in 1906. The revolutionaries in the later years of the century who became 'illegals' adopted false or forged passports.
2. Kropotkin, P., *Zapiski revoliutsionera* (Notes of a Revolutionary), p.229.
3. ibid, p.231.
4. Shashkov, S. S., op. cit., p.238.
5. Marx, Karl, *Communist Manifesto,* London, 1945, p.77.
6. Statistics from Shashkov, op. cit., p.267.
7. I have taken most of my information about women's labour in the capital in this period from Karnovich's invaluable work (see Bibliography).
8. Stasov, V., *N. V. Stasova: vospominania i ocherki.* (N. V. Stasova: Memories and Essays), p.142.
9. pianism' describes the complex allegorical literary style that veiled political comment and criticism in this period of savage press censorship.
10. Vodovozova, E., 'V. A. Sleptsov' , *Golos Minuvshego* (Voice of the Past) (see Bibliography), no. 12, 1915, pp.107ff.
11. Stasov, op. cit., p.131.
12. Bulanova-Trubnikova's biography of her mother, *Tri pokolenia* (Three Generations).
13. Tyrkova, A. V., op. cit., p.114.
14. Lemke, M., *Ocherki osvoboditel 'nogo dvizhenia '60'ykh godov* (Essays on the Liberation Movement of the 1860s), p.284.
15. Venturi, op. cit. p.288.
16. Abramov, Yuri, *Sunday Schools in Russia,* p.31.
17. Abramov, Yuri, *What to Give the People to Read.*
18. Kropotkin, P., op. cit., p.236.
19. It is not known precisely which university she is referring to.
20. Stasov, op. cit. p.317.
21. Kropotkin, op. cit., pp.234-6.

CHAPTER IV
INTO EXILE

'What we want,' wrote Bakunin in 1868, in an article 'Science and the People', '... is what people of all times and countries have sought: truth, justice and freedom. There is only one way to attain truth – science; not a metaphysical science, but one based on experience. This science does not accept God – indeed, religion has to be driven out of practical life. The positivists have done the first, but not the second. To Hegel belongs the honour of having driven metaphysics to suicide, and it was Feuerbach who best understood this ... As partisans of the revolution we are enemies of religious priests but also the priests of science. To this end schools for the people are important but not sufficient, in view of the enormous extent of the problem and the resistance of the State ... [He concludes] The way to the liberation of the people through science is closed to us. There is only one way left open, the way of revolution. The people have first to be freed, then they will learn, and it is our task to prepare for the rising of the people ... We must make the people conscious of the strength that has lain dormant in them since Pugachev.'[1]

116

Despite its intentional vagueness, this article aroused much sympathy among Russian populists. Their experiences in the Sunday schools had shown them that education would always be regarded by the people as some sort of personal gift from the Tsar, and could never be the means of producing any real revolutionary consciousness. Substitute 'women' for 'people' and the article reflects women's growing despair of the chances of getting an education within the official school system. By the late 1860s they were deciding that even the limited education provided did not justify the initial sacrifices made in fighting for it. They began to look for alternatives abroad.

Bakunin, who wrote this article in Geneva and spent most of his life abroad, would have been politically suspect merely as an *emigré*, quite apart from his political activities. But the government had not always regarded its *emigré* students with such suspicion. Both Peter and Katherine had encouraged students to gain technical qualifications in foreign universities, and students had been sent abroad, particularly to Göttingen and Strasbourg universities in Germany, returning to enrich the Russian vocabulary with a mass of foreign neologisms. Foreign degrees were coveted as much as foreign clothes and furniture. After 1796 the tendency was discouraged and after 1848 Nicholas I ordered that the number of students registered at each foreign faculty (excluding the medical faculties) should be restricted to three hundred.

Zurich University had been founded in 1839, the Polytechnical Institute shortly afterwards, and the high academic standards and the liberal atmosphere there quickly attracted a large number of foreign students. Women were freely admitted into both the university and the polytechnic, and by the 1870s there was a large student colony composed largely of women and foreigners. By the late sixties a newly opened railway line had made Zurich one of the most accessible of the foreign universities.

117

Although the 'superfluous woman' was created by many of the social conditions that brought the 'superfluous man' [2] into being, women could at least avoid the crippling 're-pentant' stage. For they had little to repent of, relatively few privileges to reject and, with courage and firmness, much to gain. Sofya Kovalevskaya, Nadezhda Suslova and Marya Bokova were among the first women to develop their exceptional abilities abroad, and they inspired many girls kicking their heels in the provinces to follow their example. When in 1867, at the age of twenty-four, Nadezhda Suslova qualified as a doctor in Zurich, many girls' eyes were suddenly opened to the real possibilities of studying abroad.

Nadezhda's father was a house serf of Count Sheremetev and an exceptionally clever man. He had bought himself out of serfdom before the Emancipation and was soon put in charge of the whole of his master's enormous estate. His daughters Nadezhda and Apollinaria were encouraged to attend day school but had little chance to develop intellectually at home. In 1860 Suslov, who was by now flourishing as the owner of a factory in Ivanovo Voznesensk, near Moscow, gave his daughters permission to attend the public lectures in the capital. Here they quickly made friends with some of the more radical students, and Nadezhda was put under police vigilance for her participation in various student circles. After her return from Zurich some time later it was even stated by the Third Department that she had connections with the International. This was a somewhat wild charge, since neither the Marxist nor the Bakunist sections of the International managed to attract many Russian members until the 1870s, and Nadezhda's visit to Herzen in London in 1863 was scarcely more than a courtesy call. Besides she was above all anxious to continue her studies.

In 1861 she filed a petition for the right to enter the St Petersburg medical faculty. Thanks to testimonials from various eminent professors her petition was accepted, but the

118

faculty was not prepared to encourage women in *any* serious scientific studies, let alone to allow them to qualify as doctors. Nadezhda was an outstanding student, and when women were expelled from the medical faculty a couple of years later she was resolved to qualify elsewhere as a doctor. She had heard vaguely of a few colleges admitting women in England and America but knew nothing of their academic reputation. In Paris, apparently, certain faculties of the Sorbonne had been opened to women in 1863, but this was not generally known. It was in Zurich, therefore, that she chose to continue her studies. She left Russia in 1863 and spent the next three years in Zurich writing her thesis.[3] This almost broke her; she had no colleagues, few friends and was generally distrusted by the local students and citizens. Franz Erisman, one of the first Swiss students to advocate the admission of women, befriended and later married her, and if she lacked the friendship of her peers, she quickly gained respect and sympathy from her professors. After she had defended her thesis her professor, Rose, said to her:

> Although I regard you primarily as a friend, I must express to you my happiness that you have achieved your goal, my great respect for your energy, and my hopes for your future ... Slavery at the present has vanished from the face of practically the entire world. Let us hope that the end of women's enslavement is in sight, an enslavement that weighs particularly heavily on the educated classes, and so weighs heavily on all of us ...[4]

She and Erisman returned at once to St Petersburg, where she was welcomed enthusiastically by the university. But her return threw the government into a bureaucratic turmoil, and it was eventually decided that she should be barred from practising until she had taken the examinations required of a foreign doctor. Erisman established himself as an ophthalmologist but, horrified by conditions in Russia, was soon anxious to return to Zurich. They left for Zurich in 1872. Nadezhda returned soon afterwards to Russia and she

119

set up a large gynaecological practice in Nizhny Novgorod, where she worked until her death. Erisman stayed in Zurich, where he joined the International and later married another young Russian student – for after Nadezhda's success more girls decided to leave Russia for Zurich.

A year after Nadezhda had qualified, Marya Bokova, born Obrucheva, arrived in Zurich. She was twenty-nine years old, and a few years before had formed part of a *ménage* that probably served as the prototype for the one described in *What is to be Done?* – a *ménage* that had inevitably earned her much scandalized slander from the reactionary press. I have described in the previous chapter her fictitious marriage to Petr Bokov and her passionate and lifelong liaison with Mikhail Sechenov. If women's education was generally regarded as an unnecessary indulgence, medicine was positively a scandal, and Marya was lucky enough to have the support of two men deeply concerned with her academic success.

Marya qualified as a doctor in 1871 with a thesis[5] that attracted a favourable review in *S. Peterburgskie Vedomosti* ('St Petersburg Gazette'). She was eventually allowed by the government to practise, establishing herself as an optical surgeon in the capital and later moving with Sechenov to Kiev.

When Sofya Krukovskaya was sixteen she was taken to Stuttgart for her health. The year 1866 was the year of Karakozov's arrest[6] and the wave of arrests that followed. A friend who met her there described her as 'electrified by progressive ideas ... She was ready to endure the test of fire, die the death of a martyr for her lofty ideals for humanity.' A year later, back in the capital, it was already clear that she would realize some of these lofty ideals with her quite exceptional talent for mathematics, which she was studying privately with Professor Strannolyubsky. She recalls:

120

What a happy time that was! We were so enthusiastic about the new ideas, so sure that the present social state could not continue for long. We pictured to ourselves the glorious period of liberty and universal enlightenment of which we dreamt, and in which we firmly believed. Besides this we had the sense of true union and cooperation. When three or four of us met in a drawing room among older people where we had no right to advance our opinions, a tone, a glance, even a sigh was sufficient to show each other that we were one in thought and sympathy.[7]

Sofya and her elder sister Anna, who played her part in the events described later in the chapter, were born in a remote estate in Palibino, near Vitebsk, and both were profoundly impressed by this first contact with the intellectual circles of the capital. Their father, General Krukovsky, was a cultured and liberal man, a close friend of Nikolai Pirogov. But ideas about women's education seem to have made little impression on the General's mind.

People lived quietly and peacefully in Palibino [wrote Sofya]. They grew up, they grew old; they argued sometimes about some article in a journal, quite convinced that these questions belonged to another world, far apart from theirs, which would never have any contact with it. And then suddenly, wherever you looked, there appeared the signs of some strange madness, which unquestionably approached closer and closer and threatened to submerge this patriarchal way of life. In this period, from the sixties to the seventies, all intelligent sections of Russian society were concerned with one problem, the family antagonism between the young and the old.[8]

Krukovsky was interested in mathematics, and he could not have foreseen any dramatic consequences when he papered the walls of Sofya's nursery with mathematical calculations in order to save money. By the age of six Sofya was already inventing mathematical problems, and it was decided to hire a young tutor for her.

When the Krukovskys visited the capital in 1867 their daughters' obviously exceptional talents were cause for some anxiety. Anna was writing poetry and short stories, and her suggestion that she and her sister study at a foreign university was regarded as reprehensible. When Sofya declared her intention to pursue her mathematical studies Krukovsky denounced such activities as unbecoming for a woman. Both Sofya and Anna signed the petition to Tolstoy without much enthusiasm; they were by now quite determined to study abroad. At that time one of their friends committed the unforgivable crime of a love marriage. The sisters were outraged – their plans were not to be compromised by any such emotional involvements. A fictitious marriage seemed to be the only way of escaping from their parents, and Anna, whose charm and intelligence had already won her many admirers and friends, had no qualms about approaching suitable candidates for such a match. The first man she approached was a young professor whom she barely knew, and she was hurt to find her naïve proposal rejected. Her next choice was Vladimir Kovalevsky, an exceptionally able young man of a good family, who owned a publishing firm and was anxious to study in Germany. He agreed to Anna's proposition with one qualification – that he should marry Sofya instead. Krukovsky was adamantly opposed to his younger daughter's marriage and immediately made plans to take the family back to Palibino. Bitterly resentful now, and terrified at the prospect of being incarcerated once more in dull provincial life, Sofya decided to elope with Kovalevsky. At the age of seventeen she was still in many ways exceptionally childish, and never for a moment suspected that passion could interfere with her friendship with Kovalevsky. A few years later, when she found herself painfully entangled in a sexual relationship with her husband, she bitterly regretted her naïvety. But in 1868 she was ecstatic about her prospects. She wrote to a friend, 'I prepare for my examinations and write my thesis. Then I study independently.

122

Later we form a colony and I go to Siberia. Anna writes a wonderful book while I make a discovery. Then we open a mixed secondary school. I have my own physics laboratory, drop medicine and take up physics and maths, applied to political economy and statistics.' [9]

The Kovalevskys decided to leave as soon as possible for Heidelberg University, where Sofya would study mathematics and Vladimir geology. They were anxious to take with them a friend, Julia Lermontova, who was battling with her parents to study abroad. Eventually in the spring of 1869 the three of them set off for Heidelberg, where they matriculated the following year. There they met Anna Evreinova, who had run away from home and entered Germany with a false passport. She was studying law, and returned to Russia a few years later, as Russia's first woman lawyer, to campaign for women's legal rights. Natalya Armfeldt was also there. She had been active in the Sunday School Movement in the capital, and when she returned to Russia four years later she was active in revolutionary circles. After the Kovalevskys had matriculated they went to Paris to join Anna who had arrived there the previous summer. She was already deeply involved in the turbulent and confusing events of the capital and had married the prominent revolutionary Jaclard. Sofya was tempted to abandon her studies and stay with her sister, but the Kovalevskys eventually returned to Germany where Sofya was able to study under the eminent mathematician Weierstrasse at Göttingen University. Her doctorate, for which she was granted the highest distinction, was awarded on the basis of three treatises, one of which, 'Zur Theorie der Partiellen Differentialgleichung', was obviously the work of a brilliant and original mathematical mind.

In 1874 she returned to Russia, along with hundreds of women who had been either intimidated by the government *Ukase* of the previous year, forbidding women to study abroad, or enticed by its specious promises of improved educational opportunities for women. Sofya hoped to teach

123

at the Vladimirsky courses, which were obviously in need of such scholarly teachers. But the government was more interested in her political sympathies than her academic achievements. She was viewed as a 'dangerous nihilist', and after her death years later the government went to the lengths of issuing a secret decree to the press forbidding any mention of her name.

Sofya's own confused and naïve political views make this attitude particularly incomprehensible. We get some idea of these sympathies from her novel *Nigilistka* ('The Woman Nihilist'), translated as *Vera Barantsova*,[10] whose eponymous heroine was inspired by one of her friends involved in the second great show trial of young revolutionaries in 1877. Vera is a romantic Turgenevian heroine basking in provincial boredom. But by the late 1860s she is already aware that the tinkling of sleigh bells is more likely to announce the arrival of the local police chief than of a potential suitor. The novel is both politically and psychologically naive, but it does reflect honestly some of Sofya's own confusions. 'We must solve the social problem,' Vera says after she has arrived in the capital in search of some socially useful activity, 'and after that we can attend to study. Why muddle our brains with talk about wages, credit, and all the rest of it, when oppression and inequality are so self-evident?' But Vera herself never becomes directly involved in any political action. She merely clings to a boundless capacity for self-sacrifice, and she ultimately finds her fulfilment in marrying, and thus saving from death the distinctly unattractive leader of the revolutionaries on trial. She departs ecstatically with him for Siberia, and the author talks vaguely of her 'useful work' there. Sofya wrote the novel in 1880, when she was becoming increasingly exasperated by the lack of creative outlets within Russia. The work was an expression both of frustration and indomitable optimism. Vladimir's financial speculations were adding to the strain of their fraught marriage, and her only consolations were her small daughter and her literary work.[11]

By 1881 it had become obvious that she could no longer live with Vladimir if she was to continue any serious study, so taking her young daughter with her she left for Berlin where she wrote him a long letter explaining her reasons for leaving him. 'You are quite right in saying that not a single woman has achieved anything as yet. But this makes it all the more imperative for me, while I still have energy and a little money, to put myself in conditions which will enable me to prove whether or not I have the brain to achieve anything.' Both her husband and her country had refused to recognize the genius who was later to be ranked among the eminent mathematicians Ostrogradsky, Bunyakovsky and Chebuishev. It was only in 1884 that her talents were officially recognized and she was appointed professor at Stockholm University. But the price she paid for her professional success was almost as excessive as the penalty of neglect. In Stockholm her intellectual assertiveness made her an object of malicious curiosity, and she even had the honour of inspiring Strindberg to write an intensely hostile article about her. She died six years after arriving in Stockholm, and for many years her name was anathema to the Russian government.

Sofya Kovalevskaya was in no sense a revolutionary. Unlike many of her friends, who were driven to take direct political action against the government, she remained determined throughout her life to pursue an academic career. It was this professional dedication that made her such a threat to the government and such an inspiration to women who heard of her achievements. Younger girls now planned their futures with the same exuberant optimism with which Sofya had embarked on her career.

Vera Figner was fifteen in 1867 when Nadezhda Suslova qualified as a doctor. In a chapter in her autobiography entitled 'A Mood' she describes her reaction to the news.

A report of this in the journal *Delo* ['The Cause'] indicated to me in what direction to turn. Not the thought of my duty to the people, nor the conscience of the repentant nobleman impelled me to study in preparation for a job as a village physician. All such ideas were of a later growth, under the influence of reading. My main moving force was a mood ... An excess of vital forces permeated my entire being and excited me with a joyous sensation of freedom. It was this superabundance of joy, an attitude to life as I first entered it, that formed the real source of my altruistic aspirations.[12]

Behind all her ecstatic descriptions of the countryside, the sun and the stars there is a growing awareness of the poverty and misery of the peasants on the Figner estate. Nadezhda Suslova's success 'seemed to extend like a golden thread, not only to me, but to the village and still further'.

Vera was born in 1852, the eldest of four daughters and two sons of a wealthy landowner from the Kazan' province. Paternalistic with his serfs and patronizing with his wife and daughters, he was, as Vera said, a man of words, not deeds. In the comfort of his drawing room he would claim to be an admirer of Garibaldi. 'If the peasants revolted,' he said once, 'I'd be there, leading them.' Actually the Figner estate was at some distance from the peasants' dwellings, and the only serfs Vera ever met were house serfs with whom the family kept on friendly terms. Vera, a beautiful child, was encouraged to mix with her parents' friends. 'Some adults, especially men, by their excessive attentions, developed in me the pretensions of a woman. Others unconsciously impelled me to seek success in life,' she recalled. Some, like her uncle Nikolai, taunted her with the success that her beauty seemed to guarantee her. 'Let's count up, Vera dear, how many pounds of rye there are hanging on your ears in the form of those earrings,' he once said to her. And there was the conversation she overheard between two of her aunts: 'Vera's a beautiful doll. She's like that pretty crimson lantern hanging in the corner. On the near side it's good to look at, but the side turned to the wall is empty.'[13].

She had emerged as a fragile anaemic creature from the Institute to which her father, who argued so vociferously in favour of women's education, subjected his daughters. The Kazan' Institute for Girls of the Nobility acted as a kind of barrier against any original thought. The girls were tormented with lessons in penmanship; they were taught to sing, draw and dance, and in all her years there Vera did not read one serious book. Any form of physical activity besides dancing was discouraged, and the girls became sickly and apathetic. When, at the age of seventeen, she left for her parents' home, she immersed herself in her father's library, where she read all the novels she could get hold of. She found unexpected support from her father in this passion for reading, and her mother tried to answer some of the religious and moral questions with which she was now struggling.

After two years it was time for her to be 'brought out' and married off. But Vera's reading had made her all too aware of her isolation from the world of science, even from the political upheavals that were threatening the stability of the University of Kazan'. For Vera the prospect of a visit to Kazan' more than compensated for the ordeals of the marriage market. At the age of nineteen she was jolted out of introspective adolescence into the hectic activities of the 'season'. Her admirers tended to be the more serious of the young students she met. The Fillipovs were close family friends of the Figners, and in Aleksei, the eldest son, she found someone who protected her from the rigorous demands made on her charm and talents. The following year they were married. Vera was certainly not consciously motivated by the desire to leave home, but although the marriage was not a conventionally fictitious one there seems to have been more comradeship than passion in the relationship; they were both primarily concerned to pursue their studies. After a year in Kazan' they moved to St Petersburg, where Vera's sister Lydia joined them, and here the three of them embarked on an almost fanatically intense programme of reading. Vera persuaded Aleksei to drop his profitable lawyer's practice, which she saw as an intolerable compromise with the Tsarist legal system, and all three began to teach themselves German in preparation for their studies abroad. They studied medicine and political economy too, and inevitably came into contact with radical student circles. But they were too idealistic about their work to involve themselves in any political activities. In a letter to a friend Vera wrote:

> In my opinion in order to be more useful one should know more, but where can you learn what you want to? I think only the university is worth so much that a woman could sacrifice everything for it ... But in Russia this way is closed to women ... Therefore, my dear Maria, I have decided to go to Zurich. We shall return to our country house and organize life in a fine way. Aleksei will leave state service and become a village doctor. I shall organize a hospital and open a school or a handcraft institute. Wonderful! I shall stop at nothing because this whole plan is not the mere product of an idle fantasy but my whole flesh and blood, and my motivation will be the three needs or targets of my existence: economic independence,[14] the formation of my intelligence, and usefulness to others.

In the spring of 1872 the three of them left Russia for Zurich, where they registered at the medical faculty.

Vera and Lydia Figner were certainly not the first Russian girls to arrive in Zurich in the 1870s, but they were better prepared than most who were leaving Russia in those years: their family was fairly wealthy. Most girls travelled light, and many could barely muster the fare to Zurich, depending, on their arrival, on financial help from the student colony. Their intellectual luggage was light too; their minds were uncluttered and receptive. Vera Pantaleeva, who arrived at the same time as the Figners, describes her ability to 'chatter away in three foreign languages, some bits of information picked out of bad textbooks, music and art – this was the normal light baggage which I too carried in the fifties and sixties.'[15]

Evgenia Subbotina was nineteen when she arrived in Zurich that year; her sister Marya was a year younger. Their father had died shortly after the birth of his youngest daughter, leaving his family a considerable fortune. His wife Sofya had always encouraged the girls' intellectual development, teaching them to dress simply and to be self-sufficient. They were sent to the First Moscow Gimnazium for Girls, where Marya quickly earned a reputation for political 'unreliability' by announcing her intention to study at the Agrarian High School. She obviously had no chance of realizing this plan, and her mother persuaded her and Evgenia to consider studying in Zurich instead. In the spring of 1872 they arrived, along with their friend Anna Toporkova. She had been an outstanding student in Marya's year at the *gimnazium*. Her father was an unsuccessful merchant and could not afford to subsidize her studies, and Sofya Subbotina had made herself financially responsible for her. She had even helped her daughters in their unsuccessful attempt to smuggle another *gimnazium* friend, Ekaterina Anserova, with them to Zurich, and they went so far as to find her a fictitious husband. Ekaterina's father, who was a priest, put paid to the plan and Ekaterina herself paid for this friendship with the sisters by being subjected to constant police supervision. A year after the Subbotinas had arrived they were joined by their youngest sister, Nadezhda, accompanied by her mother.

Berta Kaminskaya was seventeen when she arrived in Zurich in October 1871. She had had almost no formal education when she left the small southern town of Melitopol' where her father was a merchant. Her mother had died when she was very young and Kaminsky, an amiable but uneducated man, encouraged her to develop her exceptionally lively mind. He recognized her talent, but there were few doors open to a Jew born in a remote town in South

Russia. As a child she had mixed freely with the poorer Jews of the neighbourhood, and her social conscience was aroused early. She was determined to be a doctor.

Vera and Olga Lyubatovich were from Moscow, where their father was a highly placed official. They both left the Second Moscow Gimnazium without bothering to finish, and arrived in Zurich in 1871, eager to study but bewildered and insecure; Vera was seventeen and Olga was a year younger. They were immediately homesick for the political oppression and overt sexual prejudice that had justified adolescent rebellion in Russia. They agreed with Marya Subbotina that 'in despotical Russia life is easier. There is not this depressing atmosphere of routine and habit as here in "free" Switzerland.'[16] In Switzerland they had to content themselves with outraging the local burgers and students from afar. A Swiss student, Franziska Tiburtius, describes her first meeting with Olga:

> Behind the table was an enigmatic being whose biological character was not at first clear to me. A roundish boyish face, short-cut hair parted askew, enormous blue glasses, a quite youthful tender expression, a coarse jacket, a cigarette burning in its mouth – everything about it was boyish, and yet there was something which belied the impression it desired to create. I looked stealthily under the table and discovered a bright faded cotton skirt. This being took no notice of my presence and remained absorbed in a large book, every now and then rolling a cigarette ... And then it appeared that this phenomenon was a seventeen-year-old Russian girl from Moscow, Miss Lyubatovich, which fact she confirmed with a brief nod. Nominally she studied philosophy, without any preparation, and with insufficient knowledge of German ...[17]

Girls like Virginia Shlykova attracted less attention. She came from an affectionate and cultured liberal family. Her father had generously compensated his serfs after the

130

Emancipation, and had ensured that his daughter received a good education at home. Virginia was well integrated into the class she was born in, and rarely felt the pangs of aristocratic remorse. But at the age of fifteen she read *What is to be Done?* and realized that girls of her class were not inevitably condemned to romantic passivity. She recognized her feelings of frustration and, with her parents' encouragement, enrolled at the Arlachinsky courses. Here she met Vera Lyubatovich who urged her to join her in Zurich, and Virginia's father eventually gave her his permission to leave on the condition that she did not study medicine. In 1871 she set off with the governess, who was to chaperone her, and her mother, who was to find her suitable accommodation. The following year she matriculated and married a Swiss professor. She was soon joined by her entire family, who decided to settle in Zurich.

Stefania Berlinerblau and Anna Gershenstein both came from Kherson. After a prolonged battle with their parents they were eventually allowed to leave for Zurich. A large crowd, obviously realizing the significance of the occasion, gathered silently, cap in hand, to see the boat off as it left for Odessa. They arrived safely in Zurich and both registered in the medical faculty in October 1870. Anna died there the following year but Stefania remained to finish her studies.[18]

There was really only one woman who managed to unite all these disparate elements, tame some of the more unruly girls and create a real feeling of comradeship among the women who arrived in Zurich in these years. Sofya Bardina was older than most of the women there. She was twenty-six when she arrived, and her moderation and generosity inspired confidence among all who met her — academics and revolutionaries, Swiss and Russians. She discouraged the flamboyance and pretentiousness of some of the younger girls, among whom

. . . a special kind of friendship dominated, one that is best

131

described as a friendship of day school girls, because it was characterized by all the exclusiveness and exaltation one usually associates with day school girls. Not that these girls were so extremely young; some of them were almost twenty. But the mass of new, unknown and deep impressions on these sensitive souls was too great to be kept silent. Hence the desire for intimate friendship, which in the general exaltation caused by such a deep moral change naturally assumed a sort of solemnity and exclusiveness which would bring a smile to the face of a more level-headed observer.[19]

Sofya Bardina's childhood seems to have been an unhappy one. She was unwilling to talk about it, and all we know is that she was born in 1853 in Morshansk, in the Tambov province, where her father was a forester. He was a tyrannical father and husband, and Sofya withdrew into her studies at the Tambov day school, from which she graduated with distinction. She then moved to Moscow, where she soon joined in self-education circles. Here she met the Lyubatovich sisters, and inspired by their example, left Russia shortly after them for Zurich, where she enrolled in the Polytechnical Institute to study agriculture. At the end of the first semester she was top of her class, but she then came to feel that medical studies would be more compatible with her growing political awareness. She decided to join the majority of the Russian students, men and women alike, who were registered at the medical faculty. She became a close friend of the impetuous Berta Kaminskaya and of Lydia Figner.

Vera Figner too was an exemplary student, and like most of the women there wished only to continue her studies in a peaceful environment. She writes:

On my arrival in Zurich I was obsessed by one idea – to give myself entirely to the study of medicine – and I crossed the threshold of the University with a feeling of awe. For two years I had cherished this thought, for two years I had heard time and again that its execution

132

demanded enormous energy, character and industry. I was nineteen, but I intended to renounce all pleasures, however little, in order not to lose a minute of valuable time, and I set to lectures, textbooks and practicals with an ardour that in the course of three years never diminished.[20]

But already the idealistic faith in science was giving way to a more utilitarian, politically conscious attitude to education. 'Essentially, we didn't aspire to higher education as such, believing that one could develop one's mind and enrich it without the guidance of any authority. We sought specialization, and the majority took medicine in order to have at their command an instrument for social action.' With characteristic reticence she avoids any mention in her memoirs of the strains that were developing in her relationship with Fillipov. They were living at some distance from the student community, and as a married woman Vera felt constrained from making close friends with the other women there. Fillipov was disturbed by these independent young women, and he was generally disliked by the women students. Although Vera was too devoted to her studies to play much part in the political activities of the student colony, she became increasingly exasperated with Fillipov's pleas for moderation. 'One must be altogether deaf and dumb not to get involved,' she said. In fact Sofya Bardina was the only person with whom she could discuss her personal and political problems. Lavrov, who met her at this time, saw nothing in her that would lead one to believe that she would subsequently become a political activist.

Marx's International Workingmen's Association had been established in Geneva in 1864, and by 1870 the anti-Marxist Russian section of the International had cohered round the figures of Bakunin and Lavrov. Bakunin had gained much ground among Russians and workers in the Jura Canton following his final split with Marx after the Fourth Congress of the International in 1867 in Basel. He voiced many

Russians' despair of using existing political means to effect any revolutionary action. Bakunin's arrival in Zurich in July 1872 and Lavrov's arrival shortly afterwards brought the simmering political atmosphere in the colony to boiling point. Herzen had identified the typical 'young emigrant' as an inflated personality whose boundless self-esteem, unchecked by the oppressive conditions of his native country, helped to create a self-enclosed little expatriate community. Men students were able to integrate their political study groups with their university work, but most of the girls' political activity was confined merely to the reading of revolutionary periodicals. University work took up all their time. Classes were often from six in the morning to nine at night, and most of them were too exhausted by the effort of keeping up with the men students and understanding German to join political discussion groups. Kropotkin, who visited Zurich in 1872, described the student colony, centred around the Oberstrasse area near the Polytechnic.

> They lived as most students do, especially the women, that is on very little. Tea and bread, some milk and a thin slice of meat, amidst spirited discussions of the latest news from the socialist world and the last book read – that was their regular fate. Those who had more money than was needed for such a way of life donated it to the common cause . . . As to dress, the most parsimonious economy reigned in that direction. Our girls in Zurich seemed defiantly to throw this question at the population there: can there be a simplicity of dress which does not become a girl if she is young, intelligent and full of energy?[21]

The girls' spartan life-style was occasionally excessively censorious, and Olga Lyubatovich once denounced Sofya Bardina's liking for strawberries as 'bourgeois'. But they were generally respected by the professors for their enthusiasm and ability. As early as 1870, Würzburg University had canvassed Zurich on the reaction to Russian girls studying there, and the response had been extremely favourable.

Professor Frey, the histologist, had especially praised their ability with the microscope. They were not so well received by the local inhabitants or the Swiss students. They had to tread extremely carefully. The fact that they went out unchaperoned horrified the local citizens, while their tendency to avoid the men students got them a reputation for superciliousness. The Swiss students resented the fact that Russians could register without so much as a *gimnazium* diploma, and a complaint about this was sent to the rector, with a note that Russian women were demanding special privileges and fighting for the best places at lectures. Women were clearly the target for a general resentment against the Russian student community, and anatomy classes provided many opportunities for lewd asides and stupid practical jokes. One girl, for instance, anxious to resume work first thing the next day, left an embryo in a bottle to which she attached the curious little message, 'Embryo of Miss N. N.'. Next day the note was covered with predictably obscene comments. When the girls protested to the students that they would not expose their sisters to such obscenity, their reply was 'But they are our sisters. You are students.'

When Bakunin arrived he spoke to individual students rather than addressing the colony as a whole. Hermann Greulich, in a letter to the General Council of the Marxist International, reported: 'For some time Bakunin has been in Zurich, and he continues his intrigues even here. He spins his intrigues behind the scenes. Thus he has been harassing some Serbian members of our section, and also some of the Russian women who study here. With these his success is only partial ...' Among these Russian women were Sofya Bardina, the Lyubatovich sisters and Varvara Alexandrova, who were to be seen walking with him in the town. Franziska Tiburtius paints an unflattering picture of the *Kozakenpferdchen,* as these young women came to be known: 'The short-cut hair, the enormous blue spectacles, the short quite unadorned dress which resembled umbrella lining,

135

the round glossy matelot, the cigarette, the dark and supercilious countenance all came to be considered as characteristic of the "woman student".[22] Anna Rosenstein tore up her examination papers and decided to become a revolutionary after meeting Bakunin. Varvara Vakhovskaya played the piano for the 'old man', as he was called, and breathlessly sat at his feet. She was only sixteen when she arrived from Podolsk, fired by the ideas of Pisarev and Chernyshevsky. Her doting father, a highly placed official, was bewildered by his high-spirited daughter, who had formed a small discussion group at her *gimnazium*. He eventually agreed to give her a small allowance that would cover her fare to Zurich and her expenses. After that, he warned her, she would have to be financially self-supporting. She planned to study history, which would enable her to understand the past, and science, which would help her to map out the future. But she found it difficult to get down to any serious study once she arrived. 'I was astonished to learn for the first time that in the world there was already going on a war of the workers against those who did not work, of workers against capitalists. Eagerly I threw myself at the workers' periodicals, studied the labour problem, and university study moved to the background.' Bakunin had no qualms about urging his noble young initiates to drop their studies and return immediately to Russia.

Many students who had been stirred by the rousing slogans of Bakunin's article 'Science and the People' nevertheless felt removed from the real centre of the political struggle in Russia and sought in Zurich to prepare themselves for it. Vera Figner had been active in establishing the Russian library in Zurich, and it was on her initiative that works of Feuerbach and Lassalle had been translated into Russian. For students like her, Lavrov's 'Historical Letters',[23] which appeared at the same time as Bakunin's article, were more relevant to the political situation in the *émigré* community. Lavrov had chosen this title, he explained in his conclusion,

136

'because the ethical level of the individual conditions his understanding of history; understanding history means understanding the world ideas of the time worked out by the best minds, and creating the conditions for realizing them.' When Lavrov arrived in Zurich he addressed himself to the student community as a whole, persuading them to pursue their studies and to clarify their political views in informal study groups. For Lavrov, the final decision for revolution was always the result of a choice which, itself the result of argument, might produce new argument. Whereas for Bakunin the young students represented fully prepared revolutionaries, Lavrov had no illusions about his gullible and inexperienced audience. And it was these two opposing figures that brought the Russian student colony, men and women, out on to the streets with umbrellas and even revolvers. It was these two ideologies that inspired the first women's discussion group.

Rosalia Yakeshburg, after entering into a fictitious marriage in Russia with a man named Idel'son, had left for Zurich in 1871. Her *de facto* husband there was Mikhail Smirnov, and together they had made contact with most of the student discussion groups. Rosalia was treasurer of the Russian Library which, despite explosive arguments, remained fundamentally in favour of Lavrov's views. In the summer of 1872 she summoned all the women students to a meeting, asking for their support for a new society, which was to be named the Women's Club for Logical Speech. She explained to an audience of some fifty women that they were silent at political meetings not because they were ignorant, but because they were inarticulate and diffident. The Club would provide a tolerant and affectionate atmosphere in which they could air their views freely. The first meeting of the Club was well attended and the discussion was heated. A report had just come out in Russia on suicide, raising the question whether the task of social medicine was to cure symptoms or eliminate causes. There was much talk among

137

the women of definitions of 'normal' and 'abnormal' states of mind. At the second meeting Varvara Alexandrova read a paper on Sten'ka Razin, which was rather indifferently received. But the arguments from the third meeting continued to reverberate for many weeks. The speaker took a Bakunist line, arguing that culture must be destroyed along with the whole economic structure. For Bakunists, existing art was no more than a beautifully sublimated justification for the pain and anger of the world. The privileged classes, in their sufferings, had always had the possibility of expressing their sufferings and of disguising their true horror. But Bakunin had of course no theory as to how 'untamed' suffering could find its artistic expression, and the speaker was furiously opposed by women who argued that culture must be extended, rather than abolished. Vera Figner for one believed passionately that it was the role of the intelligentsia to bring to the people its knowledge. Rational arguments about the 'cultural problem' quickly degenerated into angry shouting until 'at last, really desperate, the president rang the bell so furiously that for a moment the voices grew silent. She exclaimed: "Mesdames! Think what you are doing! The whole of Russia is looking at us!" This exclamation, reminiscent of Napoleon at the foot of the pyramids in Egypt, caused general laughter ... But the debate went on in the streets, and for some time the still silent quarters of Zurich resounded with loud cries of "destroy!" "maintain" ' [24]

The Club had by now largely served its purpose, and many women felt confident enough to take an active part in men's discussion groups. At the same time, fired by their enthusiasm, many men were anxious to attend Club meetings. For some time discussions centred on the issue of their admittance. Vera Figner, arguing, as one of her friends put it, as a 'pure feminist', was against their admittance. She had been horrified by drunken scenes in the Russian kitchen, and insisted that women could not afford to compromise themselves in the eyes of the University and the local citizens.

The issue was the cause of much angry and protracted argument, and the Club finally disintegrated. But women were gradually discovering their own political and personal identity.

Most of the women students lived in a large house owned by a woman named Fräulein Fritsch. After their studies they would discuss what they had been reading, and at weekends they generally went off to the countryside together. It was Sofya Bardina who insisted that they should extend their political horizons beyond the mere reading of socialist literature. Any significant revolutionary activity, she explained, must depend on the mobilization of cadres of workers within the factories, and she decided to draw up a referendum that would transform this informal group of friends into a cohesive political circle with its own political identity. Four topics of study were formulated; socialist ideas from Thomas More, Fourier and Cabet to Louis Blanc, Proudhon and Lassalle; political economy, popular movements and revolutions; the workers' movements in the West; the trade unions and the International. The group, which became known as the *Fritschi*, now found some kind of equilibrium between their studies and their political activity. Some of the men branded them as supercilious 'aristocrats', disdainfully standing aside from the rest of the community, but it was their enthusiasm and intellectual assertiveness that most impressed Lavrov, who attended one of their meetings.

There was a sizeable group of Georgian students in Zurich, whose exuberant nationalism excluded them from the larger student community. The *Fritschi* felt the Georgians to be more approachable than the Russians, and they became natural allies. Dzhabadari, a leading member of the Georgian political study group, recalls the opening of this alliance. He was sitting in the student café one day when two unknown Russian girls approached him. 'One, blushing, asked me aside. "Could you lend me 500 francs for a few days?" she

139

asked.'[25] He readily agreed, and the girls introduced themselves as Vera Lyubatovich and Evgenia Subbotina. A few days later they returned to repay the money, and after overcoming their initial shyness they began to talk openly about their political studies. Dzhabadari urged them to attend his discussion group with a view to forming a new party. And so the basis of the Pan-Russian Social Revolutionary Party was laid.

When he arrived in Zurich, Lavrov was undecided about whether to embark on the publication of an underground workers' journal. It was chiefly the energy and enthusiasm of the *Fritschi* that eventually persuaded him to bring out his famous journal *Vperëd!* ('Forward'). Early in 1873 the first issue came out, and it was immediately recognized as the most significant underground publication of its kind. It had a readership of two thousand, and was the first journal directed at factory workers. Sofya Bardina, Berta Kaminskaya, Marya Subbotina, the Lyubatovich sisters and Anna Toporkova all severed links with Bakunin and worked as typesetters and binders for the new journal. And it was probably this that acted as a final irritant for the Russian government, already inundated with a series of distorted rumours about women students in Zurich.

The Collection of Decrees from the Ministry of National Education for the 1870s contains an interesting entry: 'In 1872 a special Commission was set up under the Ministry of the Interior and the Third Department to discuss the measures required to deal with the ever increasing flood of women leaving for Zurich, and the deplorable events taking place in their midst.'[26] On 21 May the following year *Pravitel'stvennyi Vestnik* ('Government Herald') carried an 'article' whose official context gave authority to the most shameless slander. 'In the '60's,' it said,

... several Russian girls set off abroad to attend lectures at Zurich University. At first there were only a very few of

140

them, but now there are more than a hundred women there ... Largely because of this increase in Russian women students, the ringleaders of the Russian emigration have chosen this town as a centre for revolutionary propaganda, and have done all in their power to enlist into their ranks these young women students. Under their influence, women have abandoned their studies for fruitless political agitation. Young Russians of both sexes have formed political parties of extreme shades ... In the Russian Library they hold lectures of an exclusively revolutionary nature ... It has become common practice for the girls to attend workers' meetings ... Young and inexperienced minds are being led astray by political agitators, and set on the wrong course. And to cap it all, meetings and party struggles throw the girls into such confusion that they accept this fruitless and fraudulent propaganda as real life. Once drawn into politics the girls fall under the influence of the leaders of the emigration, and become compliant weapons in their hands. Some of them go from Zurich to Russia and back two or three times a year, carrying letters, instructions and proclamations and taking an active part in criminal propaganda. Others are led astray by communist theories about free love, and under pretext of fictitious marriages carry to the most extreme limits their rejection of the fundamental laws of morality and feminine virtue. The immoral conduct of Russian women has aroused the indignation of the local citizens against them, and landladies are even refusing to accept them as lodgers. Some of the girls have sunk so low as to practise that branch of obstetrics which is judged a criminal offence, and deserves the utter contempt of all honourable people.

The article then resorts to cajolery. 'The Government will therefore create and subsidize institutions which will answer women's need for advanced education, and will grant them every opportunity of gaining an education within their own country. But it is highly improbable that the mere thirst for education would tempt Russian women home from Zurich, since most of our young people were attracted there in the

141

first place by ideas that had little to do with education.' (It would be superfluous to repeat that Russian women's singleminded search for education was only gradually replaced by a growing political consciousness.) Then there are references to 'false ideas about women's role in society', and 'the attraction of fashionable ideas which are destroying them irrevocably'. But the real sting of the article is contained in its conclusion: 'Therefore, the Government warns all Russian women attending universities abroad that those who after 1 January 1874 continue to attend courses will be deprived of employment or the rights to advanced education.'

This decree, which masqueraded as an article, had a shattering effect on the women students, who now became objects of open hatred to the conservative Swiss citizens. Many girls were to be seen sobbing in the streets, and some of the more determined among them suggested drafting a letter to the European press rejecting these false accusations – the most ludicrous one being the charge that they practised abortions, since they had not even started to study obstetrics. But most girls felt that they would be compromising themselves by taking any action. Vera Figner took very seriously the implications of the decree. 'What will the innumerable enemies of women's education say,' she remarked to Nikolai Morozov, a fellow student and poet, 'when, of hundreds of women students who came here, only a few manage to finish? Won't they say that this proves our innate inability for any form of higher study? We are the first ones. Everyone is looking at us with interest and anticipation.'[27] She herself decided to leave for Berne, where she enrolled in the medical faculty. Her sister, along with Sofya Bardina, Vera Lyubatovich and Marya Subbotina, moved to Paris, where they registered at the Sorbonne.

If, as the government claimed, they had been seeking the 'good life', the women would not have gone to Paris, where things were more expensive than in Zurich. A meagre diet and damp rooms, in which at one point they all had to take

142

turns in sleeping in the bed, sapped their energy and undermined their health. They were grudgingly tolerated by the dean of the University, who eventually asked the Russian consul, Orlov, why it was that these women could not be educated in their own country. Orlov replied that he considered it 'improper' for women to study outside Russia. 'There is no need for it,' he said, 'because there exist adequate educational institutions inside Russia. Furthermore, Russian women are all for pursuing their studies along with the men, but when they do so they have no time for study, but devote themselves to politics, which is what happened in Zurich where they were members of the International Workingmen's Association.' Orlov was lying of course; there were no adequate educational facilities for women in Russia. And it was he who later wrote a second slanderous article in the *Government Herald*. Girls came abroad, he said, merely to enjoy the delights of male company.

Probably the only male company enjoyed by the girls in Paris was that of Dzhabadari, who contacted Sofya Bardina in order to discuss the future activities of the Pan-Russian Social Revolutionary Party. The girls were as shy and withdrawn as they had been in Zurich. They were occasionally to be seen walking in the Jardin des Plantes, but they generally returned straight to their rooms after lectures. When Dzhabadari visited Sofya Bardina he found Varvara Alexandrova, Evgenia Subbotina, Vera Lyubatovich, Lydia Figner and Berta Kaminskaya all competing for her attention. One girl, he recalls, was holding her hand, another clasping her waist. Sofya gently pushed them away and insisted that they join in the discussion.

Dzhabadari was only twenty-one, a modest and respectful young man, and soon the girls overcame their diffidence and embarked on a heated discussion about their future activities in Russia. Dzhabadari found them quite the most intellectually sophisticated Russian students he had ever met, the most ascetic and the most prepared for immediate

143

political action. It was through them that he first felt able to put aside the national differences that had isolated him from the wider Russian political movement, and to enter the revolutionary arena, as he puts it, 'as a member of the Russian political family'. He spent most of his time in their company until November 1874, when on their recommendation he left for Berne to urge Vera Figner and her friend Dora Aptekman to return to Russia and embark immediately on propaganda work in the factories of Moscow. But the Russian student colony in Berne was dominated by the 'young Bakunists', from whom Vera kept her distance. Besides, Vera did not share her friends' sense of political urgency. She felt that the time was not right for immediate political action, and that she would be better prepared to serve the Russian people as a qualified doctor.

Bakunin himself had left Zurich for Zagreb in 1874 in order to work among Serbian nationalists. He had written ecstatically to the Zurich community that the war in Bosnia and Herzegovina was taking on the character of a civil war, and Olga Lyubatovich and Marya Subbotina, both staunch Bakunists, had decided to join him in Zagreb.

At the end of 1874 all Russian women students were ordered out of Paris. They were ready to go, and grateful to the government for having emphasized the political significance of their departure. After returning briefly to Zurich, where they conferred with their Georgian friends on the constitution of the new organization, they returned to Russia – to the people. Here they were joined by Olga Lyubatovich and Marya Subbotina. Bakunin had been forced to admit the failure of his attempt at fomenting partisan warfare, and they were anxious to join the 'Moscow Group', as the new organization was called. Vera Lyubatovich, along with Ekaterina Khorzhevskaya and Elisaveta Tumanova, had stopped in Kiev and Odessa on their way from Paris to Moscow. It was in Kiev that they met Gesya Helfman, who was attending midwives' courses there. She had known

Dzhabadari and was in contact with his friends, the prominent southern radicals Debagori, Deich and Mokrievich. At the age of seventeen she had run away from a poor and oppressively orthodox Jewish home and from the man her parents intended her to marry. She had worked for two years as a sempstress in Kiev, saving up the money to enrol in courses. Her meeting with these women inspired her to set up a sewing collective and a political study group. Shortly afterwards, Ekaterina Khorzhevskaya entered into a fictitious marriage with a Kiev radical student, and a flat was established for the collective. Meanwhile Vera Lyubatovich and Elisaveta Tumanova returned to Moscow.

Little is known of the constitution of the organization. The young people whose political ideology had been formed in Switzerland were more familiar with the politics of the Jura Canton than with conditions in Russia; they had no inclination to establish any form of centralized authority which, as they realized in theory, was essential to the formation of any effective revolutionary party. The women who returned to Moscow in the mid-1870s were determined only to 'merge' with the factory workers, just as the populists of the previous decade had attempted to do with the peasantry. Comradeship and equality within the organization were to be ensured by concentrating power in an *obschina* or 'community' (shades here too of the rural populist movement). This was to be democratically elected and changed every few months. Every member of the *obschina* was authorized to propagate, infiltrate and agitate among the workers at his or her own risk. Many of the women, understandably nervous about the prospect of working among predominantly male factory workers, demanded that a formal renunciation of marriage be included in the regulations of the organization, but this proposal was eventually turned down. It was this unusual demand, however, that earned them their reputation as 'Moscow Amazons'.

145

There are no records of any meetings, and most of the women were anxious to start work right away in the factories. So Sofya Bardina, Lydia Figner, Berta Kaminskaya, Alexandra Khorzhevskaya and the Subbotina sisters, all equipped with false passports, embarked on their first political work. After three years in Zurich, the insecure adolescents who had been so avid for knowledge and liberty were now self-confident women, mature in matters of political theory. But they were totally unprepared for the realities of Russian factory life. Vera Figner, who was well aware of her physical limitations, realized that political ardour would never compensate for physical weakness. And even the women who did not succumb to the backbreaking labour, the infested beds, the overcrowded dormitories and the miserable diet were frustrated that, after fifteen hours of soul-destroying work, the exhausted workers generally had no energy to get angry about their working conditions.

Sofya Bardina and Berta Kaminskaya both got jobs in large textile factories where there was a large proportion of women workers – Sofya in the Lazareva factory, Berta in the Nosovye factory. Lydia Figner rented a small room in the city, where she lived under the passport of a soldier's wife and got a job in the large Gubner factory. Varvara Alexandrova, Marya Subbotina and Anna Toporkova all worked in factories in nearby Ivanovo-Voznesensk and lived in a communal flat leased by Anna Toporkova. On their first day at work they were greeted with the normal barrage of obscenities to which women workers were subjected. They were horrified by the demoralization and promiscuity of the workers, and tried at first to make contact with the women workers, who worked and lived apart from the men. But the women they found interested only in clothes, their sexual adventures and malicious gossip. It was obviously not long before some of the more curious workers began to question them about their presence there, with their undeniably refined ways and speech. They explained, to the workers' satisfaction, that they were Old Believers of peasant origin, who had just left their villages. Gradually they began to gain the workers' trust and respect.

Sofya Bardina was soon on friendly terms with a woman worker who confided her family problems to her, and she ended up going to the woman's home, taking with her populist fables and the latest periodicals. Her humour and persuasive narrative gifts began to win her friends, who dogged her heels, begging her for the 'latest news'. She began going with them to bars where they could show off their new literate friend, who was now urging them that the only way of improving their work conditions was to take immediate strike action. A small study group, the first of its kind, was formed within the factory, and a nucleus of literate workers was provided with literature to read and distribute among their friends. There was nothing very subversive about the literature – stories by Tolstoy and Sleptsov, the odd periodical.

The only openly revolutionary literature distributed among the workers was Bakunin's paper *Rabotnik* ('The Worker'), published in Berne and smuggled into the country by various 'young Bakunists'. It first appeared in January 1875 and was the first Russian-language paper to focus serious attention on the urban proletariat. Although it was widely distributed in the factories, its actual propaganda value was slight, making as it did unrealistic political assumptions about a largely illiterate and totally unorganized proletariat. Its vaguely idealistic collectivist spirit did not inspire immediate sympathy among the workers, and the paper soon lapsed into the sloganizing vocabulary of international revolution. The personality and intellectual power of the Moscow women far outweighed the influence of the periodicals they were distributing, and this was both their strength and their weakness. Workers were risking their jobs by inviting the women into their dormitories, where they listened reverently as the propagandists talked about the French Revolution and

147

the International Labour Movement. By the spring of 1875 their work had begun to bear fruit in a series of strikes, culminating in a particularly large one at Serpukhov. By the spring, most members of the 'Moscow Group' had been arrested and transferred to the capital to await trial.

The English manager of the Lazareva factory had been told by a police informer about Sofya Bardina's discussion group, and she had decided to leave in order to avoid arrest. Berta Kaminskaya was also in danger, and together they moved into a flat where they continued living under false passports. It was not long before the flat was raided and they were arrested. In August Varvara Alexandrova, Marya Subbotina and Anna Toporkova, together with five others, were arrested in their communal flat in Ivanovo–Voznesensk. Lydia Figner was arrested shortly afterwards.

Elisaveta Tumanova and the Lyubatovich sisters, who had been helping to smuggle illegal literature into the country and who had held workers' discussion groups in their flats, were arrested that summer. Alexandra Khorzhevskaya's flat in Kiev, which had become a meeting place and mailing address for local radicals, was raided soon afterwards, and she and Gesya Helfman were taken along with the Moscow women to the capital to await trial.

They were to wait for almost three years in preventive detention before the first of the great Russian show trials, the 'Trial of the Fifty', or the 'Trial of the Moscow Women', was held. In these three years of almost total solitary confinement most of them succumbed to what was known as 'prison sickness'. Solitude, isolation from their comrades and the painful awareness of the failure of their propaganda activities induced in them a state of torpor, and most sat listlessly in a virtually comatose state in their cells. Olga Lyubatovich went on hunger strike for seven days just in order to get a needle and thread to vary life a little. Imprisonment put an intolerable strain on Berta Kaminskaya. She began to suffer from hallucinations, and in the delusion that she was the victim of a conspiracy among her comrades began to rap out insane messages on the walls of her cell in an attempt to warn her neighbours of traitors. Her incessant weeping and raving was having a seriously demoralizing effect on the other prisoners, and the prison authorities, anxious to be rid of her, handed her over to her father's protection. Marya Subbotina too was finally released in a state of total collapse, having tried to kill herself.

Vera Figner was meanwhile still in Berne. She had only two months to go before she qualified as a doctor, and despite her anguish at the fate of her friends and her sister she was determined to finish her course before she returned. But at the end of 1876 she received a letter from Mark Natanson begging her to return and lend moral and practical support to those in prison and to help resuscitate the flagging revolutionary movement. She decided unhesitatingly to return, dismissing her studies as mere selfish professional ambition, convinced now that she could serve the people just as well without official medical qualifications. On her return to Moscow she spent whole days writing coded messages to friends in prison, meeting various dubious characters in bars and arranging meetings with venial policemen and prison warders in an unsuccessful series of attempts to free prisoners. It was an intensely depressing period for her. She had left Berne thinking that 'the beautiful science of socialism was applicable to all peoples and periods, no matter what level of development these people had reached. Socialism could be established anywhere, and it was only necessary to convince people of its necessity and then everything would be easy.'[28] Capitalism she had regarded as a 'fortuitous phenomenon'; like her friends in prison, she had gravely underestimated the monolithic proportions that Russian capitalism of the 1870s was beginning to assume.

The government, however, had seriously underestimated the moral influence the Moscow Women were to have at their trial, which opened in St Petersburg under special Senate

149

supervision and without jury on 14 March 1877. The women emerged not as 'dangerous nihilists' but as dedicated diffident young women who welcomed the opportunity of a packed courtroom to defend, most of them in silence, the dignity they had been fighting for as women and revolutionaries. They made an indelible impression on those in court, and among liberals and conservatives alike they began to take on a semi-mythical significance. Kravchinsky's account of their appearance was characteristically ecstatic: 'Before this trial only young people had known socialists. Now an amazed public witnessed the radiant faces of these girls, with their childishly sweet smiles, calmly going to where there was no return, no hope – they were going to the central prisons, to long years of hard labour. "Apostolic times are returning," people said; "a new strength is born." ' [29]

The central moment of the trial was Sofya Bardina's speech to the prosecutors. Arrested, like her friends, for little more than reading a few pamphlets to factory workers, she was able in her speech of self-defence to take advantage of a packed courtroom to defend an entire cause. Her speech suggests no very subversive goals, and yet her methodical exposition of her case gave dignity and plausibility to the entire revolutionary movement. A century before her Babeuf, in his 300-page summary of the ideals of the French Revolution, had asserted the same basic human aspirations. Happiness, he had said, was a new idea in Europe. 'But today we know that it is the unhappy who are the really important powers of the earth; they have the right to speak as the real masters of the government that neglects them.' There is a modesty about Sofya Bardina's speech that recalls some of the greatest speeches of self-defence.

The Moscow Women had been accused of attempting to destroy the sacred foundations of property, the family, religion and the State. Sofya Bardina carefully dismantled each one of these accusations, and used them as the basis for a positive statement of her comrades' aims. After her speech

150

people in court were heard to murmur, 'They are angels!' The speech,[30] which was printed and widely circulated, made a deep impression on liberal sections of society; the Moscow Women might not be angels, but they were certainly not bloodthirsty nihilistic desperadoes – misguided perhaps, but certainly not 'dangerous'.

All of these accusations against us would be terrible if they were true [began Sofya at the top of her voice]. But they are based on misunderstanding. I do not reject property if it is acquired by one's own labour. Every person has a right to his own labour and its products. So why do our masters give us only one-third of our labour-value? As for the family, I also do not understand. Is it the social system that is destroying it, by forcing a woman to abandon her family and work for wretched wages in a factory, where she and her children are inevitably corrupted; a system that drives a woman into prostitution through sheer poverty, and which actually *sanctions this prostitution* as something legitimate and necessary in any well-ordered society? Or is it we who are undermining it, we, who are attempting to eliminate this poverty, which is the chief cause of all our social ills, including the destruction of the family?

As to religion, I have always been true to the principles established by the founder of Christianity, and have never propagandized against these principles. I am equally innocent of attempting to undermine the State. I do not believe any one individual is capable of destroying the State by force. If it is to be destroyed, it will be because it bears within it the embryo of its own destruction, holding as it does the people in political, economic and intellectual bondage. I am accused of inciting riot, but I believe that revolution can only be the result of a whole series of historical events, and not instigated by any one group of individuals.

We do not stand for anarchy if this means chaos and dictatorship; what we want is a social system that would establish harmony and order in all social relations. And if

151

to attain this we must have an armed revolution, this is because in the present circumstances this is unfortunately an unavoidable evil. Whatever my fate, lords of the bench, I do not beg for mercy and I do not desire it. Persecute us if you want to, but I am deeply convinced that this vast movement which has already been existing for so many years cannot be checked by any repressive measures. It can be suppressed briefly, but then it will renew itself with even greater force, as always happens after such a reaction. Persecute us for at the moment, gentlemen, you have the material power on your side. But we have the moral power, the power of historical progress, of ideals – and ideals, I fear, you will not kill with your bayonets.

She sat down, leaving her defence council to mouth a lengthy apology for his rebellious client. Her speech to be sure was one of minimum demands (although the terms minimum/maximum demands were not yet part of revolutionary vocabulary). Marx had written in the Manifesto that 'with the end of capitalism, personal property is not merely transformed into social property. It is only the social character of property that is changed – it loses its class character.' But Marx had made little impression on Russian radicals of the period, who believed that the land could be equally distributed among the people without being forcibly expropriated.

There was little the lords of the bench could do but deal out savage sentences. Sofya Bardina and Olga Lyubatovich were both condemned to nine years' hard labour in Siberia. Lydia Figner, Alexandra Khorzhevskaya and Gesya Helfman all got five years' hard labour in factories, Anna Toporkova got two years' hard factory labour – their fates were typical of those of their friends in the trial; their treatment struck almost everyone as an outrage and an anomaly.

It was in reverential tones that poets like Nekrasov, Polonsky and Turgenev referred to the Moscow Women.

Turgenev was inspired to write a short prose poem (found posthumously) called *At the Threshold*. A young girl is standing outside a great door, waiting to be admitted. 'You who enter,' says a voice from within, 'do you know what awaits you? Cold, hunger, hatred, mockery, contempt, shame, prison, illness, death.' 'I know,' says the girl, 'I am ready.' 'Not only from your enemies, but from your family and friends ... So you are ready for the sacrifice. You will perish and nobody will even know whose memory to revere.' 'I need neither gratitude nor pity. I do not need a name.' The girl crosses the threshold, and a heavy curtain falls covering the door. 'Fool!' sneers someone. 'Saint!' calls out someone else. This fragment makes its intense restrained appeal to the emotions, rather than making any political statement.

Nekrasov's voice, in his poem *The Trial of the Fifty,* is that of the 'citizen poet':

> The honourable are silent, they have fallen gloriously.
> Their lonely voices, crying out for the wretched, are silenced.
> But cruel passions have been unleashed,
> And the whirlwind of malice and madness has swept over you, land of the meek.
>
> All that is alive and honourable is crushed.
> In this night without a dawn of the gloom you have spread,
> We hear only the voices of our enemies, exulting among themselves.
> Like bloodthirsty birds flocking around the corpse of a slaughtered giant,
> On whom venomous reptiles are crawling.

Polonsky laments the fate of the young heroines in his poem *The Girl Prisoner:*

> What is she to me? Neither wife, lover nor my own daughter.
> So why does her accused life haunt me night and day?
> How old is she? Seventeen perhaps?

153

Is it true what they say, that this girl, who has never
known happiness,
Will never be released?
That they will punish her for her poverty? For speaking
freely?
For her boundless love?

Vera Figner was quick to deny that she was the object of this
somewhat embarrassingly effusive poem; it was probably her
sister Lydia's appearance in court that inspired it. Ever since
her return to Russia Vera Figner had been desperately
anxious to talk to her friends in prison and to share their fate,
and she had been arrested almost immediately for trying to
talk to some of her comrades through the windows of the
prison. On her release she strongly urged her friends to
concentrate all their energy on arranging the escape of Sofya
Bardina and Olga Lyubatovich. Her eagerness to accept new
ideas and her scrupulous honesty immediately impressed all
who met her. Mikhailovsky, the populist writer, was struck
by her force of character. 'One was enchanted by her
integrity, which informed every gesture, every word. For her,
indecision and doubt did not exist.' Actually she was as beset
by doubts as all her comrades, waiting in trepidation for the
next arrest, and her macabre meeting with Berta
Kaminskaya, by now seriously deranged, did little to raise
her morale.

Berta had not returned to the custody of her father, but
had stayed illegally in the capital. She visited Vera, totally
distraught by the failure in the factories, and determined now
to 'go to the peasants'. In preparation for her solitary
pilgrimage to the people, she was learning to make boots. She
had lost all hope in meetings, discussion, long-term
propaganda work, indeed in any form of joint action. Vera
recalls her[31] glassy-eyed and deaf to all of Vera's less
catastrophic interpretations of the situation. She was bent on
leaving, and begged for Vera's help. The next day Vera

154

reluctantly accompanied her to the market, where they bought her a peasant skirt and a great pair of peasant boots. Berta wandered off 'to the countryside', without any provisions or literature, scarcely knowing where she was going or what she was doing. The following day she turned up again at Vera's house; she had apparently arrived at a large river and could find no way of crossing it. Vera found her pitifully disorientated, and it came as no great surprise to learn a few days later that her friend had committed suicide.

Most of the sentences of the Moscow Women were commuted by a few years. But Sofya Bardina had spoken for all her friends when she rejected mercy. She also refused any financial help in exile from her parents or from prisoners' aid organizations, and she existed for three years in a Siberian village in utter poverty. In December 1880 she managed to escape to Kazan' where, broken in spirits and health, she wandered for a few months around the countryside. All her old optimism had gone, and she was unwilling to return to her friends who were so eagerly awaiting her in the capital. In three years political events had moved far beyond her moderate socialist ideals, and she felt totally isolated from the revolutionary movement. In the spring she left for Geneva, and this time she did not return. A few months later she shot herself in the head.

For Olga Lyubatovich, the prospect of exile was not so daunting. She had lost none of her reckless optimism, and was quite confident of eventually escaping. She was able to make a little money by sewing, and became very popular among the local villagers. After a year or so she was allowed to stand in for the local doctor, who was a notorious drunkard. The police, however, were not so well disposed towards her, and decided to withhold some literature that she had ordered, a work of Spencer's. She demanded it from them and was immediately put under house arrest. Barricading herself into the house, she announced that she would meet any violence from the police with armed resistance (she was armed, in fact, with nothing more than a wooden stake). One night she managed to slip out, and throwing some of her clothes into the river to suggest that she had killed herself, she caught the first train to Moscow. She arrived in the capital in 1879 as an 'illegal'.[32]

Here I shall digress a little by resuming my narrative of women in emigration and exile, and turn from the ferment of the *émigré* colony in Switzerland and their fates on their return to Russia to the turmoil of Paris in 1871, where two remarkable women, Elisaveta Dmitrieva and Anna Krukovskaya, the sister of Sofya Kovalevskaya, were living. Elisaveta and Anna had known one another in emigration but had not been on friendly terms, and subsequently had had occasion to disagree in Paris. Both were Internationalists, but by background and temperament they were very dissimilar. Elisaveta Dmitrieva was a militant organizer and spokeswoman and, in letters to various friends, wrote that she daily expected death on the barricades. Anna Krukovskaya was fondly remembered by a friend at her funeral in 1887 for her qualities of devotion and courage and for the intelligent support she showed her husband and friends in their political struggles. There is of course much more than this to be said about her. But let us look first at the more militant of the two women.

After the collapse of the Commune and Elisaveta Dmitrieva's escape to Berne, the Council of War had an almost blank dossier on her: 'It has been impossible to ascertain what the Dmitrieva woman was doing before 18 March,' it admitted. This amounted to a serious lapse on their part, since they were anxious to establish the direct influence of the International on the Commune, and Elisaveta Dmitrieva made no secret of her Internationalist connections. People recalled only her exotic elegance – her riding habit, her felt hat trimmed with red feathers and her silk scarf. Lissaragay, in his *Huit Jours de Mai,* remembers the 'tall, golden-haired, wonderfully pretty woman, her dress soaked in blood, who worked unstintingly at the barricades, finding unbelievable strength in her noble heart.' But by 1897 the same writer had obviously found some sort of axe to grind against this angel of mercy, now transformed into a bloodthirsty harpy. 'She left her husband in the lurch in Russia,' he says, 'and whether it was that the "bare-armed people" were not *in camera* very pleasing to her or that love for her was an exclusively feminine sport, no man could ever melt this iceberg.' And he continues by describing her life in exile: 'In her salons there was a brilliant society of "hard labour", with a sprinkling of death-sentences and other exotica.' It is difficult to imagine the cause of this intense hostility, which provoked him to conclude his hatchet job by declaring that she had helped her lover to poison her husband. The fact is that after the death of her husband she fell in love with a political prisoner, whom she followed to exile in Siberia, where she died.

But these are mere anecdotes. It is remarkable that the Council of War had no information on this woman, for the Union des Femmes pour la Défense de Paris et les Soins aux Blessés, of which she was secretary, represented the French section of the Marxist International, whose direction of the Commune the Council was so keen to prove. The other main target for reaction was of course the common women of Paris, the thousands of wretched women arrested and shot merely for carrying a shopping-basket or crying in the streets. Elisaveta Dmitrieva was clearly not one of the mythical *pétroleuses*. At the age of twenty she was the youngest and most dedicated member of the Marxist International and a close friend of the Marx family. Marx himself had selected her to visit Paris in order to keep him informed of activities there; he had given her almost no advice on what to do when she arrived. A few things are known about the chain of events that brought her into contact with Marx.

Dmitrieva was a revolutionary pseudonym, adopted in Paris. She was born in 1851 the illegitimate daughter of a tyrannical Pskov landowner named Kushelev and the wet-nurse of his elder children. This woman, whom he subsequently married and from whom he demanded the servility befitting her class, was a gentle and affectionate mother who felt deeply uncomfortable in her master's home. As a child Elisaveta associated almost exclusively with the children of the estate serfs, and became painfully aware of the discrepancies between her father's pampered life-style and the wretched existence of his dependants. By the age of fourteen she was already reading Chernyshevsky and the progressive journals, and entertained dreams of going to the people and donating her fortune (her father had awarded her a generous allowance) to establish a mill on collective lines. She was soon to make friends with several radical students from Pskov University who fired her political enthusiasm by encouraging her to read Marx and Tkachev. At the age of fifteen she had read Marx's *Outlines for the Critique of Political Economy,* described by Tkachev in his introduction to it when it appeared in 1865 as 'common property of all thinking honest people; hardly any intelligent person will find any objection to it'. By 1867 she was determined to go abroad to extend her political horizons. But although financially independent, she suffered from the double disability of being illegitimate and a woman. An arranged marriage was the obvious solution, a relationship that in her case apparently represented little of the idealistic comradeship of the conventional 'fictitious marriage'. The brother of her step-sister's husband, Vladimir Tomanovsky, was the willing victim of this arrangement, and in 1867 her money, 50,000 rubles of it, bought her a passport and a cultured, ailing, elderly husband whom she urged in vain to travel with her to Geneva. He preferred to stay in Russia, and the following year she set off on her own.

She arrived in Geneva without any experience of revolutionary circles, exile, imprisonment or conspiracy. The people she met there were politically experienced exiles who

158

had much to teach her. Natalya Korsini we have already met as the first woman to enrol in St Petersburg University in 1860; branded inevitably as a nihilist, she had been arrested shortly afterwards for her part in the Sunday School Movement. The following year she had become involved with a young professor, Nikolai Utin, who had been imprisoned for encouraging the student disturbances at the University. When he escaped to London in 1863 she had followed him there, and they were married three years later in Geneva. Utin, described by Herzen as a 'typical young emigrant', was nevertheless a political realist. He and Natalya were Elisaveta's teachers, and their good sense enabled her to ride the storm of Nechaev's dramatic arrival on the scene the following March,[33] when he managed to persuade Bakunin to donate half his funds to one of Nechaev's typically mythical ventures. (The pamphlet he subsequently produced indirectly justified this confidence trick: 'The robber is the true and only revolutionary,' announced the *Revolutionary Catechism,* 'the revolutionary without phrases or wordy rhetoric.')

Elisaveta Dmitrieva had never known the moral support of political discussion groups, nor had she faced the problems of the delimitation of power *vis-à-vis* the State which had gone so deep in most Russian *émigrés.* Her confidence and ambition were boundless. In the year 1869 Bakunin's eloquence swayed most of the exile community in Geneva, but Russians like the Utins felt the necessity of maintaining a Marxist line in the face of Bakunin's often wildly inconsistent behaviour and tempestuous propaganda. That September Elisaveta and the Utins left Geneva to attend the Basle conference of the Marxist International. Keeping as much money as she needed for herself, she donated the rest to the Central Committee, and the following year she was asked by her friends on the Central Committee to visit Marx in London. The purpose of her visit is explained in the letter she was to present to him. 'Dear Citizen,' it ran, 'allow us to present to you our best friend, Elisaveta Tomanovskaya, who

159

is sincerely and profoundly devoted to the revolutionary cause in Russia. We should be happy if, through her, we might know you better, and if at the same time we could acquaint you in more detail with our activities, of which she will be able to speak to you.'

She was warmly welcomed by the Marx family when she arrived in London in the summer of 1870, and became especially friendly with Jenny and Laura. Her letters to Marx, many of which have been kept, are affectionate and unpretentious. This letter, dated 7 January 1871, shows how seriously she took her duties as an International liaison officer:

> Regarding the alternatives that you foresee in the problem of how communal property will fare in Russia, unfortunately it is very probable that it will be transformed into small communal holdings. I venture to send you this copy of *Narodnoe Delo* ['The People's Cause'], in which this problem is examined. Certainly you know of the study by Hoxthausen, which appeared in 1847, describing communal systems in Russia.[34] If by any chance you do not have it, let me know; I own a copy and could send it to you at once. In the articles on landed property which you are reading at the moment, you will see that Chernyshevsky mentions it often and quotes passages from it . . .

Marx was deeply impressed by this young woman. In the spring of 1871 he asked her to go to Paris on a mission of investigation.

In Paris Elisaveta's political intuitions compensated for her inexperience. She realized at once that the working women of Paris could shatter the illusion that the emancipation of their sex could occur only as a side-effect of the class struggle. Her mind was unencumbered, too, by the debilitating influences of Proudhon and Michelet. Proudhon's collectivist ideals had encouraged the growth of supply co-operatives, in which

160

women, true to their traditional role as feeders, had been able to participate in the political movement. But most of them would have been unable to reconcile Proudhon's socialism with the absurd views expressed in *Amour et Mariage*. Were the women who were later so ready to defend the Commune really suffering from a triple inferiority to men? Was their physical strength really in the ratio of two to a man's three? And where did this ratio come from anyway? Did they in fact lack men's 'cerebral tension' and commit 'irremediable errors of judgement' ? If, as Proudhon claimed, virtue was directly proportionate to strength, then women's virtue must be in her chastity.

Such ideas need not concern us too much, as they did not directly concern Elisaveta either, but it was against such deeply ingrained and sophisticated prejudices that many of her women comrades were struggling, and this explains the existence of the numerous women's clubs in Paris. Even the bourgeois wives and mothers who founded the Société des Citoyennes Révolutionnaires in 1793 had been branded as 'lost women dragged out of the mud', 'hideous jades' and 'shameless viragos'. The Directory had banned all women's associations, and only in 1848 were women allowed the right of assembly. La Voix des Femmes was one of about three hundred women's clubs founded in this year alone, and it asserted women's right to participate fully in the Revolution. Collectives and phalansteries began to proliferate. Two women who emerged from literary activities and figured as prominent defenders of their sex in the Commune were Louise Michel and André Léo, who formed the Société pour l'Egalité des Femmes. For the goals of the Commune, propounded in the Declaration to the French People, took virtually no account of the existence of women, apart from a few concessions: the stigma was to be removed from the numerous *'unions libres',* and a pension of 600 francs was to be awarded to widows, legal or not, and to members of the National Guard killed in the defence of the Commune: the

Roman *macula bastardiae* was also removed, and all orphans were to be granted 365 francs.

It was to Louise Michel and André Léo that Elisaveta turned on her arrival in Paris in March 1871. She hoped, she told the Society, to 'help to unite women *communards* into one active society, to give the Commune valuable help, and create a centre of support for the emancipation of women'. 'At this hour,' she told the Executive Commission of the Commune, 'when danger is imminent, and the enemy is at the gates of Paris, the entire population must unite to defend the Commune, which stands for the abolition of privilege and inequality, the distinctions maintained by the necessity of the antagonism on which the privilege of the governing classes has rested.' On 7 April the official paper of the Commune, *La Sociale,* carried a proclamation written by her that was posted all over Paris. 'To all women citizens of Paris,' it read: 'Finish with the old world. Not only is France rising up, but also Russia and Germany are fired with the breath of Revolution . . .' This was followed a few days later by the first meeting of the Union des Femmes pour la Défense de Paris et les Soins aux Blessés, of which Elisaveta was the moving force. *La Sociale* described this as a 'responsible organization of Paris *citoyennes,* resolved to give support and defend the cause of the people, the Revolution and the Commune . . . to give assistance in the work of government commissions, and to serve at ambulance stations, field-kitchens and barricades.' The Union requested the Commune to give it a hall in every *mairie,* in which to establish centres open to the public. 'The Government Commission need only turn to the Central Committee of Citoyennes to have a necessary number of women ready to serve in medical centres or, if need be, at the barricades.'

But the Union, despite its militant vocabulary, could not claim to speak for the majority of Paris *citoyennes,* who saw their power in their ability to neutralize the Fédérés, and increasingly favoured an armistice. Elisaveta voiced her fears in a letter to Marx in the middle of May. 'It is feared that the female element of the Parisian population, revolutionary for the moment, will return, because of continual privation, to the passive and more or less reactionary stance to which it clung in the past.' It was vitally urgent to organize women into collectives, based on socialist rather than charitable principles, and to ensure that they were freed from the repetitive undemanding tasks to which they were condemned in most collectives. In each *arrondissement,* the Union declared, women were to organize centres to receive raw materials; workshops subsidized by the Commune Finance Committee were to be set up to be responsible for the distribution of their products. Daily meetings were to be held, and the committees were to be available day and night. Money was to be collected for medical provisions, petroleum and weapons, which last two, it was stressed, were to be used purely defensively.

Despite her success in realizing many of these plans, Elisaveta was becoming increasingly pessimistic about the situation. The National Guard had not attacked Versailles and had given Thiers time to concentrate his forces. Marx's letters to her gave few grounds for hope either; it was, he said, a 'useless struggle'. Organizational work and active defence were taking their toll on her strength and she was suffering badly from bronchitis. Nevertheless it was she who on 23 May led a detachment of women in the battle for La Batignolle. G. Lefrance recalls, in his *Mémoires d'un Communard:* 'At dawn, a detachment of women fighters, with guns on their shoulders and red cockades on their heads, appeared to defend the building of the regional municipality. At their heads was E. Dmitrieva. In a loud but gentle voice she announced: "Now, when our brothers are going to fight on the barricades, we demand the honour of defending the national municipalities. We shall defend it to the last drop of our blood." ' A hundred and twenty women held the barricade at the Place Blanche, and halted General

Clinchant's troops for several hours. When at eleven o'clock they withdrew, exhausted and out of ammunition, the women who were captured were killed on the spot. Elisaveta then issued a last order to the Union Committee of the eleventh *arrondissement:* 'Muster all the women and the committee itself, and come here immediately to go to the barricades.' She then left with Louise Michel for Montmartre, and from there they went to the Faubourg Saint-Antoine, which was being held by Frankel.

During the entire week of 'bloody May' Elisaveta fought and urged the women in the Union to follow her example. It is hard to know precisely what her movements were in this chaotic week. The Union by no means controlled the activities of most of the women fighters who were largely disorganized and thus easily branded later as roving bands of writhing, sweating, bare-breasted women, urging the men to drink while they threw petroleum into cellars and conducted obscene bacchanals among the burning houses. For this was the vocabulary of the Council of War in its indictment of the working-class *communardes* – the mythical *pétroleuses.* Middle-class activists like Louise Michel were described by the Prosecutor, Captain Jouenne, rather differently:

If they were uneducated one might perhaps grieve as one damned them, but among these women – and I blush to give them the name of women – we find some who are unable to summon to their aid even the paltry resource of ignorance. While lofty minds speak out for the important benefits of education for the people, what a bitter deception this is for them and for us! For among the accused we shall see schoolteachers. These women cannot pretend that the notion of good and evil was unknown to them ...

Elisaveta Dmitrieva managed to avoid the fate of most of the women fighters, 850 of them, who were shot or imprisoned indefinitely in unspeakable conditions. In June she was back in Geneva again. But her allegiance to the

Marxist International had been shaken by her experiences in Paris, and when she attended the London conference of the International in September 1871 she was tempted to go over to the Bakunists. Her indecision was shared by most of the other *émigré* communards. Later that year she was able to return to St Petersburg. Russia, even radical Russia, had little idea of the significance of the Commune, and it was relatively easy for ex-communards to be repatriated. In Russia she was astonished to find that even the radical journal *Delo* ('The Cause') had been most superficial in its accounts of the events in Paris. In St Petersburg she began to make friends with Bakunists, among them a man named Davidovsky. We know little of her subsequent activities. We know only that after the death of her husband she married Davidovsky and followed him to exile in Siberia, where she died.

Anna Krukovskaya was led to Paris by a rather different chain of events. In 1866 Dostoyevsky proposed to her and she rejected him. At the age of twenty-two she, like her younger sister Sofya, was intoxicated by her first contact with the intelligentsia of the capital. For two months Dostoyevsky had been a constant visitor to the Krukovskys' St Petersburg house, and the two had argued passionately and sometimes angrily about socialism. Dostoyevsky had a very high opinion of Anna, regarding her neither as a bluestocking nor as an affected nihilist – high praise from him. 'She is one of the finest women I have ever met in my life,' he records in his memoirs, 'a girl of high moral qualities. But her convictions are diametrically opposed to my own; she is too singleminded.' Marriage between them would obviously have been catastrophic. Anna confided to Sofya, 'I am sometimes astonished that I am unable to love him. He is so good, so intelligent, so kind. But he needs a woman who would devote herself utterly to him, and I cannot do that.' Anna's friend, the writer Natalya Gizetti, also knew Dostoyevsky, and put rather more succinctly the 'single-mindedness' that made it impossible for Anna to accept

Dostoyevsky: 'In those days, it was a question of the honour of defending and actively struggling for women's equality and independence, not a question of "happiness". And these questions were not determined by mere "single-mindedness".'

Anna herself was also a writer. For the past few years she had been secretly and actively rebelling against the stultifying conventions of family life in Palibino, and had been writing short stories and poems. 'The Dream', her first published story, was written when she was twenty in a conscious act of defiance against her father's refusal to allow her to leave home. Lizen'ka is a poor sempstress, the daughter of a poor German teacher. She leads a featureless isolated life in the provinces, surrounded by people without hope or imagination. One day she has a dream in which she meets an idealistic young student, and with him she embarks on a life of happy, hard-working poverty. Without love she is unable to transform her impoverished existence, and she dies soon afterwards, despairing of her wasted youth. The writer's spelling and grammar were faulty, the story was tentative and unstructured, but these very defects gave it its peculiar power; the authenticity of the despair was unmistakable. She sent it to the literary journal *Epokha,* edited by Dostoyevsky, and he decided to publish it. It appeared the following year, anonymously of course, and Dostoyevsky encouraged this unknown young girl from the provinces to continue writing. Her next story, 'Mikhail', published shortly afterwards, exudes the same feelings of frustration and pessimism. The idealistic young hero decides to enter a monastery, but quickly disenchanted by its cynical and inhumane atmosphere he leaves in despair. He then falls in love with a girl and once more is able to dream of leading a simple and useful life. His happiness is short-lived; she falls in love with another man, and abandoning all hope he returns to the monastery, where he dies soon afterwards. Dostoyevsky was captivated by the story; it is more than likely that Mikhail served as the

166

model for Alesha in *The Brothers Karamazov*. 'Now you are a poet!' he wrote to her, and their correspondence became increasingly frequent and intimate. Meanwhile Krukovsky had discovered that Anna was writing to 'some unknown man', and Anna had to defend her right to correspond with the great writer. 'Mikhail' was published, anonymously again, in the ninth issue of *Epokha* in 1864.

When the Krukovskys visited the capital at the end of 1866 Anna was naturally anxious to meet Dostoyevsky. But more important for the sisters than any new personal relationships was the urgent desire to leave home, to go abroad, to study and to write. For Anna the obvious way of escaping from her parents was through a fictitious marriage, a relationship without all the tangles of guilt and self-doubt she experienced in her conversations with Dostoyevsky. Sofya thoroughly approved of the plan: 'We are seeking people like us, wholly committed to the cause, whose principles are identical to ours, who would not marry us but free us, knowing that we are necessary and useful in the present situation.' For her the 'cause' meant the political problems that her new radical friends in the capital were debating so passionately. She had met Marya Bokova and her *de facto* husband Sechenov, the eminent physiology professor who was helping Sofya with her studies. Sechenov had even proposed a fictitious marriage to her, a proposal she had rejected for fear of becoming emotionally involved. Through Marya Bokova however she met Nadezhda Suslova, who had just returned from Zurich and strengthened her determination to study abroad. Tkachev gained much support from women readers. In his important article 'People of the Future and Heroes of the Petit-Bourgeoisie', published in *Delo* in 1868, he defined the 'new woman' in the context of the novels of George Eliot, André Léo and George Sand.[35] When Anna met Tkachev she was impressed by his literary tastes and his lucid exposition of Marxist theory.[36] Like Elisaveta Dmitrieva, she was inspired by him to read Marx's

Outline for the Critique of Political Economy, and in May 1868 she was writing to a friend; 'Only through a scientific and economic revolution can we realize our projects for the future, in which our associational beginnings can serve as a transitional stage for the masses.' She and her friend Anna Evreinova were learning to type, in order to be able to support themselves and to save time on letters, and were vaguely discussing the idea of wandering around the countryside as pilgrims, staying at monasteries, in order to write about conditions in the countryside. After all, this was how Flerovsky had written his valuable *Conditions of the Working Classes in Russia.* But Anna was too sophisticated to be a populist, too politically uninformed to interpret what she saw around her. She was temperamentally suited to the politics of the city, and her desire to leave Russia took on a new urgency. Sofya was married now to Kovalevsky, and they were free to go abroad.

Anna and her friend accompanied Sofya and Vladimir to Heidelberg, but there was little for Anna to do there and she longed to write and see more of the world. She and Anna Evreinova decided to leave for Paris. Kovalevsky agreed to give them translation work for which he would pay them an annual salary of a thousand rubles, enough to live on and enrol in the Sorbonne. She was to communicate through Sofya with her parents, who still believed the sisters to be together. Anna had never joined any political group, and her ideas were occasionally unsupported by theory. Sofya recalled her in those days, 'reading revolutionary brochures in secret, and determined, no more and no less, to overthrow the whole bourgeois structure and turn Europe upside-down.'

When she arrived in Paris in the winter of 1869, Anna found that socialism and women's emancipation combined much more harmoniously than in Russia. Tkachev and Pisarev had written her a letter of introduction to André Léo, and through her Anna was soon on friendly terms with the writers Marie Desraismes, Noémie Reclus and Louise

168

Michel. André Léo herself was still writing, far from the turmoil of Paris, and could not help Anna to find her feet. With Louise Michel, who had already dropped literary work for exclusively political activity, Anna was rather out of her depth. She felt more drawn to the polemics of Marie Desraismes and Noémie Reclus. Marie Desraismes, enraged by an offensively mysogynistic article by Barbey d'Aurevilly, had taken up her pen in 1865 and embarked on a lengthy survey of women's historical, legal and family conditions, a survey that ended only with her arrest after the collapse of the Commune. Anna herself was too confused by the multitude of new impressions in Paris to be able to adopt any definite political position. She was simultaneously discovering work (she was employed as a typesetter), poverty and an embryonic workers' revolution. 'When I left for France,' she wrote, 'I never suspected that the dream of the overthrow of the bourgeois regime was so close to being realized.' [37] Her guide through all the confusing events of the Commune was to be a young medical student whom she had met at a Blanquist meeting, and whom she was later to marry. Victor Jaclard, subsequently a hero of the Commune, was sentenced to deportation shortly after she met him. Together they left for Geneva, from which Elisaveta Dmitrieva had just left for London. Here they stayed with the Utins, who gave them the latest information on the International.

When the Empire collapsed the Jaclards hurried back to Paris, where Victor played an important part in the crucial battle of 31 October and was then appointed colonel of the Seventeenth Legion, member of the Central Committee of the National Guard and deputy-mayor of the seventeenth *arrondissement*. Anna joined Jules Allix's Comité des Femmes in the eighteenth *arrondissement*.

The Committee's priorities were work, education, social welfare and women's rights. Allix proposed the establishment of communal workshops and kitchens, and the Committee took over a large house in which a workshop was set up.

169

Various political tendencies were contained within the Committee, and Elisaveta Dmitrieva for one worked briefly with Allix on her arrival in Paris. But the Committee tended to regard the Union des Femmes as a dictatorial monolithic organization, and prided itself on representing all political aspects of the Commune. There were to be frequent altercations between the two groups. Anna's ideas about the new society were in many ways Utopian. She and Noémie Reclus were responsible for superintending girls' schools, and some of the plans they drew up for their improvement were able to be used as a guideline by the bourgeois Republic. Her chief concern was that the Commune should uphold moral standards, and she was outraged by the excessive drunkenness and brutality of many of the communards. She was convinced that the raising of family allowances would eliminate prostitution, and wanted to see all prostitutes detained and then trained as nurses. Since many of the National Guard found the idea of being nursed by former prostitutes repugnant she suggested, in a letter to the Central Committee of the Commune, that these women should be sent to the eighteenth *arrondissement,* where there were 'spirits generous enough to let such women be welcomed'. 'Drunkards who have lost all self-respect should be arrested,' she continued in the same letter; cafés should be closed at eleven pm and smoking in concerts should be forbidden. These proposals were never carried through of course. The Central Committee was as anxious as she to abolish the last vestiges of the decadent Empire, but had more urgent tactical problems on its hands.

The Comité was particularly anxious to destroy the stranglehold of the Church on public institutions. Nuns were monopolizing all the jobs in hospitals and prisons. Charity was an obstacle to solidarity; alms must be replaced by communally sponsored relief committees. On 13 April the Central Committee issued a decree calling for the organization of a medical corps. Several sections in every *arrondissement* were to be ready day and night, and the Comité demanded the right of all women to put themselves at the disposal of the Commune and to form first-aid committees. Here Anna and Jaclard were to run up against the almost universal contempt of the Commune surgeons for women doctors and nurses. Many women, after making enormous sacrifices to be accepted as ambulance nurses, were to find they were given inadequate medical provisions and little co-operation from their male colleagues. Jaclard proposed that ambulance stations should be entrusted only to the more open-minded doctors, accompanied by three or four women doctors. 'The women who had the courage to force open the doors of science will surely not fail to serve humanity and the Revolution,' he exhorted them. At a time when, as André Léo put it, all must move towards 'that responsible alliance of men and women, that unity of feelings and ideas which alone can create, in honour, equality and peace, the Commune of the future', it was vital that these prejudices be abolished, and the Jaclards played an important part in encouraging co-operation between the men and women fighters and the doctors.

After the downfall of the Commune, Jaclard was one of the more prominent victims of the Council of War. Poor General Krukovsky, shattered first by the news of Anna's clandestine literary activity, then of Sofya's unfeminine interest in mathematics and unseemly elopement, bore bravely the final blow. He had imagined that Anna was living quietly and chastely with Sofya in Berlin, and when Sofya wrote to him begging him to go to Paris and intercede with his old acquaintance Thiers for the life of his revolutionary son-in-law he was on the point of disowning Anna altogether. But eventually he agreed, and on arriving in Paris together with Sofya and Kovalevsky he managed to strike a gentlemanly bargain with Thiers for Jaclard's life. Kovalevsky gave Jaclard his passport, and they all left for Berne.

171

It was obvious that the Council of War had as little information about Anna's activities as they had of Elisaveta Dmitrieva's. On 29 December she was sentenced to hard labour for life, a sentence hardly justified by the cryptic, curiously apolitical charge of 'complicity in the fraudulent removal of various objects at the expense of M. de Polignac'!

In 1874 the family returned to Russia, where Jaclard got a job teaching French at the Mariinsky Gimnazium for Girls. He took his job extremely seriously, and as well as contributing articles to various journals on political events in Europe, he compiled a two-volume French anthology for the benefit of his pupils. Anna had resumed her writing and her friendship with Dostoyevsky, who was now embarked on writing *Crime and Punishment*. Their arguments about Christianity and socialism were as heated as before, but Anna was now becoming interested in spiritualism, and read all she could in English, French and German on the subject. In 1886 the literary journal *Severnyi Vestnik* ('Northern Herald') published her long short story, 'Notes of a Spiritualist'. The story is narrated by a man dying in a madhouse. He recounts the time when he had possessed supernatural powers, and had been employed by a wealthy count to attend a congress in America and to bring back a message from the dead countess. He travels to America and is overwhelmed by all he sees there; he returns to Russia, his task completed, to find that the count has lost interest in the message from beyond the grave. The young man suddenly becomes horrifyingly aware of the cruelty of Russian society, and of his own physical powerlessness against it. This awareness inevitably brings on the insanity that condemns him to the madhouse; the story's obvious references to travelling and conferences show very clearly how alienated Anna felt from Russian society after her return. Her next story, published the following year in the same journal, has a bleakly optimistic message. The heroine in 'The Young Nurse' is pregnant and unmarried. She is on the verge of

172

committing suicide when she meets a young doctor who urges her to continue working and to look forward to the birth of her baby.

Anna's stories express with even greater intensity the poignant confusions of her younger sister's novel *The Woman Nihilist*. She had contracted a serious liver condition and was preoccupied with her own imminent death. After a brief stay at a Paris clinic she died in 1887, attended by her sister, her husband and her friends. At the funeral André Léo spoke lovingly of her friend and comrade. Sofya, shattered by her death, was increasingly drawn to spiritualism, and hoped that Anna would appear to her in a dream.

These girls who lived and studied abroad in the seventies set an inspiring example to their Russian sisters. Their experience of political events was as important, on their return to Russia, as their educational acquirements.

NOTES

1. I have paraphrased this article, contained in the first issue of *Narodnoe Delo* ('The People's Cause'), which came out on 1 September 1868, and which Bakunin reluctantly agreed to edit.
2. The 'superfluous man' and the 'repentant nobleman' were cruelly apposite stereotypes of the mid-nineteenth-century Russian, whom Turgenev and Chekhov described particularly convincingly. Turgenev's 'superfluous man', abandoning some of his inherited social privileges, lapses into impotence, while Chekhov's 'repentant nobleman' attempts ludicrously and often drunkenly to make amends for his privileges.
3. Her thesis was entitled *Beiträge zur Physiologie der Lymphe*.
4. Tyrkova, op. cit., p. 173.
5. Her thesis topic was *Zur Lehre von der Hypophasis Keratitis'*.
6. See Glossary of Names.
7. Leffler, C., *Sonya Kovalevskaya*, p. 3.
8. Kovalevskaya, S., *Vospominania detsva* (Childhood Memories), p. 25.
9. Polubarina-Kochina, S., *S. V. Kovalevskaya. Her Life and Work,* p. 75.
10. First appeared in Swedish in 1888; translated into Russian in 1890.
11. She was writing her memoirs (Childhood Memories).
12. Figner, V., *Work Completed,* Complete Works, vol. 1, p. 63.

173

13. ibid., p. 35.
14. ibid., vol. 12, pp. 535-6.
15. Pantaleev, op. cit., vol. 1, p. 638.
16. *Obschina* (Community), 1828, pp. 6-7.
17. Meijjer, J. M., *Knowledge and Revolution 1870-3,* pp. 59-60.
18. Chudnovsky. *Iz davnikh let* (From Bygone Years), pp. 226-7. (Not available but quoted in Meijjer, see above).
19. S. I. Bardina (Obituary), pp. 61-2.
20. Figner, V. *Student Years,* Complete Works, vol. 1, p. 76.
21. Kropotkin, P., op. cit., p. 256.
22. Meijjer, op. cit., p. 99.
23. In *Nedelya* (The Week), 1868-9.
24. Figner, V., *Work Completed,* Complete Works, vol. 1, p. 167.
25. Dzhabadari in the journal *Byloe* (The Past), September 1907, pp. 169 ff.
26. Stasov, op. cit., p. 240.
27. Morozov, N., *Povesti iz moei zhizni,* (Stories from my Life), vol. 1, pp. 481-2.
28. Figner, V., *Work Completed,* Complete Works, vol. 5, p. 99.
29. *Iz vospominanii Kravchinskogo o dele 50'i,* (Kravchinsky's Memoirs of the Trial of the 50) in Kovalensky's work (see Bibliography), vol. 1, p. 157.
30. I have summarized the speech. The full text is in Dragomanov's *Le Proces des Socialistes de Moscou* (in Russian). See Bibliography.
31. Figner, V., Complete Works, vol. 5, pp. 157 ff.
32. Kravchinsky, in *A Female Nihilist,* describes her escape.
33. See Glossary of Names.
34. The German economist Baron Hoxthausen had engaged on a study of the Russian peasantry, and had brought out the first authoritative treatise on the Russian peasant commune. The work echoed much of what Herzen had said on the subject, and made a deep impression on Russian radicals, since it emphasized that Russia's future lay not in artificial imported Western concepts of 'progress', but in its own neglected countryside.
35. Tkachev, *Selected Works,* vol. 1, p. 173.
36. Tkachev was the leading, if not the only, Marxist writer at the time.
37. Thomas, Edith, *Women Incendiaries,* p. 76.

CHAPTER V
TO THE PEOPLE

The revolutionary activities of the 1860s and 1870s in Russia itself were generally spontaneous and sporadic. By the late sixties the aspirations of those belonging to what is nebulously described as the 'revolutionary movement' had cohered somewhat with the formation of the Land and Liberty Party, whose development I shall attempt to trace later on. But for the twenty years or so preceding this there were few people who did not discuss with increasing pessimism the State's ability to bring about any fundamental social change. Intensified police vigilance was making committed revolutionaries of people who had merely sought to bring some enlightenment to the people in the Sunday School Movement or indulged in vague socialist speculations.

The first known 'movements to the people' by the early populists coincided with the closure of the Sunday schools in 1862. In the years following the student disorders of that year small groups of students began to set out rather haphazardly for the villages, armed with the Bible and various folk tales, whose ethical precepts they hoped to impart to the peasants in their homes and schools. But unlike the early Sunday school teachers, these pioneer populists did not regard

175

themselves as an enlightened élite, capable, indeed duty-bound, to propagandize among the people. Bakunin rather than Marx was their guide; the peasantry, they believed, must only be made aware of the strength that had lain dormant in them since the Pugachev rebellion. These young militants set out as pupils, as 'apostles', rather than as teachers and leaders; for the leaders were to be found among the peasants themselves. In 1863 a group of students from Kazan' University set out for the local villages. But they betrayed their ignorance of an almost totally illiterate peasantry; the literature they carried, their accents and vocabulary, not to mention the bewildering and inexplicable fact of their presence there, set up an insuperable barrier between these early 'apostolic pilgrims' and their peasant 'teachers'.

Men began to transfer all their filial love and duty to the peasants, and the peasant commune acquired for them a kind of religious significance: 'the sacred and redeeming heritage bequeathed to us by our past life, the poverty of which is atoned for by this one invaluable heritage'.[1] Women could accept this new faith without confronting such immediate problems of leadership and authority, and many of them set out as teachers in the mid-sixties.

Marya Kuvshinskaya had no definite political ideology to propound to her pupils. She set out, carrying with her the works of Pisarev, Dobrolyubov and the latest copies of *Sovremennik,* to a little village near Vyatka in the Urals, where she got a job as a teacher in a girls' school. This was an area that for centuries had boasted of its independence from Moscow; an area of small, cultured, hard-working communities. There was also a sizeable colony of political exiles there, of whom Charushin and Khalturin, later prominent in the revolutionary movement, had a considerable influence on Marya Kuvshinskaya's ideas. She soon became a much-loved teacher and was welcomed into her pupils' homes, where parents and children read and discussed the books she brought with her.

176

One of the homes she spent some time in was that of the local priest, Yakimov, a hard-working man with a large family to support. He had no great love for women's education but was anxious that his children should be able to support themselves after they left home. His eldest daughter Anna had entered the school at the age of eleven, and was already entertaining dreams of becoming a village nurse or midwife. For her and her friends Marya Kuvshinskaya was an ideal and an inspiration. She and a group of friends began to meet secretly after school in the library, where they would discuss the ideas of Chernyshevsky and Dobrolyubov. Then Charushin began to accompany Marya Kuvshinskaya to the school, and from him they learnt for the first time about the French Revolution and the International Workingmen's Association. The school, which had prided itself on its liberal reputation, was now finding Marya Kuvshinskaya's presence an embarrassment, and these rather irregular activities were reported to the police, who immediately searched the place and ordered Marya Kuvshinskaya's dismissal. Anna Yakimova now considered herself a staunch Bakunist, and the action of the police merely strengthened her resolve to 'go to the people'. When she left school in 1872 at the age of sixteen she announced her intention to enrol in pedagogical courses in Vyatka in order to become a village teacher, and threatened her reluctant father that she would leave home for good if he did not give his consent. Her two closest friends, she reminded him, had run away from home, one of them under the pretext of a fictitious marriage. Anna was determined at all costs not to compromise her independence by committing herself to such a relationship. With a small allowance from her father she went alone to Vyatka and enrolled in pedagogical courses. After a year there she was ready to support herself as a teacher, and she got herself a job in a school in Orlov. Her father, seriously fearful now that she would suffer the same fate as Marya Kuvshinskaya, begged her to return home, offering to build her a school in

177

his house. But for Anna there was no question of going home; she had gone to the people, never to return.

Marya Kuvshinskaya, along with hundreds of disillusioned populists, returned to the cities and to the 'circles' in whose companionable atmosphere crucial political questions could be asked. For an important choice now faced all populists: they had to go beyond Bakunin's hazy formulations about the immediate fomentation of peasant uprisings and decide whether to embark instead on long-term propaganda work. The revolutionary intelligentsia was still unprepared to assume the responsibilities of leadership and was temperamentally antagonistic to any form of authority; they had no real tactical or ideological basis for a revolutionary organization: the choice was a painful one. A few, it is true, compromised with their political beliefs and became engulfed in the professional bourgeoisie. But for most populists, Bakunin was now being ousted by Lavrov. His appeal to the intelligentsia, his insistence that the future revolutionary leaders must first concentrate on their own education, was more appropriate for the disillusioned activists than Bakunin's impetuous philosophy of agitation.

In these radical self-education circles women were making their presence felt. Those who had stayed in Russia and graduated from the day schools in the 1870s were more materialistic than their predecessors in the Sunday School Movement. To be sure, education was gained in many cases at the cost of breaking with parents and husbands, but the practical advantage of a teaching diploma seemed to offer a new, officially approved kind of security. It was not long however before they realized that their diploma opened few professional doors. Men teachers, even without qualification, were generally preferred to women, and there was now less demand than ever for governesses; in 1870 in Moscow, for eight women's teaching places there were over a hundred applicants. Women now looked increasingly for support to the radical student circles.

178

In 1869 Olga Shleisner and her husband Mark Natanson, together with a group of dissident students from the St Petersburg Medical Faculty, began to meet regularly in order to define a 'revolutionary ethic', a satisfactory ideology that would enable radicals to embark on serious practical activities. After the arrest of Natanson three years later, his place was taken by Nikolai Chaikovsky, and the group became known as the 'Chaikovsksists'. But this group 'could not be described as really complete until the spring of 1871, when it was joined by a small group of women, all destined to take an active part in the Underground'.[2] Sofya Perovskaya, the Kornilov sisters and the friends they made at the Arlachinsky courses were to be an inspiration to women hitherto fighting for their independence in isolation. It was not for nothing that the government had feared the effects of women's education. By 1874, of 808 political arrests, 188 were women.

One small girl unfailingly sat in the front row at lectures at the Arlachinsky courses. She had small features and a large forehead and always wore a simple brown dress. Since she was too shy to ask questions she attracted little attention. She was Sofya Perovskaya, and she was sixteen years old. The Perovsky family could boast an unblemished noble lineage: her great-grandfather, Kiril Razumovsky, had been the last hetman[3] of Little Russia, and her grandfather had been governor of the Crimea in the reign of Alexander I. On the basis of this her father, Lev Perovsky, was securely ensconced as a governor-general of St Petersburg, where he and his wife and four children occupied a mansion in the Ministry of Internal Affairs building. It was in this house that his youngest daughter Sofya was born in 1853. Lev Perovsky was an arrogant, capricious man, and his presence at home provoked constant scenes. He spent most of his time drinking and playing cards with his friends. He felt that his wife Varvara had betrayed him by not being able to modify her simple provincial ways so as to scintillate at her husband's side at social gatherings. She was a sensitive, deeply religious woman, passionately involved with her children. She was especially concerned not to inflict on Sofya and her sister Marya the stupefying classes in French and deportment that had passed for education in her day. A German governess was engaged for the two girls, and Lev would occasionally treat the family to dramatic renderings from *Les Misérables*. Sofya was a reserved child, deeply attached to her mother and outraged by her father's offensive criticisms of his wife; these criticisms inevitably extended to her too, sometimes in the form of offensive banter, sometimes as outright abuse. When she was twelve she and her mother visited Geneva where Sofya became close friends with the daughter of a Decembrist, Alexandra Poggio. Together they discovered the pleasures of reading, and when she returned to St Petersburg she started to read avidly.

In 1866 Karakozov's attempt on the life of the Tsar had dramatic consequences for the Perovsky family, although as a cloistered girl of thirteen Sofya was barely able to grasp the political significance of the act. Her father lost his lucrative sinecure and was demoted to a less lucrative position in the Ministry of Internal Affairs. He grudgingly consented to modify his lavish tastes, and after much argument with his wife agreed to give up the St Petersburg house and to settle with his mistress in a smaller apartment, allowing his wife and children to settle on her estate in the Crimea. Released at last from her father's watchful and critical eye, Sofya could indulge her taste for reading and study, and between the ages of thirteen and sixteen she immersed herself in her grandfather's library. There was no money for a teacher, and she profited by her solitude to teach herself maths.

In 1869 she returned to the capital with her mother and sister to visit her father. On the boat from Odessa she struck up a friendship with a girl who at the age of twenty-four had decided to leave her home in the Crimea and enrol in the Arlachinsky courses. Her name was Anna Vil'berg, and

Sofya was immediately attracted by her impetuousness and independence. By the time she reached St Petersburg Sofya had decided to enrol too; she was especially anxious to attend Strannolyubsky's mathematics lectures. Her brothers Vasili and Nicolai were a great encouragement to her. They were attending the renowned Mendeleev's physics courses at the university and with Mendeleev were moving in radical circles – nothing more radical, actually, than the student groups in which Pisarev and Chernyshevsky were discussed, but radical enough to get Vasili expelled from the university that summer for his political 'unreliability'.

Lev Perovsky was now implacably opposed to Sofya enrolling in the Arlachinsky courses. He detested her new 'nihilist' friends, and Anna Vil'berg's somewhat slovenly dress and offhand manners provoked many unpleasant scenes at the dinner-table. Her mother invariably took Sofya's side, and was excited at the prospect of her further studies; in the heated political atmosphere of the capital she felt her religious faith wavering, and listened sympathetically to the young students who accompanied Vasili home, and read aloud the works of Dobrolyubov, Mill, Buckle and Büchner. As her capital was under the direct control of her husband she decided to sell some of her personal possessions in order to meet Sofya's fees.

With Anna Vil'berg, Sofya started to attend Strannolyubsky's mathematics lectures, and then lectures on inorganic chemistry, geometry, Russian literature and pedagogics. Gradually, she overcame her shyness, and was introduced by Anna Vil'berg to Sofya Lecherne, who had been active in the Sunday School Movement some nine years previously. She also met Anna Korba, later prominent in the revolutionary movement, and the Kornilov sisters, Alexandra and Vera. Sofya's subsequent 'downfall', her rapid involvement with the political movement, was attributed by the official *Khronika Sotsialisticheskogo Dvizhenia* ('Chronicle of the Socialist Movement') to her attendance at

181

these courses, where she formed 'evil friendships'. The charge is obviously as ludicrous as that common reference to her as a 'man-hater'; 'it is not surprising that she acted rather coldly and restrainedly towards men, as towards activists in general; she considered herself superior to men and did not really like them,' notes her generally sympathetic biographer,[4] pointing to her father's coldness towards her. At the age of sixteen she was as insecure as all her young friends, anxious to take advantage of their first chance of intellectual independence. In Alexandra Kornilova, who was to become her closest friend in these days, she found a similar passion for independence.

Alexandra, Lyubov, Nadezhda and Vera Kornilova were the daughters of a wealthy merchant who had sent them all to a Mariinsky Institute. Their great-grandfather was a wealthy peasant who had accumulated the capital to establish one of the largest porcelain factories in Russia, the Kornilov Brothers. Their father, deeply imbued with all the traditional prejudices of the merchant class, took a utilitarian view of his daughters' education; 'after all, I can't hire them four governesses,' he explained. Their mother had died when they were young and their family life was simple and unpretentious. But the activities of the eldest son, Alexander, had shaken some of the comfortable assumptions that had created this harmonious atmosphere. In the early 1860s he had been a Sunday school teacher in the provinces; his red shirt and his stock of literature had proclaimed him a materialist, rejecting all ideas of philanthropy through education. His arrest and early death had made a profound impression on the whole family. Old Kornilov was sympathetic to his daughters' friends, and Sofya became a frequent visitor to the house, where she would stay until late into the night discussing with her friends questions of philosophy, economics and politics. Here she met Olga Shleisner, who was attending Sechenov's lectures on physiology and persuaded Sofya to accompany her to them.

This group of studious young girls began to attract the attention of progressive professors, including Professor Engel'hardt.[5] He invited them to his *dacha* in Lesnoi where he gave them the free use of his laboratory. In Sofya he found a remarkable student; she was quick to learn and speedily outstripped the other girls. But she was not taken with practical laboratory work – she preferred abstract mathematical problems. By now she was finding Strannolyubsky's lectures too slow, and was studying algebra on her own out of a French textbook.

The summer of 1869 she spent in a fever of discussion and reading at the Kornilovs' house. This became a meeting place for a number of friends from the Arlachinsky courses. They took long walks in the country together, and began tentatively to work out a systematic reading programme. When she returned to her father's place after the summer, however, she was met with a barrage of criticisms. No longer the lofty government official, he was now a whining old man whose sons had disgraced the family name and whose indomitable daughter's open contempt for his authority exposed the tattered remnants of his dignity. But Sofya's studies pushed these domestic arguments to the background. Strannolyubsky, who was giving geometry courses at Anna Korba's house for the more gifted women students, remarked on 'Sofya's remarkable ability for mathematics'. Her brother Vasili had encouraged her to believe that women would soon be admitted to the universities, and Sofya was all set to apply to the technological institute for admission. She must have realized that such reforms were on the very distant horizon, however, and unlike Alexandra Kornilova and Anna Vil'berg she never involved herself in the campaign for women's educational reforms. She was more interested in the radical students she was meeting. She and Alexandra Kornilova once visited a student 'commune', where they were welcomed rather as victims in search of their liberation; one student actually proposed a fictitious marriage to Alexandra on the

183

spot, but both girls felt that this would be an unnecessary compromise, and talked to him instead about the miseries of being a student mother. Vera Kornilova however had managed to establish an equitable relationship with a fellow-student whom she married fictitiously in order to set up her own flat in the city.

Sofya was by now seriously worried by her father's threats to put an end to her studies, and she decided to move in with Vera. There were no protracted domestic arguments. She acted immediately on her decision, apologizing profusely to her mother for the repercussions this would have on her. The break was inevitable. She was warmly welcomed at Vera's flat, and continued her studies as seriously as before. But by now Lev Perovsky, half-demented, his social position hopelessly compromised, decided to exert some of his old influence to ask Trepov, Governor-General of St Petersburg, to usurp his role as father and produce a full-scale police investigation of his daughter, who must be either mad or a criminal. Varvara Perovskaya began to visit Alexandra Kornilova late at night, begging her to tell her where Sofya was; but Alexandra would reply calmly that Sofya's duty was not to comply with threats but to study. Old Kornilov was bothered by the police too, but he refused to give them any information; he enjoyed watching the young people fighting for their independence. Sofya's elder brother Nikolai, however, felt responsible for bringing about some sort of reconciliation. He supported his sister's move in principle, and realized that she had the full support of all her friends, but as a seventeen-year-old girl she had had little experience of the tactics of police persecution. He talked to a policeman working on the case who warned that his sister might 'fall into the trap of certain unprincipled men'. The whole affair grew increasingly ridiculous, and Lev Perovsky eventually became so debilitated that his doctor seriously advised him to wash his hands of the business and give his daughter a passport. This he finally did, with a small allowance, which Sofya received through her brother.

Sofya was far too involved with her new independent life to be much concerned about her father's manoeuvres. She and her friends were combining their studies with wide reading. In the spring of 1870 she moved into a communal *dacha* with Alexandra Kornilova, Anna Vil'berg and Sofya Lecherne, and here they began to discuss seriously a systematic reading programme. Sofya was especially anxious to read consistently and to discuss every point fully. When a young student, Alexandrov, suggested they read *Capital* they refused, as they wanted first to grasp the foundations of political economy on which the work was based, a work that 'for many years was extremely difficult and almost impossible to understand', as Sofya said. And so they read Mill and Lassalle, whose eloquent presentation of economic structures fascinated them. 'We did not accept any authority, we did not want to take on faith, from another's mouth, a philosophy we could not study independently, critically,' wrote Alexandra Kornilova[6] succinctly expressing the mood of the group. And as a group of assertive young women who accepted nobody's authority they began to attract some unwanted attention from passers-by in their walks in the country. In order to be able to go around unmolested they decided to wear men's clothes. Sofya put on some wide trousers of her brother's and a rough peasant shirt. Alexandra revelled in her new 'nihilist' appearance in a rather strange jacket and trousers; she grew attached to her men's boots too, which she wore from then on. They enjoyed their time off from serious conversations and reading, exploring all the possibilities of this new life in which suddenly authority counted for nothing. They learnt to ride, picked mushrooms and berries and went for long walks. There is a photograph of them, just returned from a riding expedition, looking alert and yet supremely indifferent to the spectator.

185

It was this group, with its seriousness and its spontaneity, that inspired the first communal Chaikovsky group. We have few specific details of the young people who were to comprise this first major revolutionary group. Many of them were immediately inspired to go to the people and carry their enthusiasm to a wider audience. But most of them were anxious to form a united circle in which they could better prepare themselves for this task. The Chaikovskists are best considered as a group of about thirty friends, with a nucleus that formed in the spring of 1871 when Mark Natanson and his wife Olga Shleisner rented a couple of cheap *dachas* in the village of Kushelevka, near the capital. There were about ten young people there, most of them students and four of them women. Natanson drew up a programme that seemed to him to evolve from the university courses; questions of political economy and psychology were to be discussed. But he was very much the teacher, and Alexandra Kornilova recalled feeling like an incompetent schoolgirl when asked to give a little speech on Mill. Both women and men had to endure the cooking test, however, and life was cheerful and spartan. They got up at dawn, did gymnastics and rowing (at which Sofya Perovskaya excelled), and lived on a diet of black bread and horse meat. Soon Natanson was arrested, and his successor, Nikolai Chaikovsky, did not try to impose the same kind of programme on the group. There is no doubt that the women had reacted strongly against any attempt to *organize* a 'programme' that seemed to them to evolve quite naturally from their discussions and reading together.

At about this time there was a students' meeting at the Forestry Institute to discuss the 'women's question'; the meeting expressed very clearly three distinct phases in the history of Russian women. The first speaker enunciated some rather florid commonplaces about women's life-enhancing qualities; the second proposed, rather more concretely but anachronistically, the establishment of women's collectives. The third speaker said: 'It is impossible to isolate the

186

women's question from the general problem of the emancipation of the proletariat'. The Chaikovsksists were in a majority at the meeting and the last speaker was warmly applauded. The 'women's question' was thus neatly disposed of, and men and women could now happily contemplate an equal partnership in future political activities together. But the temperamental differences between these men and women revolutionaries account for the extraordinary combination of recklessness and caution, ruthlessness and compassion, that they brought to their activities in the seventies and eighties.

Sofya Perovskaya's moral authority over the Chai-kovsksists was not mere romantic invention; it was absolutely essential to the formation of the group. We must, however, immediately discount the overflattering portrayal of her intellectual and political influence; as an inexperienced girl of eighteen she still had much to learn politically. But it was she more than anyone else who insisted on the absolute integrity of every member of the group, and this personal preference was in the end the only real criterion for membership. Her own disciplined and ascetic life was universally admired; she always slept on bare boards (a habit she kept through most of her life) and insisted on taking on the most strenuous of the household chores. Kropotkin visited the *dacha* in 1871 and recalls her returning from the river Neva, dressed in rough peasant clothes and laughing as she carried two buckets of water on her shoulders. 'We were excellent comrades with all the women members of the group, but Sofya Perovskaya we all loved. When we saw her our faces always lit up with a broad smile, although she paid us little attention,' he said.[7] If she paid little attention it was because she spent most of her time reading. He recalls her sitting absorbed in a book while her friends were discussing a comrade; she briefly glanced up to remark, 'he's a philanderer' and then returned immediately to her book. They were probably discussing Klyachko; it was Sofya who insisted that Klyachko, torn between political commitment

187

and a tormenting love affair, be excluded from the group. Another comrade, Lermontov, who wore gloves and a starched shirt, she accused of 'frivolity', while Dmitry Klements she rebuked for wasting his exceptional talents by excessive drinking. These criticisms, although in themselves relatively minor, helped to encourage the spirit of mutual self-criticism that became the chief unifying factor within the group. Nor did this self-criticism make the Chaikovsksists exclusive; they were as anxious to recruit new members as they were accessible to new ideas. Already they had established important contacts in Moscow, Kiev, Odessa and Kherson. Dmitry Rogachev came from the same group of artillery officers in St Petersburg that had given Shishko and Kravchinsky to the revolutionary movement. He was in close touch with the St Petersburg Chaikovsksists, and in 1870 he travelled with Kravchinsky to do propaganda work among young radicals there.

Tatiana Lebedeva was one of many young radicals who were stirred by these men's eloquence to establish a Chaikovsky group in Moscow. She had enrolled in pedagogical courses, initially intending to become a village teacher. But, as she and her friends were only too well aware, idealistic populism had outlived its day, and she was now looking for more concrete political goals. What was said at the meeting attended by Tatiana and her friends we do not know, but their speeches inspired her, at the age of twenty, to break with her family and commit herself to a life of political action.

Vasily Lebedev had been a moderately wealthy magistrate in the Moscow region, whose wife had died shortly after the birth of their sixth daughter Tatiana in 1850. The eldest girl was sent to a Moscow Institute and the younger girls were packed off to an orphans' home, whose spartan barrack-like atmosphere Tatiana could never remember without horror. The girls were trained in a hard school; they cooked, washed and sewed and were perfunctorily taught some Russian and foreign literature. These lessons were Tatiana's only consolation and she developed a passion for Russian romantic poetry, a passion that was to sustain her through many years of hardship and illness. At the age of eighteen she left the orphans' home and moved in with her brother Pëtr and his wife Vera, who had a great influence on Tatiana. Widely read and generous with her ideas, she encouraged Tatiana in her reading, and soon both of them started reading classes in the house for illiterate workers. Pëtr was a judge, well known for his radical views. When his father died he had rejected his claim to the inheritance, which he had redistributed equally among his six sisters and an elderly aunt.

Although Tatiana was now financially independent, her break with Pëtr and Vera was nevertheless a painful one. But she was determined that they should not be in any way implicated in her activities. She decided to stay in Moscow for a while to 'fill in the gaps in her revolutionary education' and to form new contacts in the movement. She moved into a squalid little room in the Skvortsov building, a five-storey tenement, a real 'nest of nihilists' with at least a thousand inhabitants. She was soon running the students' library at the agricultural faculty of Moscow University, which under her direction acquired a large stock of illegal literature and became a popular meeting place for radicals.

One of the St Petersburg Chaikovsksists' most important visible achievements was their thriving underground publishing business. Alexandra Kornilova had donated her considerable fortune to the 'cause of the book', and most of the books were published with her money, although they did occasionally manage to negotiate contracts with sympathetic publishers. Among the books published and then distributed to members who were going to the people were Louis Blanc's *History of 1848* and the works of Bervi-Flerovsky, whose *ABC of Social Sciences* and *The Position of the Working Classes in Russia* had caused such a stir among Russian

189

radicals. Marya Kuvshinskaya was one of the people who visited the *dacha* briefly to collect works to take to the people, and Anna Yakimova used these works in her discussions with the peasants she was meeting.

Immediately after leaving her pedagogical courses in Vyatka, Anna Yakimova had embarked on her wanderings in the Orlov area, and from 1872 to 1874 she taught in local schools and learnt to give smallpox vaccinations. She had plenty of opportunity for discussing political questions with the populists she met on her solitary travels; they gave her Chaikovsky books and pamphlets which she distributed and discussed with the peasants. But although she found the peasantry eager to listen to her explanation of the injustices under which they laboured, they seemed incapable of applying what they learnt to their own lives. The fault, she concluded, lay in herself; she was isolated from any central revolutionary organization.

The St Petersburg Chaikovsksists were facing an isolation and an ideological crisis of a rather different kind. Tikhomirov, of the St Petersburg Chaikovsky circle, spoke for most revolutionary circles in Russia when he said:

> We understood our programme in a very anarchist sense. Anarchy was then flourishing. Were we anarchists? I really do not know. But all the undefined formulae of anarchism reconciled themselves very easily to the undefined nature of our ideas. Apart from a few convinced anarchists, most of us were content with vague expressions about the future, about unconditional freedom and unbounded equality. But this wasn't a programme; these dreams replaced for us both our future life and our lost faith.

It was Kropotkin who first brought out some sort of systematic revolutionary programme, although the great play subsequently made of it by the government was hardly warranted by its contents; its importance was that it united much of the thinking of the Bakunists and the Lavrists. 'We

190

should be concerned to spread our ideas about the future society,' it said, 'and this should be done by means of literary propaganda and systematic agitation.' The programme went on to emphasize that industrial strikes merely diverted attention from long-term propaganda and study, but that local conflicts between peasants and landlords were to be encouraged as useful preparation for later large-scale insurrections. Kropotkin was optimistic that the revolution could be speedy and humane, and rejected all Bakunin's talk of brimstone and bloodbaths, his irrepressible urge to destroy.

In fact, by the mid-seventies the importance of practical organization had outweighed the life-and-death conflicts between Bakunist and Lavrist theories that had come to such a violent head in Zurich, and Bakunism and Lavrism combined to form an appropriate revolutionary ethos for the period. But Bakunin's *State and Anarchy* was the most widely read statement of faith among the revolutionaries. According to this work, Marxist theory envisaged a population doomed to await patiently the unfolding of the historical process; by teaching the masses theory, Marx would succeed only in stifling the revolutionary ardour that is present in everybody. Bakunin's brand of 'purely instinctive socialism' accepted the basic Marxist class analysis to be sure, but it also gave a major role to the primitive peasantry, the *Lumpenproletariat,* and the fragmented unassimilated bourgeois elements of Russian society, rejected by Marx as 'a bunch of *déclassés,* lawyers without clients, doctors without patients, petty journalists, and poor students with no role to play in the class struggle'. It was precisely among these people, who had no stake in the present order, that Bakunin felt the revolutionary impulse must be strongest. By rejecting the conspiratorial Jacobinist *coup d'état* as a 'heresy against common-sense and historical experience' he left some room in his philosophy for the Lavrist insistence on preparation and self-education. His passionate call for universal upheaval

191

had gained support in southern Europe, and it was in Italy and Spain, rather than in the more prosperous industrialized countries of northern Europe, that he had managed to establish Bakunist branches of the International. In Russia his influence was more ephemeral; his 'holy instinct of revolt' lent its mystique to the still amorphous revolutionary movement in Russia. Bakunin was the 'true seeker', the man who 'cleaved to no system'; he confirmed a disillusionment with ideologies, a need for immediate action.

After a year of intensive self-education the Chaikovsksists in the capital were now beginning to emerge from their isolation to share some of their revolutionary enthusiasm with a wider audience. Sofya Perovskaya in particular feared that the circle was tending towards a kind of political and intellectual élitism that must be avoided by going directly to the workers and peasants. Many populists who had abandoned their faith in the peasantry were now anxious to talk to dissident workers, and it was the Chaikovsksists, before any other group, who helped to create radical cadres of workers in the capital. Sofya Perovskaya had had no experience in the countryside, however, and at the age of nineteen she was already conscious of the limitations of her theoretical revolutionary education in the city. She decided to explore conditions in the villages.

In the summer of 1871 a short-haired lady had arrived in the village of Stavropol' in the Samara region. She wore men's trousers and a straw hat, and her strange appearance immediately attracted a gang of the local children, who trailed after her chanting 'short-haired lady, short-haired lady!' She was in fact Marya Turgeneva, the wife of a wealthy local judge and she had settled in the village in order to train young girls as teachers. A little school was built next to her own house, and soon local girls were crowding in to learn maths and literature. The school began to make a name for itself in the capital, and in the spring of 1872 Sofya Perovskaya decided to leave for Stavropol'. A fellow-teacher

192

described the sensation she caused by her appearance, her inexhaustible energy and wit. Although she looked like a peasant child in her kaftan, her short skirt, her boots and her hair in pigtails, in her classes in Russian language and literature she revealed a mature and sensitive mind. She would talk to her pupils long after classes were over, then slip off to the nearby beechwoods with a book. Rumours began flying through the village about this strange creature, who slept most nights out alone in the woods. Some of the peasants regarded her as a witch, and the more sophisticated of them ascribed her behaviour to 'socialist' tendencies. Her pupils warned her that there were plans to murder her, but she laughed off their anxieties and continued to roam about the countryside.

In her wanderings she met and talked to peasants and learned about their life. In August she asked the local doctor to teach her to do smallpox vaccinations, and then set off with another teacher to visit the neighbouring villages. For most peasants vaccination was a mark of the devil, and impassioned arguments against such superstitions put any sort of direct propaganda completely out of her head. In these arguments she gained the trust of many of the peasants she met, and she started to share with them her books and pamphlets – mostly simple religious fables, as used in the Sunday schools. By the autumn the police had already grown interested in the school and the 'subversive activities' in the area, and Sofya decided to leave. The school was searched and the books removed, but no arrests were made. Sofya moved on to the Tver region, where the following spring she received her diploma as a village teacher.

This was probably the happiest year of Sofya Perovskaya's life. She carried much of the spontaneity and optimism of these days into her later activities, and through all her life as a revolutionary continued to be regarded by many of her friends as a naïve populist. By the end of a year, however, she began to feel isolated from her comrades, and

193

grew anxious to learn about their activities among the factory workers. When she returned to the capital in the summer of 1873 she discovered that the original movement had already disintegrated as a result of wide-scale arrests. She now found twenty-four members of an organization that was already conspiratorial in character. Some members were working in the factories, some were holding discussion groups for workers in their flats, some were spending their time in cheap cafés talking to workers. Sofya moved into a flat with Shishko near the textile factories, and was put in charge of visiting political prisoners and arranging for suspects to leave the country. To her prison-visiting she brought the same delicacy and consideration that made many of her men comrades say regretfully 'She would have made an ideal nurse!' – or, as her biographer said, 'Perhaps her true calling was as a doctor.'[8] Perhaps, on the other hand, she was finding her true calling in the revolutionary movement. Anyway, she was too good a teacher and propagandist to be consigned to mere prison-visiting, and when Sinegub asked her to help him with the classes he was running for textile workers in what they called ' 'eography and 'eometry' she moved into a flat with Rogachev as his 'wife'. Her special pupil there was a worker named Alekseev, who subsequently in his speech of self-defence at the first great show trial revealed a political maturity that Sofya had helped to develop. But rumours of these classes reached the ears of the police, and in January 1874 Sofya was arrested, along with Sinegub. According to the official *Chronicle of the Socialist Movement* she had 'appeared before the workers as a prophet of new ideas', but in fact there was little hard evidence against her. She was confined to her mother's estate in the Crimea, where presumably it was hoped that she would provide the alerted local police with enough incriminating evidence to convict her properly. In her three years in the Crimea she worked tirelessly in the Simferopol' hospital where she eventually qualified as a *fel'dsher*. Even Vin'berg, the president of the local *zemstvo*[9] council, was struck by her devotion, and managed to get her a surgery of her own. In the autumn of 1877, at the outbreak of the Russo-Turkish War, a military hospital was set up in Simferopol' for returning soldiers. By then however Sofya Perovskaya and thousands like her had been detained; dossiers had been compiled and prisons built in preparation for the second great show trial of the 1870s, the Trial of the 193.

Tatiana Lebedeva and Anna Yakimova were also arrested. In early 1874 there had been rumours of a police raid on the Moscow students' library, and Tatiana Lebedeva broke her resolve never to see her family again; she immediately rushed to her brother's house carrying with her all the illegal books, but the house was searched and she was sentenced to eight months in prison. After serving her sentence she was handed over to her brother's protection under a kind of house-arrest. With the outbreak of the Russo-Turkish War she volunteered as a nurse, for which she passed the necessary exam, but on the very day she was due to leave she was arrested again and taken to the capital, to join hundreds of other women in the St Petersburg Women's House of Detention. In 1875 the school in which Anna Yakimova had been teaching was searched and she was arrested. She spent a year in solitary confinement in the local prison before being taken to the capital, where she was to wait another year before the Great Trial.

In the years of police terror and imprisonment the woman described by the government as 'the most wanted woman in Russia' was Ekaterina Breshko-Breshkovskaya, the 'housekeeper' and guiding spirit of the famous Kiev Commune. After the Great Trial the turbulent politics of southern Russia played an important part in the politics of the capital. In Odessa, Bakunists and Lavrists were all more or less united in the Bashentsy group, which directed most of its energies to protecting the local Jewish population against

195

constant pogroms; the Odessa groups were the only ones that consistently refused to make any use of religion in their propaganda, for obvious reasons. Many workers, especially plasterers and carpenters, unable to find work in the capital had moved to Odessa and formed *artels* and co-operatives in which future revolutionaries like Andrei Zhelyabov were active. In Kherson too groups of differing persuasions existed in mutual tolerance and co-operation.

Anna Makarevich had arrived in Odessa with her husband straight from Zurich in 1873. She soon left for the more politically exciting Kiev, where she met the Lyubatovich sisters, Ekaterina Khorzhevskaya and Elisaveta Tumanova, who were all on their way back from Zurich to European Russia. In Kiev she found two organizations of very different outlook, not unlike the circles they had known in Zurich – the Kiev Chaikovsksists and the famous Kiev Commune. Many students expelled from St Petersburg during the riots of 1869 had moved to Kiev and established a circle among the radical students there. Long after the St Petersburg Chaikovsksists had lost interest in propaganda work in the universities, those in Kiev still tended to concentrate their attention on the young intelligentsia. Self-education circles began to proliferate, and co-operatives, collectives and communes were established on the lines of those in the capital. By 1873 one commune had established its own arsenal and such a reputation for terrorism that even the local police chief was initially inhibited from taking any action against it. This was the centre of the *buntari,* the 'rebels' – those populists, that is, who believed that along the Volga and the Don the spirit of Pugachev and of Sten'ka Razin was still alive in the people's collective memory, and who anticipated that local insurrections in these areas would spread to the whole of Russia.

The Kiev Commune was an asylum for those preparing to work among the people in these areas or those just returning – for anyone, in fact, who believed that local agitation must be the first priority. Money and possessions were shared, and like the St Petersburg Chaikovsksists the only real requirement for membership was mutual affection and sympathy. People seeking admittance were merely asked, 'Are you ready to go immediately to the People? If so, you're one of us.' The girls who had just returned from Zurich, with no experience of the Russian peasantry, asked members of the Commune; ' "What is this People, so powerful and mysterious?" and the Kiev Populists replied, "They are good, simple, eager to learn, and they greet us as friends." ' [10]

The communards were often naive, impatient of theory and openly contemptuous of the Chaikovsksists' reverential attitude towards learning and self-preparation. But the Chaikovsksists saw the communards as dismissing problems 'with the self-confidence with which Alexander the Great cut through issues he could not solve'. [11] Study was for them a waste of time; Russia's overwhelming social problems could never be resolved by theories, and any delay in going to the people was a criminal outrage. Debagori-Mokrievich, who was closely associated with the Commune, clearly expressed the views of its members when he said, 'Each of us felt for a million peasants. With such a faith, one could rely on success and ignore society– which is what we did ...' [12] Lavrov adds: 'Young people stood with one foot on the revolutionary path. All they needed was a push, a sanction, a word. And there was such a word. The slogan "To the People" was the spark which ignited our revolutionary movement. It meant breaking with the past, with study, with parents. Hard labour? But the People endure that for a mere crust of bread. Chains? But are the People free? They are slaves like us – miserable slaves of a worthless tyranny.' [13]

Many used the Commune as a meeting-place, and there was always a great coming and going of different people. Some dressed conventionally, some put on a kaftan or peasant boots to show solidarity with the cause, and some dressed entirely in peasant clothes. There was also a number of genuine peasants and workers from the local factories,

197

who taught the young people to make boots or to dye – the usual skills young populists were taking to the people. Occasionally some liberal aristocrat, prompted by curiosity, would leave his carriage at home and pay a visit. There seem to have been no security precautions at all; the passport-forging machine was right under the window in the main room and Mokrievich recalls with amusement the furtive behaviour of one visitor recently arrived from a St Petersburg conspiratorial circle.

The one person round whom this shifting and often immature population of 'rebels' revolved was the 'housekeeper', Ekaterina Breshko-Breshkovskaya, described by the government in these years of political terror and imprisonment as 'the most wanted woman in Russia'. She was twenty-nine when the Commune was established, and had already had some experience in populist and revolutionary activities. Her parents, the Verigos, were liberal cultured landowners from Vitebsk who had welcomed the emancipation of the serfs and who had encouraged her at the age of sixteen to open a peasant school on their estate. But all too soon she became painfully aware that scattered round her parents' home, which was 'modelled on that of the Tsar', were 'long streets of miserable huts ... Men would come to the master begging for bread; women would come weeping, demanding back their children of whom they had been robbed. These things tormented me as a child, pursued me into my bed, where I would lie awake for hours, unable to sleep thinking of all the horrors that surrounded me.' The condition of the serfs was obviously a fraught issue for her parents too, since she was always sent out of the room when 'politics' were discussed – 'politics' including for them some of Pushkin's more committed poetic statements. Meanwhile she was reading Voltaire, Rousseau, Diderot and everything she could find on the French Revolution. Of her parents' virtues she always spoke eloquently: 'If there is anything good in me, I owe it all to them.'

198

But her peasant school was soon attracting unwelcome police attention, and besides she now regarded such ventures as essentially charitable. At the same time, she was still too close to the peasant mentality to be able to envisage any alternative. 'Now that the peasant was free, he was no longer bound to the land. He was shown a little strip of the poorest soil, there to be free and starve. He was bewildered – for centuries past an estate had always been described as containing so many "souls". It was sold for so much per "soul". The "soul" and the plot had always gone together, so the peasant thought his soul and his plot would be freed together ...' Her father was appointed as local arbiter to persuade the peasants of the wisdom of the emancipation, and she was able to witness the confusion and misery of her father's former serfs. 'In one village near ours,' she recalls, 'where the peasants refused to leave their plots, they were drawn up in a line along the village street. Every tenth man was called out and flogged, and some died. Two weeks later, every fifth man was flogged ... I heard many heart-rending stories in my little school house. The peasants would throng to our house night and day ...'

After a year of running the school Ekaterina began desperately to search for some more general political solution to the local misery she saw around her, and at the age of seventeen, after some conflicts with her parents, she set off alone for the capital. In the train to St Petersburg she found herself sitting next to a man who started talking to her of the early populists. They had gone to the countryside, he said, without any idea of social reconstruction in their minds; they simply wanted to teach the peasants to read, to interest them in new ideas, to give them some medical help and to raise them in any way they could from their darkness and misery. In the process, these young people had been able to formulate some of their ideals for a better society. What he said corresponded astonishingly to Ekaterina's own experiences; the man she had been talking to turned out to be no other than Prince Pëtr Kropotkin. When they arrived in the capital he introduced her to various radical circles and helped her to get a job as a private teacher – much to the distress of her parents. In her two and a half years in the capital she regularly attended study groups in which politics and the natural sciences were discussed. The girls she met in the city, who like her 'had won their personal freedom, now wanted to make use of it, not for their own personal enjoyment but to carry to the people the knowledge that had emancipated them'.

Eventually Ekaterina succumbed to her parents' demands that she return home, where she opened another school, this time for peasant girls. A few years later she met a local wealthy landowner who was anxious to set up a model estate with her. Breshko-Breshkovsky soon became her husband. Together they established a co-operative bank and a peasant agricultural school on his estate. Her experiences in the revolutionary circles of the capital had taught her to be pessimistic about such reformist ventures, however, and when she visited her sister the following year in Kiev, she found again the sort of uncompromising attitudes she had first encountered in St Petersburg. Axel'rod, a prominent Marxist theoretician of the time, particularly impressed her with his revolutionary enthusiasm, but in general she was horrified by the students' inactivity, and striding one day into the students' canteen she shouted at them, 'Why are you all such idlers? Why do you let academic affairs screen your eyes from reality?' These were the very questions students were asking themselves, and she quickly attracted a circle of Bakunist students. In the discussions they were having together, she found that women were expected merely to listen respectfully. She herself had no qualms about speaking out, speaking, as Kravchinsky said, in a way that was 'passionate and prophetic'.[14] At the first meeting at which she stood up to argue against a male comrade her words were greeted with a stunned silence, and the meeting collapsed; this

200

was apparently the first time a woman had ever spoken so assertively. But essentially everyone was in agreement. 'Hunger is the best teacher,' Bakunin had said. 'Tell the peasant why he is hungry, and show him how to feed himself, and he will learn quite readily.'

There were some problems, though, for which Bakunin had no answer. By the time Ekaterina was six months' pregnant she had already committed herself irrevocably to the revolutionary movement. She tried to explain this to her husband, asking if he was prepared to sacrifice his property and security for a life of revolutionary activity; he declined, and she was on her own. She saw no alternative but to leave her child with her sister-in-law, and wrote a heartbreaking account of the separation in her memoirs: 'I felt that in my child my youth was buried, and that when he was taken from my body, the fire of my spirit had gone out with him. But it was not so ... I knew that I could not be a mother and a revolutionary. Among the women involved in the struggle for freedom in Russia there were many who chose to be fighters rather than mothers of the victims of tyranny ...' Her son Nikolai, brought up in an aristocratic *milieu,* grew up as a fairly successful 'victim', a popular novelist with little sympathy for his mother's political activities.

In 1873 she was in the capital again but, growing impatient with meetings and with the theoretical deliberations of the Chaikovsksists, she soon moved back to Kiev. There, a large house on Zilianskaya Street had been set up on communal lines and among the inhabitants she met her old comrades Mokrievich, Kovalik and Marya Kolënkina. She talked with the people who were making daily ventures into the countryside or preparing for longer excursions. With them she discussed their programme for the new society: 'It is a poor patriot who will not thoroughly try his government before he rises against it. We searched its laws and edicts. We found certain scant and long-neglected peasants' rights of local suffrage, and then we began by showing the peasants

201

how to use the rights they already had.' Anna Yakimova, affectionately nicknamed 'Bas'ko' (which means 'Okay' in some Little Russian dialects), stayed briefly at the Commune, supporting herself by giving private lessons and urging the others to set off on their own to the countryside. She soon left for the villages, where she gave smallpox vaccinations and read stories to the peasants.

It was to Marya Kolënkina that Ekaterina Breshkovskaya was most closely attached. She was without any of the death-defying bravado that typified most of the commun-ards and remained in the background among her more boisterously self-sufficient comrades. Her devotion and her beauty made her an object of adoration among her friends, but she was oblivious to all admiration: 'I am in love with the cause,' she would say. At the age of twenty she had left her home town of Temzhuk on the Azov Sea and had enrolled in midwives' courses in Kiev. Her father was a speculator who after three years as a factory-owner in Tambov had gone bankrupt. He was a religious hypocrite and an excessively despotic father who grudgingly admitted that his daughter should at least be trained to read and write. Marya was educated at the home of a family friend, and immersed herself in nineteenth-century Romantic poetry. Nekrasov developed in her the passionate longing to serve humanity, and throughout her life she would recite passages from his work. A year after she started her midwives' course she met Ekaterina Breshkovskaya, who introduced her to revolutionary ideas; in 1873 she dropped her courses and moved into the Commune. Ekaterina 'had never met anyone of more steadfast mind, or greater resolve in a pursuit once taken. Her "it must be done" was a reasoned and deeply felt imperative.'

By July 1874 Ekaterina, Marya and Yakova Stefanovich, a young cobbler, were ready to go out to the people; they decided to go to the large villages around Kherson and Podolia, where there were large sugar factories. Marya had taught Ekaterina to dye, and the three of them set off with passports that described them as peasants from the Orel Province. Their first stop was Belozeria, where they opened a dyeing workshop. Marya made friends easily with the peasant girls, while Ekaterina and Stefanovich visited people in their homes. But the soil was bad and the peasants listless; their chief topic of conversation was speculation about the Tsarevich's future bride. They decided to move on to the small town of Smela, where they had more success, visiting peasants and reading them *Moses and his Four Brothers,* the popular story that Sunday school teachers and populists had been using ever since the first pilgrimages. However, their Great-Russian accents and their eagerness to discuss the peasants' grievances with them attracted the attention of the police, and it was decided to separate. Marya hid out with some relatives, while Ekaterina moved to the Kherson area, where there was a large colony of Christians who had rejected all the rituals and excesses of Orthodoxy and were systematically persecuted for their beliefs; these were the Stundists. Ekaterina, with her thorough biblical training, was able to talk very frankly with the Stundists, disputing and reinterpreting passages from the Bible with them. By mid-September she had already given away all her literature and was writing her own proclamations. She did not know that by now she was the object of the most intense police search in South Russia.

When she was finally arrested she was staying in the small town of Tulchin, a centre for itinerants, gipsies and contra-banders and the base of the Cossack raider Karmeluk. The peasants were living in a perpetual state of intimidation and harassment from all sides; one of them had decided to go through her pack, and had handed letters and documents over to the police. She was arrested immediately and taken to Kiev, where she was held in solitary confinement in the unspeakable Kiev Prison for a year. She was then taken to the St Petersburg House of Preliminary Detention, which had

203

just been built to contain women who were to figure in the Great Trial of the populists.

The Trial of the 193 is a misnomer; thousands of people were arrested and detained for several years. How many women there were in this number is not known, but in Ekaterina's section there were thirty-seven, all of whom had carried out 'revolutionary propaganda in the thirty-seven provinces of the Empire'. Many, like Ekaterina, had already spent a year or more in provincial prisons ruled by regulations that dated back to the seventeenth century. But despite this, the women, according to Ekaterina, were less prone to commit suicide or go insane than the men. They managed somehow to establish contact with each other through the 'water-closet club', tapping messages to each other along the drain-pipes about their revolutionary plans and their conduct at the coming trial.

One of the first people Ekaterina met through the 'club' was Anna Yakimova, whom she described as 'firm as a rock, untouched by storms, despite her year's solitary confinement'. She also contacted Sofya Ivanova, known to her comrades as 'Shusha'. She was the daughter of a wealthy captain, who had died when she was nine. The dazzling social life of her three elder sisters did not appeal to her, and when she was sixteen she had begged her brothers to take her to Moscow, where they were about to enrol in the university. She had read little, had almost no political convictions and knew only that she wanted to be self-supporting – which she was, living in terrible poverty for a year as a seamstress. Then she saw Ippolit Myshkin's advertisement for a typesetter. Although Myshkin was not directly attached to any organization, his press produced most of the literature for the Moscow Chaikovsksists. He was virtually unknown in revolutionary circles, and decided to employ Sofya chiefly because her lack of political commitment would create less of a security hazard. At first she could barely understand the literature she was working on, let alone her own part in its production, but it was not long before she moved into Myshkin's small, friendly socialist commune on the Arbat, and became deeply involved in the works they were producing. They were arrested together.

Varvara Vakhovskaya was there too. As a young girl in Zurich she had sat entranced at the feet of the old Bakunin. She had been arrested almost immediately after her return to Russia, and had not actually been able to put any of her Bakunism into practice. This, plus her rather too elegant appearance, alienated her from many of the women, especially when her doting aged father obstinately insisted on treating her subsequent release from prison as a sort of 'coming-out' ceremony. Ekaterina Breshkovskaya, however, had a very high opinion of her political judgements.

In the years between the first arrests and the opening of the Great Trial, the government had been desperately trying to formulate some effective policy to deal with the revolutionary movement. New prisons had been built, and thousands of people were under close police surveillance. Nobody was in any doubt that this was a political trial, and the prisoners had to decide whether to adopt a policy of total non co-operation or to use the courtroom as a political forum. In the event, the majority were 'protesters'.

Optimistic conversations about the trial were not yet marred by the knowledge of what was actually happening to many of the prisoners in the same building. Of the thousands detained, evidence could be found to arrest only some 300 people, and of these only 193 were able to stand trial: the rest had died from malnutrition, exposure, suicide or insanity.

The Trial of the 193 opened on 18 October 1877 in St Petersburg under the special supervision of the Senate – that is to say, without a jury. Ekaterina Breshkovskaya described her first impression at the trial. 'In the courtroom, packed to overflowing, what did we see? Deathly pale faces, greenish-yellow, some of them swollen, some emaciated,

205

others coughed terribly. And yet these people, who were approaching death, looked eagerly round, as if seeking support from their comrades who were in better health.' Indeed for many people arrested on the dubious charge of 'propaganda' this was an occasion of joyful reunion with old friends. Many of them who emerged from their isolation could now see themselves as members of a movement officially described as 'revolutionary'.

For it was in the years 1874 and 1875, when naive rural populists were being arrested as 'revolutionaries', that 'Land and liberty', the 'pilgrims' slogan of the sixties, had begun to assume the proportions of a party. Little is known about the formation and precise goals of *Zemlya i Volya* ('Land and Liberty') Party; this itself testifies both to its conspiratorial nature, and to the diverse political currents contained within it. What is known is that such 'jacobins' as Mikhailov and Daviden'ko, who had both been Chaikovsksists, tried to unite Chaikovsksist dedication with early populist enthusiasm to form a centralized political organization. This organization cohered in the years of police terror preceding the Great Trial.

The prisoners were divided into seventeen groups, all accused of 'spreading revolutionary propaganda in the thirty-seven provinces of the Empire'. The St Petersburg Chaikovsksists were tried first, and as 'protestors' had to be brought in by force. Sofya Perovskaya, who had been brought up from the Crimea to stand trial, was the first to be questioned. She refused to make any statement before consulting her comrades, and the others followed suit. She was subsequently acquitted for lack of evidence, but continued to attend the trial, chatting and laughing with her friends. Then at the end of October it was the turn of the Kiev group. Ekaterina Breshkovskaya, the first of the Kiev prisoners to be examined, stood up and proudly announced herself a member of the Russian Socialist Revolutionary Party. She anticipated history of course; such a party did not

206

exist. But in the chaotic conditions of the courtroom she felt the movement to be threatened by feelings of isolation and despair, and her statement had a rousing effect on the prisoners' morale.

When the Moscow group came up for trial Ippolit Myshkin calmly strode up to the 'Golgotha', the prisoners' stand, and delivered himself of a speech that proved to be the central moment of the trial. He had taken no part in the debates between the 'protesters' and those who wanted to make political capital out of a packed courtroom, but in his speech he combined an eloquence with a contempt for official procedure that challenged the very assumptions of the trial. Nechaev's speech of self-defence comes to mind, a speech in which, according to the Third Department, it was 'not society and not the State which, in the person of the judge, are the accusers, but on the contrary, they are the accused, and they are being accused with all the force and fanaticism that seem to cry out for martyrdom'. Although Myshkin provided the name and some component characteristics for Dostoyevsky's heroic martyr in *The Idiot,* he was no martyr. He spoke with a moderation that even his accusers could not fail to appreciate. As he started, his words were virtually drowned by the murmured support of his comrades, and the chief prosecutor, Zhelikovsky, was heard to mutter: 'This is Revolution!' As policemen started to surround him, he shouted: 'For every word, the accused has his mouth shut. I can say now that this is not a tribunal but a futile comedy; or rather, something even worse than a brothel. There, girls sell their bodies out of necessity. Here we have senators . . .' At this point policemen tried to drag him off the dock, but prisoners rushed up to fight them off. '. . . senators,' Myshkin was dragged off shouting, 'who trade with the lives of others, with truth and with justice; trade, in fact, with everything that is dearest to humanity, out of cowardice, baseness, opportunism, and to gain large salaries.' For this speech Myshkin received a ten-year sentence of hard labour, a sentence he never lived to complete since a few years later he was shot in prison for some misdemeanour.

The majority of the 193 were acquitted. Myshkin's speech had a dramatic effect on liberal public opinion, and the government had already realized before the trial began that it was dealing with a movement that could not merely be rounded up and eliminated. Forty of the accused were sent to exile in 'the remote provinces', and eighteen of them were sentenced to hard labour – sentences of three to ten years. Most of the women were acquitted for lack of evidence. Tatiana Lebedeva, whose health was now rapidly failing, and Anna Yakimova both refused to speak in their own defence; they were set free. Ekaterina Breshkovskaya was one of the six women to be sentenced; her statement at the trial had compounded her guilt, and she was condemned to five years' hard labour in Kara, Siberia. Until her emigration after the 1917 revolution her life was a series of escapes, rearrests and prolonged sentences, and she spent most of the rest of her life in prisons and labour camps. At the mercy of an arctic climate and a near-starvation diet, surrounded by death and despair her optimism and resilience was truly unimaginable. Her passionate letters from prison bear comparison with Wilde's *De Profundis,* about which she so aptly comments: 'How much are to be pitied those who have never known the solidarity of minds and hearts.'

NOTES

1. Chernyshevsky, *Complete Works,* vol. 4, p.341.
2. Venturi, op. cit., p.480.
3. A hetman, in the Polish-Lithuanian state from the sixteenth to the eighteenth centuries, was the supreme commander of the armed forces.
4. Asheshov, N., *Sofia Perovskaya: materialy dlya biografii i kharakteristiki.* (Material for a Biography and Character-Study), p.237.
5. Engel'hardt and his wife, Anna Makarova, were active in forming the Society of Women Translators. See p.96.
6. Kornilova Moroza, A., *Perovskaya i osnovanie kruzhka Chaikovtsev*

(Perovskaya and the Establishment of the Chaikovsky Circle), *Katorga i Ssylka,* no. 24, 1926, pp.14ff.

7. Kropotkin, op. cit., p.194.
8. Asheshov, op. cit., p.177.
9. *Fel'dsher* was a doctor's or surgeon's assistant, somewhere between a nurse and a doctor. The *zemstvo* was the elective district council established after the Emancipation.
10. Kravchinsky, *Peasant Russia,* p.87.
11. Lavrov, *Narodniki–propagandisty 1873-8* (Populists and Propagandists 1873-8), p.177.
12. Debagnri-Mokrievich, *Memoirs* (unavailable in England but widely quoted), p.38.
13. Lavrov, op. cit., p. 175.
14. Kravchinsky, *Peasant Russia,* p.65.

CHAPTER VI
UTOPIA ABANDONED

The women who were acquitted in the Great Trial now had to overcome their distrust of political organizations in which they were so outnumbered by men. Vera Figner had, by some miracle, escaped arrest altogether. In the spring of 1876, the *Zemlya i Volya* Party organized its first demonstration, outside the Kazan' Cathedral in the suburbs of the capital. The number of demonstrators fell short of expectations, but nevertheless 250 workers and students turned up under a red banner bravely proclaiming 'Land and Liberty'. For Vera Figner, who had played an active part in organizing the demonstration, this was an inspiring experience, 'bearing the first fruits of the attempt to unite populists with the proletariat'. The government, recognizing the seriousness of the event, had ordered the police to disperse the demonstrators with violence. Numerous random arrests were made, and Vera Figner set to work organizing a Red Cross section within the Party, which would be responsible for visiting prisoners and working for their escape. Sentences were savage, especially those meted out to the students. One Emelyanov, a twenty-four-year-old student arrested under the name of Bogolyubov, was sentenced to fifteen years' hard labour, a particularly vicious sentence considering that he had had no part in organizing the demonstration and was not active within the Party.

While awaiting deportation, Bogolyubov was put in the St Petersburg House of Detention, already crammed with those who were to figure in the Great Trial. By July 1877 the atmosphere in the prison had already reached boiling-point when Trepov, Governor-General of St Petersburg, made his tour of inspection. The political detainees watched from their cell windows as Trepov, who was in a particularly vicious mood that day, examined prisoners in the yard below. Suddenly, over-reacting to some imagined misdemeanour of Bogolyubov's, he ordered him to be flogged savagely. Bogolyubov went insane as a result of the beating, and within two years was dead. That night the prison resounded to the shouts of the detainees. In the women's section Tatiana Lebedeva, whose health had been seriously undermined by prison conditions, vociferously urged her friends to shout out their support for Bogolyubov. Prison officers made savage reprisals, and many women were dragged out of their cells by their hair and flogged.

Public opinion was outraged by the event, and although the Party was agreed that Trepov must be 'punished', it was unwilling to jeopardize the fate of the 193 by taking any precipitous action. Mikhailovsky and Osinsky, who had moved to the capital from Kiev to attend the Great Trial, agreed between them that the 'requisite measures' should be taken, but most party members were not informed of this, and the 'requisite measures' were never actually spelt out. Vera Figner for one was in the dark, and it was at about this time that she met Marya Kolёnkina who had moved to the capital with her Kiev friend Vera Zasulich. They were both infuriated by the apathy that seemed to have hit the radical circles of St Petersburg after the great wave of arrests. Immediately they arrived in the capital they bought guns and taught themselves to shoot. They had plans for establishing a

211

revolutionary cavalry detachment of women, but this amazing project was quietly ignored by the Party, and they had to content themselves with working for the release of political prisoners. Between them they managed to raise 1,500 rubles, which they gave to Osinski who was to use it to arrange the escape of the Kiev prisoners. In Kiev Vera Zasulich had attracted little attention; she was known as a dedicated and reliable worker. Now in St Petersburg she worked inconspicuously as a typesetter for the party paper. But both she and Marya Kolënkina grew increasingly impatient with their modest roles; were women always to be condemned to humdrum office jobs and working for the release of prisoners? They began to argue heatedly about the need for immediate reprisals, and Vera Figner was reluctantly forced to agree that action must be taken against the 'tsarist hangmen'. In Vera Zasulich she found someone who had experienced all her doubts about terrorism, perhaps more painfully than she.

Little is known of Vera Zasulich's family and background. She was born in 1851 into an aristocratic Moscow family and was educated at a second-rate *pension,* which she left at the age of fifteen as a qualified governess. After supporting herself for a year as a judge's clerk in Serpukhov, she left for the capital, where she lived with her mother and attended teachers' courses. Vera's education had been haphazard; she was neither well read nor politically experienced. But she was drawn to the radical students she met at these courses. And among these students was Nechaev,[1] who was desperately looking for contacts to give some plausibility to his great organizational fantasy, the People's Vengeance Party. Nechaev recognized guilelessness when he saw it, and at the age of seventeen Vera became, quite against her will, involved in the sordid events surrounding Nechaev's trial.[2]

In February 1869 she received two letters through the post. The first read: 'I was walking on Vasilevsky Island this morning and I passed a police cart, the kind they use for transporting prisoners. As it went by, a hand appeared at the window and threw out a piece of paper, and I heard a voice saying, "If you are a student, send this to the address given." I am a student, and feel it my duty to fulfil this wish. Destroy this note.' The other letter was in Nechaev's writing and said: 'They are taking me to prison. Which prison I do not know. Tell the comrades I hope one day to see them all again. May they continue our work.'

In fact Nechaev had ignored the police summons for his arrest and had fled abroad. But Vera Zasulich was not wise to the kind of convoluted manoeuvres for which this 'revolutionary bandit' was later notorious, and anxiously asked her friends what she should do. Now that Nechaev had eluded them, the police were especially anxious to detain his associates, and Vera was one of 152 people to be arrested. When told by the police that she could buy her freedom by divulging information about the Party, she replied in all honesty: 'But I don't know what I am being arrested for.' Throughout her two years of imprisonment in the Peter and Paul fortress she remained convinced that her arrest was merely the result of some misunderstanding. She was released, with two rubles in her pocket and the clothes she stood up in, to spend the next four years in exile in Khar'kov.

She was twenty-four when she arrived in Kiev in 1875, politically at sea but anxious to contact radical circles. She never actually moved into the Kiev Commune, but worked there as a typesetter and messenger. It was her qualities of modesty and dedication that drew her to Marya Kolënkina, and the two became close friends. These qualities also made her an invaluable organization worker; temperamentally she was never suited to active populism, and her venture to the people was one of the more ludicrous episodes in the populist movement.

Frolenko, an important South Russian revolutionary, had arrived from Odessa that year and was looking for a nominal

213

'wife' with whom to go to the countryside. The two had never met, but Vera volunteered for the job; their failure is partly explained by their mutual incompatibility. It was decided to set up a little teashop in the village of Tsibulevka, near Kiev. Unfortunately Vera, who was to act as the proprietress, was barely able to make a cup of tea and flatly refused to do any cooking or cleaning. She was quite incapable of playing roles, and hobbled about in her peasant boots and kaftan, betraying her class with every gesture. While she spent all her time reading in the filthy shop, Frolenko desperately got drunk with the local peasants and police in order to allay their suspicions. Stefanovich and Marya Kolënkina passed through Tsibulevka once and tried to help, making Easter cakes and cleaning up, but the peasants were obviously suspicious and contemptuous of this strange couple. The police grew intrusive, and they decided to leave.[3]

After this demoralizing episode Vera Zasulich left Kiev for St Petersburg, where she contacted Marya Kolënkina, who was also dispirited by her visit to the countryside. They moved together to a flat on the Angliiski Prospect. A comrade recalls the flat, with its cluttered smoke-filled rooms, packed with workers, students and occasionally such 'revolutionary generals' as Kravchinsky and Mikhailov.[4] Vera would sit immersed in a book, her head covered with a velvet shawl, smoking incessantly and paying little attention to her comrades' discussions and laughter. Although only a year older, Marya Kolënkina exerted an enormous influence over her. Her mobile expressive face, her halo of red hair and her angry criticisms of the Party's inactivity made her the centre of attention. She was sarcastic and impatient, often exasperated by Vera's plodding ways. Vera always defended herself patiently against her friend's often cruel attacks; they both knew that these conversations never resulted in any concrete plans. Like most party members they were trying to talk themselves out of their feelings of despair and confusion.

This confusion was shared by Vera Figner, who visited the

214

flat after her second visit to the countryside. After the Trial of the Moscow Women she had been convinced by her friends that she should go to the people, but she had none of the moral certainties of the early populists. 'The Populists regarded the people as a blank sheet of paper on which they were to inscribe socialist characters. For the insurrectionists, the people were socialist by their very conditions. Nobody knew the hour of the people's vengeance, but so much inflammatory material had accumulated that a small spark could easily flare up into a flame and then into a gigantic conflagration.'[5]

Active populism now seemed to demand the more impetuous propaganda of the insurrectionists, but Vera Figner could contemplate working among the people only as a doctor. She went to Yaroslavl', where she passed the midwives' exam − as a male student, for some inexplicable reason. Her comrades Solov'ëv and Bogdanovich had been staying for the past few months in the Samara region and had been sending her encouraging reports of the colonies of dissident Old Believers among whom they were staying. When she arrived as a *fel'dsher* in a little village nearby, however, she was immediately overwhelmed by feelings of inadequacy. 'I confess I felt lonely, weak and helpless in this sea of peasants. Moreover I had no idea how to approach the common people.'[6] She was not one to identify and 'blend' with the people, relying on her influence as a *fel'dsher* to make contact with them. But after a day spent travelling round the countryside, fighting desperately against filth and ignorance, she would drop exhausted at night on to the straw in some peasant's hut and ask herself, 'Were not all these prescriptions a hypocrisy? There was no chance of looking into their souls. My mouth could not open for any kind of propaganda.' She spent three months there before she was forced to return to the capital, in order to avoid arrest; a friend of her sister's had just been arrested, and a letter had been found on her that compromised Vera.

215

After three months in which she had painfully realized the futility of curing even the most elementary ills, Vera Figner was happy to meet her old friends in the capital again. The Great Trial was in progress, old comrades were gradually returning and there was a general atmosphere of hilarity in St Petersburg. She met Sofya Perovskaya for the first time and was immediately enchanted by her democratic tastes, her simplicity and the gentleness of her behaviour. They talked to one another about their ambivalent attitude to the Party; the conflicts between the insurrectionists and the populists were preventing them from committing themselves to the organization. And yet, despite her comrades' insistence that she was better suited to literary work in the capital, Vera was determined to go to the people again. In her conversations with Vera Zasulich and Marya Kolënkina she became converted to the insurrectionist 'rebel' politics of South Russia, which in the North went under the name of agrarian terrorism.

For Vera Zasulich and Marya Kolënkina, meanwhile, the Trepov affair of the previous year had been their signal for action, and when Marya said, as she so often did, '*Now* is the time to act!' Vera's silence confirmed her words. But they had to restrain themselves until they could deal with Trepov, along with Zhelikovsky, chief prosecutor at the trial. They threw dice, and it fell to Vera to shoot Trepov. Karpov recalls the evening of 23 January, the last day of the trial. A group of friends and comrades sat round the samovar, talking softly and singing melancholy folk songs. Vera sat with her head on Marya's shoulder all evening, and everybody left early. 'We all knew that the next day Vera would go to Trepov and Marya to Zhelikovsky,' said Karpov. The next morning Vera set off for Trepov's office where, with her revolver hidden under her cloak, she mingled with the other petitioners awaiting their place in the queue. When Vera's turn came she faced him and shot him point blank, wounding him seriously. She then dropped her revolver and calmly awaited arrest.

Marya had not been so fortunate. Zhelikovsky was not receiving petitioners that day, and mortified by her failure she returned home and anxiously awaited news of her friend.

Vera Zasulich's arrest as a common criminal for a crime that was obviously political, and her subsequent acquittal, show what a very deep impression the young prisoners at the Great Trial had made on liberal public opinion, already enraged by the outbreak of the Russo-Turkish War. When her trial opened in March the courtroom was packed to overflowing and the atmosphere was one of restrained tension; there were few there who did not favour her acquittal. Vera herself sat in total silence throughout the trial, but her defence council, the popular liberal lawyer Alexandrov, excelled himself in his defence, which in fact was not so much a defence as an indictment of the entire system, of which Trepov was merely a particularly horrible example. After a long speech in which he summoned up all his powers of persuasive pathos and irony, even the judge could find little to expiate Trepov; and the bland words of the prosecutor, who feebly demanded what would happen if *everyone* took the law into their own hands, made little impression on the jury. Witnesses were called from the Great Trial, and the chief prison warder Kurneev was mercilessly interrogated. Vera was pronounced not guilty, but on her acquittal she felt nothing but anguish. 'I could not understand this feeling then,' she said later, 'but I have understood it since. Had I been convicted, I should have been prevented by main force from doing anything, and I should have been tranquil, and the thought of having done all I was able for the cause would have been a consolation to me.'[7] Until the end of her life, she was to reject the general use of terrorism; her own action she regarded as an act of necessary self-defence.

Vera Zasulich was free, but it was now extremely probable that she would be re-arrested. She was taken from the court in a police carriage, which was immediately thronged by a crowd of supporters and *agents provocateurs*. The carriage was eventually halted by a mob of policemen, and a young student who leapt on to the vehicle to defend her was shot dead by the police. She managed to slip away in the ensuing turmoil, and hid with a friend for the next few days before being spirited off to Geneva, where she was soon to play an important part in the exile community of Russian Marxists there.

Vera Zasulich's action initiated a series of individual and sporadic acts of terrorism. Many revolutionaries regarded the shooting of Trepov as a disastrous and untimely importation of South Russian extremism into the Party. But for both tactical and ideological reasons the Party was unable to denounce an action by one of its most dedicated members, and its immediate task now was to formulate an interpretation, if not a policy, of individual and organized terrorism. Kravchinsky's jubilation over her acquittal was characteristically melodramatic: 'Russian absolutism has been killed,' he wrote from the Balkans, where he was fighting as a volunteer in the Russo-Turkish War. 'The 31st of March was the last day of its life.' But his words certainly reflected some of the bravado that stormed into the movement in that tempestuous year, the 'year of the attempted assassinations' as it was called. Kravchinsky depicted a new species of revolutionary: 'On the horizon appeared the outlines of a sombre figure, illuminated by some kind of hellish flame, a figure with chin raised proudly in the air, and a gaze that breathed provocation and vengeance. Passing through the frightened crowds, the revolutionary enters with proud step on to the arena of history. He is wonderful, awe-inspiring and irresistible, for he unites the two most lofty forms of human grandeur, the martyr and the hero.' [8] Kravchinsky's mythologized terrorist characteristically embellished reality; for young revolutionaries gazed now with panic, rather than provocation, at the horrifying wave of arrests that followed Vera Zasulich's action.

Meanwhile, Vera Figner had lost interest in literary work in the capital, and it was as a convert to agrarian terrorism that she set off once more, in the spring of 1878, this time with her sister Lydia, to a village of Old Believers on the banks of the Volga in the Saratov area. She still felt that she had neither the knowledge nor the experience to justify her insurrectionist stance, and once again she looked to the people for some confirmation of her old populist leanings. In the event her doubts became irrelevant. They moved into an area ravaged by a cholera epidemic; faced with a mortality rate of five per cent, any propaganda seemed increasingly futile. Their very appearance there caused a sensation among the peasants. Since they certainly did not conform to the stereotype 'nihilist' image, the only explanation must be that they had the 'healer's' touch. In the ten months they were there they received over five thousand patients, as many as a city doctor with several assistants would receive in a year. Hundreds of peasants arrived daily on foot from remote parts of the province to see these mythical creatures and to beg for healing charms. In their time off the women would go to the peasants' homes, taking with them the populist tales of Sleptsov and Tolstoy, and advising the peasants on child care and hygiene. Lydia opened a school, and they became known as the 'darling little teachers'. Vera no longer suffered from the feelings of utter futility that had so tormented her during her first venture to the people, but she was assailed by a more generalized sense of political isolation. Once again misery and poverty were putting all thought of revolutionary propaganda out of her head. 'In such conditions,' she asked herself, 'is it possible to even think about protest? Is it not ironical to tell a people totally oppressed by physical disasters about resistance and struggle?' [9] The priest had been accusing them of denouncing the faith and they were now under the watchful eye of the police, but this time they were determined to stay, despite their realization that vague talk of 'agrarian terrorism' would have to be replaced by a more

219

consistent terrorist policy. This meant, as they knew, drastic changes within the Party.

Zemlya i Volya had long contained a 'disorganizational group', whose task was to encourage strikes and work for the release of imprisoned comrades. Under the leadership of Natanson this had developed into the 'troglodyte' group, which after the arrest of Natanson had given birth to a conspiratorial group, now emerging as a powerful secret faction within a secret organization. Morozov and Tikhomirov were the chief spokesmen for an inner circle of revolutionaries, armed with daggers and revolvers and bent on disposing of 'harmful' officials and defending its members against the police. For them the struggle was fundamentally political rather than economic; their means were to be terrorist. This group came to be known as the 'politicians', while those who still concentrated their energies in the provinces became known as the 'country group'.

Few party members can have felt the conflict between these two trends as keenly as Sofya Perovskaya. Despite her feelings of isolation in the countryside, she would always value what she had learnt there, alone, without the dictates of the organization. And yet she, like Vera Figner, desperately wanted the Party to maintain its unity and broaden its base, and she was resigned to going with the majority of her comrades. Her immediate concern after the Great Trial was the release of the prisoners, and this was to bring her into conflict with the 'disorganizational group'. For she believed, quite naïvely, that once important members were restored to the Party, revolutionaries could continue their propaganda work in the towns and the countryside. She could still not accept the fact that most of her men comrades now regarded violent means as an inevitable political weapon. However, whereas the men revolutionaries, once decided on their goal, could pursue it with a singlemindedness that admitted no obstacle, the women, being more vulnerable, found themselves constantly forced to adapt to new situations. Both

220

Vera Figner and Sofya Perovskaya embarked on their tasks with an intensity that enabled them to put aside the deep ideological conflicts coming to a head within the Party.

Sofya was especially concerned about the important prisoners Myshkin, Rogachev, Kovalik and Voynaral'sky, who at the Tsar's personal request were to spend the next ten years in chains; their loss to the Party was a personal tragedy for her. The government was strangely lenient, however, towards prisoners' relatives, and Sofya had no difficulty in visiting Tikhomirov as his fiancée. (Sofya's mother, not yet wise to such ploys, congratulated her on her impending marriage, much to her fury.) Sofya was one of the only revolutionaries who never had any qualms about exploiting official venality for her own ends, and her childish appearance usually averted any suspicion. She managed to bribe some prison officers to keep her informed about the fates of the four 'special prisoners' and learnt that they were to be moved to the notoriously foul Khar'kov prison. It was she who informed her comrades of this move, and urged that all energy and funds be concentrated on releasing Myshkin. As she had little support for her plan for his escape on the way from the prison to the St Petersburg station, the project fell through. Immediately after this she set off herself for Khar'kov, to await the train carrying the prisoners.

Once there, she contacted the small local Zemlya i Volya group and moved into a comrade's flat as a chambermaid. When the train carrying the prisoners arrived Sofya was there at the station with three armed comrades in a carriage that was to bear them away. But the whole thing had not really been carefully thought out; the prisoners were immediately transferred to a police carriage, and Sofya and her comrades took chase. They fired three times at the carriage, which galloped off, leaving Sofya to curse at her comrades' 'Russianness' − (a term much used by re-volutionaries to describe the kind of drunken undisciplined behaviour that jeopardized quite a few projects). The police were now hot on her tracks, and she left at once for her mother's estate in the Crimea, where she was arrested within a few days. Mezentsev, head of the St Petersburg Third Division, had recently been raging about the lenient treatment of those acquitted at the Great Trial, and as an ex-prisoner Sofya was sentenced to two years' imprisonment in Obolensk, near Siberia.

Sofya never had any intention of serving her sentence, but had every confidence that she would be able to escape along the way and return to Khar'kov. For the first part of her journey she was escorted by two considerate young gendarmes from whom she could easily have slipped away, for her appearance and behaviour gave no reason to suppose that she might be 'dangerous'. But escape from them would have been too easy and she had no wish to 'cheat'. Further north they were replaced by two 'wolves' about whom she had no such qualms. As they were dozing in the station waiting room, she quietly formed her baggage on the seat to resemble a body and then slipped out, draped like a peasant-woman in a shawl. She waited several hours behind some bushes for the next train to St Petersburg, and had a pleasant journey back, entertaining the people in the carriage with invented anecdotes of peasant life.

As an 'illegal' Sofya was to play many parts. When she arrived in the capital the Party provided her with a false passport, and from that moment she became officially 'illegal', and a member of the Zemlya i Volya Party. She made it clear that she had joined the Party only in order to carry through the Khar'kov plan, and that she had little time for party matters in general. Coldly she described to the comrades the recent failure, and demanded inexorably that all the Khar'kov prisoners be released. This time she was provided with a generous sum of money when she returned to Khar'kov.

The Party in the capital was soon receiving enthusiastic letters from her; she had joined midwives' courses in order to

222

recruit supporters, and was visiting the prisoners daily, buying them food and clothes and attending to their needs. The passionately maternal affection she lavished on the prisoners was barely comprehensible to most of her comrades. But although she was bringing her gaiety and humour into the lives of the prisoners, she was interested in more than mere prison-visiting, and was soon accepted as the leader of the growing Khar'kov revolutionary circle. In her letters to the Party she began to complain bitterly of lack of support for the release, and the Party responded by sending Tatiana Lebedeva to join her in the spring of 1879.

Tatiana Lebedeva had been acquitted at the Great Trial and ordered back to her brother's protection in Moscow, but she had now broken all ties with her family for good, and she stayed on in the capital as an 'illegal'. There she had taken over the radical students' library at the Agricultural Faculty. Sofya had deliberately removed herself from the politics of the capital and had allowed herself little time to ponder over future party tactics. Tatiana's news from the capital, and her sombre account of the increasingly terroristic stance of the Party, only strengthened Sofya's resolve to carry through a project that, as she well realized, must now be of secondary importance to the Party. It was actually with some cynicism that the Party had sent Tatiana Lebedeva to work on a project from which they had already decided to withdraw support and funds. When Sofya finally learnt that her efforts in Khar'kov were no longer supported she almost collapsed in despair. Tatiana recalled her sobbing for three nights in her room after the news came through. In public she was formal and cold, deaf to her friend's insistence that the only practical possibility now was to support the growing demand for an open commitment to terrorism. Events in the capital were now forcing the Party to extricate itself from the provinces.

In August of the previous year Kravchinsky had returned from the Balkans to the capital, where, in broad daylight, he had stabbed to death Mezentsev, the head of the St

223

Petersburg Third Division. Natanson, Mikhailov and Marya Kolënkina were among hundreds imprisoned in the inevitable spate of arrests that followed, and the Party had now to put its survivors before its victims. Kravchinsky seems to have been a natural survivor. He enjoyed tempting fate by openly roaming the streets of the city, and in his walks he was often accompanied by Olga Lyubatovich who had just escaped from exile after the Trial of the Moscow Women.

Olga had arrived in the capital on the very day of the assassination. Wandering round the streets penniless, passport-less and disorientated, she heard the same words on everyone's lips, 'He's been killed!', and she immediately assumed people were referring to the Tsar. Obviously in such a situation she had no wish to compromise any of her old friends, who must all be 'illegals' by now. She eventually managed to contact her old school friend Sofya Lecherne, who provided her with a false passport and proudly introduced her to her old friends. Olga related her experiences diffidently and enchanted everyone she met. For Kravchinsky she represented a new kind of woman: 'Her freedom was the happy prophecy for the imminent freedom of everyone.'[10] Olga still had a lot of her old flamboyance and enjoyed her walks in the city with Kravchinsky but Nikolai Morozov, who had known her in Zurich, found her much changed. There she had been nicknamed the 'wolf cub' for her scowl and her oaths against the devil and the bourgeoisie. Now he found that the typical 'nihilist', with her rough manners, slovenly dress and abrupt speech and gestures, had become a serious and reflective young woman. For the men of the capital still entertained with some awe the myth of the 'Moscow Amazons' – young women who had grown up in aristocratic homes, enjoyed all the pleasures of their intellectual freedom at a foreign university and then returned to work in the factories. Their subsequent martyrdom had sustained the myth. Olga's first experience of revolutionary politics on her return was that propounded by Morozov and his terrorist friends. He spoke to her passionately about the need for immediate revenge against the oppressors.[11] They came to love one another very deeply and were soon married. Shortly afterwards Morozov was forced to leave for Finland to escape the police.

Morozov and Tikhomirov were now openly calling for the assassination of the Tsar in their new paper, *Listok Zemli i Voli* ('Land and Liberty Leaflet'), which diverged sharply from the established *Zemlya i Volya* newspaper. It was to their terroristic circle that Anna Yakimova was drawn after her return to the capital early in 1879. After serving three years of preliminary detention before the Great Trial, she had been acquitted for lack of evidence. She had gone to meetings at the house of the Kornilova sisters where she had met Sofya Perovskaya and others released after the trial. Now, after three years in prison, she felt the need to get back to the countryside, so she and a couple of women friends set off for the Tver region, dressed all in black and living on a diet of black bread and onions (they had learnt to do without tea in prison). Anna soon parted from her friends and moved to Nizhny Novgorod, where she got a job in a textile factory. She did this in order to find out about factory conditions rather than to engage in any active propaganda work, but she was rapidly exasperated by the workers' apathy, and went along to the manager to complain about the discrepancies between the men's and the women's salaries – an issue not unconnected with the men's shameless pawings and obscene remarks. Her affrontery aroused the manager's suspicion, and she was forced to leave before he reported her to the police as a 'propagandist'.

When she returned to the capital in early 1879 she went to the address of two people she did not know, Osip Aptekman and Georgi Plekhanov, who were running a 'workers' flat' and trying to revive the flagging spirits of the urban populist movement. But Anna found that the workers who visited the flat were sadly embourgeoised and she argued incessantly with Plekhanov, who insisted that the struggle must be an economic rather than a political one. Exasperated by these arguments, she tried without success to contact Tikhomirov and Morozov, who were by now virtually inaccessible to most party members. She did however manage to meet Shirayev, Isaev and Kviatkovsky, who shared with her some of their expertise in explosives.

For Anna Korba, who had returned to St Petersburg the previous May, there seemed no way of contacting revolutionary circles. She had been in Rumania for the entire course of the Russo–Turkish War, and after two years of evacuating and nursing soldiers on the front she had no sympathy for terrorism. She wanted above all to contact the kind of revolutionary groups in which she had moved so freely as a student. Now, at the age of twenty-nine, she felt out of place with the flamboyant young revolutionaries. Two years earlier she had been reading Dostoyevsky and Uspensky; now she read Lassalle and Marx; but she still clung to the old Slavophil traditions, and started going to Slavophil discussion groups in which she tried to urge prominent writers like Kireevsky, Khomyakov and Samarin to take some political stand in their writing. Although her two years on the battlefield had been a radicalizing experience, Anna had no real political direction. She decided to attend *fel'dsher* courses in the hope of meeting radical students, but her heart was not in it and she brooded endlessly about her political inactivity. Then in August came Mezentsev's assassination, and for her this was the 'turning-point'.[12] It became easier now to attend meetings and her chief concern was that the Party should use the radical journals as a forum for its views, not so much in order to convert journalists to the cause, but to use all available literary channels to increase the influence of revolutionary politics.

Most party members felt that this was the sort of work best suited to Vera Figner, too, for she was also on friendly terms with the populist writers Uspensky and Mikhailovsky, although she was impatient with the enclosed world of political journalism. By early 1879 she was also becoming increasingly pessimistic about her activities in Saratov. In the spring Alexandr Soloviëv visited the sisters on his way to the capital. He told them that experience in the countryside had taught him the futility of trying to instil the spirit of revolution into a passive and dying peasantry. By the time Soloviëv had left, she had come to accept his reasons for doing so; he was returning to assassinate the Tsar. Mikhailov and Morozov were already back in the capital when Soloviëv made his unsuccessful attempt on the Tsar's life in April. Although they had supported him, they could not ask the Party simply to endorse this support without some major policy decisions. Soloviëv's own justification, arguing against his two rivals for the job, Goldenberg and Kobylianski, both of whom subsequently turned out to be police agents, could hardly stand as a political programme: 'Only I satisfy all the conditions. I must do it. This is my job. Alexander II is mine and I won't give him up to anyone.' On 28 May he was hanged before a large crowd, and the government put through an edict dividing Russia into six districts, each ruled by a governor-general with plenary powers. The Emperor left the capital for Livadia in the Crimea, and arrest followed arrest. The Party was now overcome by a sense of urgency that made the assassination of the Tsar the primary issue for every member.

Conspiracy, revolution and the conquest of power were on the agenda of the crucial meeting planned to be held in Voronezh in the summer of 1879. But in order that there should be a majority of terrorists at this meeting, a preliminary conference was to be held in Lipetsk. Members of the newly formed terrorist Death or Freedom Party now set out in search of recruits for this conference.

Most of the women were kept in ignorance of this preliminary meeting. Little effort was made to contact them and persuade them of the necessity of this new move, and anyway most of them were conveniently engaged in relatively peaceful activities. Anna Yakimova was an exception. After Soloviëv's assassination attempt Plekhanov's flat had been liquidated; Anna was urged by her friends Shirayev and Kviatkovsky to leave for Kaluga, to 'await orders', but she found this uncertainty intolerable, and soon hurried back to the capital where she eventually sought out Morozov and begged to join the Death or Freedom Party. It emerged that she had accumulated considerable knowledge of dynamite and nitroglycerine, and Morozov agreed that she and Shirayev should set up a conspiratorial flat in which they could have their own laboratory. They were shortly joined by Kviatkovsky and Kibalchich.

When Ekaterina Breshkovskaya was awaiting trial in 1877 she had received some curiously naïve and pedantic letters from a total stranger who had developed a passionately platonic attachment to her. He was Nikolai Kibalchich and was twenty-one years old, and he described to her in detail his disillusioning summer in the countryside round Kiev. It was partly as a joke that she had answered his letters, but they became increasingly serious, and in the last one she received before being transferred to the St Petersburg prison he wrote: 'I give you my word that I shall devote all my time and powers to helping on the revolution by terrorist means. I possess a certain amount of knowledge which will enable me and my comrades to exploit my capabilities in the cause of the revolution. Very possibly it will require years of study before my knowledge is sufficiently complete to be of real help. But anyhow I shall go on working until it is ... ' Censorship prevented him from explicitly stating the nature of this knowledge, but it hardly needed to be explained. For the next two years Kibalchich escaped arrest by taking little active part in politics and by concentrating on an intensive study of explosives. By 1879 he was a brilliant technician and the Party's undisputed explosives expert. People said that it

228

was he who provided the Russian Revolution with dynamite. The flat became the headquarters of the Death or Freedom Party, and Kibalchich, despite his shambling, shifty ways, his ludicrous top hat and his infuriating habit of spending the housekeeping money on technical books, was an invaluable teacher. The four of them amassed large amounts of dynamite and occupied themselves with what Anna described as 'home industries'.[13] Despite her active commitment to terrorism, however, Anna Yakimova was excluded from the Lipetsk conference.

Anna Korba did not know anything about the conference either, although she had been directly instrumental in organizing it. It was she whom Mikhailov had sent to Finland shortly after Soloviëv's attempt, in order to summon/back Morozov. They returned together, both fully in sympathy with Soloviev's action. While Morozov busied himself with organizing the conference, Anna was sent to visit Uspensky to urge him to take some sort of political stand in his writing, but since Uspensky's entire life was given up to his search for the 'perfect individual' this was rather a pointless mission. Besides, he was by now too shattered by recent events to write anything at all. Anna Korba could be no more than a party liaison officer and messenger; she was not an 'illegal', and had yet to prove her devotion to the cause by undertaking any propaganda work on her own initiative. Shortly after her return from Finland she was told to move into a conspiratorial flat in Lesnoi and await orders.

Also awaiting orders in a nearby conspiratorial flat in Lesnoi was Sofya Ivanova. At the Great Trial she had been sentenced to five years' exile in Archangel for her part in the Kazan' Cathedral demonstration, but had escaped to the capital early in 1879. There she contacted Anna Yakimova and stayed briefly at the flat, but the politics of dynamite were not for her. It was Sofya Perovskaya, who had made an indelible impression on her at the Great Trial, who was her guiding spirit. 'I think I would have done anything she suggested,' she was once heard to say. She was now working as a messenger and typesetter for the party paper. In Lesnoi she had little chance to keep in touch with the latest developments in the Party, and knew nothing about either of the conferences.

The Party decided that Frolenko, who had been living in Odessa, should tour southern Russia in search of recruits. The first people he contacted there were Alexander Barannikov and his wife Marya Oshanina. Barannikov had been doing populist propaganda work in the Nizhny Novgorod region before moving to Khar'kov where he had worked briefly with Sofya Perovskaya. After this he had moved to Orël, where he met Marya Oshanina, a cultured wealthy girl living in exile on her family estate. Whereas Barannikov was a fighter, Marya was more interested in questions of political organization. She and Morozov were probably the only declared Jacobins in the organization. Her views had been formed over ten years earlier by her political teacher Zaichnevsky, who gave a clear account of his Jacobinism in his inflammatory *Young Russia* pamphlet. She had been banished to Orël in the spate of arrests that followed the pamphlet, but had returned to the capital as an 'illegal' to make contact with Zemlya i Volya. She remained a convinced centralist however, and although disillusioned now with Zaichnevsky's dreams for a 'perfect organization' she still believed that power must be seized by a conspiratorial group, which would then take over the machinery of the State to direct political and social revolution from the centre. She was intolerant of the politics of the capital. Both she and Barannikov, unable as 'illegals' to make any contacts in the district, had become sceptical and bored. When Frolenko told her of the discussions in St Petersburg and of the future plans for the Party 'she at once understood that the time for isolated *coups* was over. Something new was coming into being, something closer than that which was dear to her heart'.[14] After some ten years of political isolation, Anna

230

Olovennikova, as her illegal name was, emerged as one of the more energetic and shrewd of the 'politicians'.

Frolenko's major discovery was in Odessa. Andrei Zhelyabov had been a minor figure in the Great Trial. Since his release he had been working quietly as a gardener, living with his adoring wife and small child. He had little confidence in his abilities as an activist. He was of the people, and so could hardly 'go to the people'. He had had a turbulent boyhood in Odessa, always managing to urge his friends to rebel against authority at school. He read omnivorously and was a great day-dreamer. He had no class guilt to impel him to seek an ascetic life, and he was in fact flamboyant, even overbearing. But Frolenko found him disciplined, responsive and unhesitatingly in favour of terrorism. After talking with Frolenko, Zhelyabov left Odessa for good, never to see his wife and child again. He asked for a divorce and became an 'illegal'.

In his tour of southern Russia Frolenko had deliberately avoided Khar'kov. He was not interested in confrontations with party members, even the most dedicated. He regarded Sofya Perovskaya and Tatiana Lebedeva as naïve populists, living in some arcadian socialist Utopia of their own invention. In fact Tatiana, unlike Sofya, would have been quite prepared to commit herself to the new programme. Both women were later enraged to learn of Frolenko's unscrupulous behaviour, and this enabled them to take a rather more detached view of subsequent events.

Barannikov and Maria Olovennikova both had high hopes of the Lipetsk conference. They arrived before anyone else, but on 13 June the first members of the new faction started to arrive in the quiet little spa town of Lipetsk. Morozov and Tikhomirov were there; Kviatkovsky arrived a little later, followed by the 'southerners' Frolenko, Zhelyabov and Kolodkevich, a Kiev 'rebel'. There were no formal meetings. Marya Olovennikova, the only woman present, recalled that there were no real political disagreements, only a difference of

231

emphasis. To avert any suspicion the group went on picnics, and most of the discussions were held sitting under the trees in the nearby woods. Zhelyabov did most of the talking, clarifying many of his own and his friends' confusions in the process. He had once remarked to a friend; 'History moves too slowly. It needs a push, otherwise the whole nation will rot and go to seed before the liberals get anything done.' 'And what about a constitution?' his friend had asked. 'All to the good,' was his reply. Even if his ideas about the future constitution remained very vague at Lipetsk, he was recognized by everyone there as the leader after the first day. Once the present government was toppled and a constitution granted, the real ideological battle could begin; as long as basic freedoms were denied to the people there was no point in propaganda. He spoke for everyone there when he declared any means to bring down the government as valid. 'The more resolutely we act, the sooner we shall have power on our side,' he said. He was not yet by any means a confirmed centralist, but he now put all his organizational abilities into the formation of the new party. The primary goal of this party, implied at Lipetsk rather than stated, was the assassination of the Tsar.

A Directive Committee was formed consisting of Zhelyabov, Mikhailov, Tikhomirov and Frolenko, and under this was to be a 'Strong Fighting Organization', in organized reality the Executive Committee of the party; this was to be ratified at the 'official' Voronezh conference. Vera Figner, Anna Yakimova and Sofya Ivanova were the only women to be co-opted on to this committee. All candidates for the Executive Committee were to be carefully scrutinized at Voronezh; they were to be informed of every point in the new party programme, and every point must meet with their approval. In fact, no such programme ever existed, and in practice, as Morozov later admitted, 'when admitting a new member, we never asked his views on socialism or anarchism. We merely asked, "Are you ready to offer your life, your personal freedom and all that you have?" and if he said yes, we took him on.' Discipline and total devotion to the Party were the only real requisites for membership. Like the Chaikovsksists, the early Zemlya i Volya Party and even the Kiev Commune, this subjective criterion did not enable the new faction to exert the effective centralized authority of a true party. It could only ensure that comrades were welded still closer by demanding that they reject all 'outside' friendships and family ties, and that if arrested they should concentrate on saving their own skins. However, as Morozov later confessed, 'the heroic spirit was too strong'; subsequently, under police interrogation most comrades would seek only to protect each other. It was their very lack of programme, or rather the knowledge that one could be developed only through intense argument and self-criticism, that created an indissoluble bond between the 'politicians'. Later, Anna Yakimova was to estimate that five hundred terrorists could be counted on to initiate a popular uprising. There is no way of checking this figure. Certainly in the summer of 1879 there can not have been more than five. Few present could fail to realize that the imperial colossus was not going to be toppled by a mere five, five hundred or five thousand individuals. The conferences that summer brought home to many revolutionaries their numerical and physical weaknesses.

When the Lipetsk vanguard arrived in Voronezh a few days later they found Plekhanov chatting amiably to Sofya Perovskaya and the Figner sisters about the importance of cultural work among the peasants. None of them had any idea of what had been prepared behind their backs. Vera Zasulich, who was to have been Plekhanov's chief ally at the meeting, had just returned to Russia from Switzerland to attend. She had no idea of the impending confrontation, and, gullible as ever, she was urged, possibly by her 'political' friends, not to court rearrest by attending; she stayed instead with Anna Korba at Lesnoi. Plekhanov had few of his supporters with him, and little proof of the active support he claimed for the 'country group' in the provinces. Like many others there, he had assumed that the meeting would unanimously reject a policy of terrorism. His speech was greeted with total silence, and he walked out soon afterwards, saying angrily, 'And these people call themselves revolutionaries!' Vera Figner tried to stop him, but Mikhailov said 'let him go' : now that Plekhanov had gone he could afford to be more lenient with the 'compromisers' and the populists.

For Sofya Perovskaya and Vera Figner the Voronezh conference was a tormenting experience. Excluded from the decision-making by their own conflicts and by the apparent unanimity of their leaders, there was little they could say. Olga Lyubatovich too was saddened by the events there. She had just returned from Geneva, where she had been in hiding with Morozov. When Morozov returned she had stayed and associated with the Russian community, recognizable at once, as she said,[15] for their poverty and their harassed air. There she met Plekhanov, whose ideas did not attract her, and Vera Zasulich, whom she found 'oppressed by self-criticism'. It was for Kravchinsky, who was staying in Switzerland to care for his sick wife, that she reserved her most biting criticism, 'doomed', she said, 'to a fruitless waste of his talents'. She preferred the company of such leading anti-terrorists as Deich, Stefanovich and Vera Zasulich: 'We are not family people,' she announced. It was with them that she returned to Russia, and together with Kviatkovsky moved into Sofya Ivanova's flat at Lesnoi. There she soon received a letter from Morozov, urgently asking her to come to Voronezh. She may not have been a 'family person', but her political views had been very largely formed by her husband, and had been seriously shaken by her friendship with the anti-terrorists. Although she always gave Morozov her support in public, she was increasingly distressed now by his Jacobin views. For she felt that 'the revolutionary idea is only productive when it is the antithesis of all social, State, or personal compulsion, be it Tsarist or Jacobin'. She had no positive alternative to propose to the conference. Chiefly she was saddened that the new politics were turning old comrades into implacable enemies, and there seemed no hope now of reconciliation. Zhelyabov she considered overbearing and lacking in depth: 'He had not suffered enough,' she said. 'For him all was hope and light.'

For Sofya Perovskaya and Vera Figner too it was not only friends who would have to be sacrificed to the Party split. 'We were asked to take part in the political struggle, we were called to the city, but we felt the village needed us, that without us it would be darker there. Reason told us that we must follow the course chosen by our comrades, political terrorists who were drunk with the spirit of strife and animated by success. But our hearts spoke otherwise ... it drew us to the world of the dispossessed,' she wrote,[16] and went on: 'Of course we did not take this into account then, but subsequently this attitude was properly defined as the desire for a pure life, for a kind of personal sanctity ... But we put aside our feelings and bravely stood alongside our comrades, whose political instincts determined ours.' Both she and Sofya were coming to see the necessity of retaliatory terrorism, but were still desperately anxious to avoid a split in the Party. For both of them the fundamental virtue of the new party lay in its stringent moral demands. 'If the demands of the Party had been less exigent, if they had not stirred one's spirit so profoundly, they would not have satisfied us. But in those days, by their severe and lofty nature, they exalted us and freed us from petty personal considerations. One felt more vividly that in one of its members lived, must live, an ideal.'[17] It was just these 'petty considerations', the moral scruples and family ties that beset everyone, that were most keenly experienced by the women in this organization of men; the party code seemed consolingly to minimize their intimate conflicts with male authority.

235

During the conference Vera said little, Olga spoke occasionally in support of Morozov, but Sofya demanded clarification and definitions from all who spoke. She was afraid that the peasants were being left in the background, 'as if all their old wounds had been healed', as Vera said. Zhelyabov's proposal for a constitution enraged her, but his peasant origins forced her, as a high aristocrat, to respect his experience. 'I know many peasants,' he announced, 'practical men who refuse to risk all they have for a mere will o' the wisp. A constitution would give them the chance to come out into the open. They'd have a tangible objective to work for. That is the way to build a popular party.' For Sofya the constitution issue subsumed that of terror. She was able to put aside, publicly at least, her antipathy to terror, which she recognized as a crucial agitational factor, signalizing the beginning of a mass uprising. For her, any sort of constitution meant putting power into the hands of the politicians and the financiers of her own despised class. What she wanted to see was a free association of peasant communes, established after a national uprising, and this view was supported by most present. For although most revolutionaries were tacitly agreed that the new order, whether constitutional or not, could be brought about only by the assassination of the Tsar, there was a general distaste for the kind of despotic Utopia suggested by a constitution.

After Sofya had spoken against Zhelyabov, he refused to make any more speeches, preferring instead to speak informally to his comrades. In fact he spent most of his time arguing with Sofya, whom he found intransigent. Eventually he gave up in despair, saying 'One can do nothing with this woman!' Frolenko had no wish to talk to her; she had openly accused him of deliberately excluding her and Tatiana Lebedeva from the Lipetsk conference, and he had retorted that she was an inveterate populist, and 'too argumentative' into the bargain. Kibalchich found her lacking in essential feminine qualities, while at the same time ascribing infantile motives to her behaviour; 'It was as if she was taking her revenge on Alexander II for taking her away from her peaceful work among the peasants,' he said.[18] Zhelyabov, though, was more offended than angry. She had made a powerful impression on him at the Great Trial, where she had been barely aware of his existence, and it must be said that Zhelyabov was used to exerting a strong influence on all he met, especially women. He had a long black beard of which he was inordinately proud; 'They can catch me if they can, but I won't have my beard touched,' he used to say. Vera Figner implies that she found him arrogant, but nevertheless recognized him as 'our leader and our tribune'. Sofya distrusted his flamboyance, but was gratified that of all the comrades he should be so especially concerned with her views. For many he was a hero, inspiring sometimes fanatical devotion, and his unerring convictions often made it hard for him to adapt to the will of the majority. A comfortable conventional marriage simply had not prepared him to argue with women like Sofya Perovskaya, but he was as anxious as she that the views of individual members should be incorporated into the programme of the emerging party, of which he was now the undisputed leader. When Sofya returned to the capital she was still uncommitted to the new party, and determined to make contact with Plekhanov's group, which became officially known as the Chërny Peredel or 'Black Repartition' Party.

Soon after the conference Anna Korba was told to expect an extremely important 'illegal' guest at her Lesnoi flat. This turned out to be none other than her old school-friend Sofya Perovskaya, whom she had not seen since the days when they had done experiments together in Engelhardt's laboratory in Lesnoi. They had much to talk about, and Sofya spoke vehemently about pernicious local governors. About the new party she said little, apart from remarking 'Above all we are people, and must not feel that we stand above the laws of morality and humane conduct, and so are free of them.'

When Anna made up a bed for her guest, Sofya insisted that Anna take the bed; she had kept her old habit of sleeping on bare boards.[19]

Vera Zasulich was still staying in Sofya Ivanova's flat nearby, and through her Sofya Perovskaya was able to meet Plekhanov, Deich, Stefanovich and other leading members of the anti-terrorist Chërny Peredel faction. Still hoping desperately for some reconciliation between the two factions, she began to spend most of her time with Plekhanov's supporters. However, she found Plekhanov's suggestion that she leave the country in order to avoid arrest both personally and politically offensive and it provoked her into angry arguments with him about the need for some kind of terrorist programme. Zhelyabov, said Vera Figner, had 'swept Sofya off her feet', and a new passion lent conviction to her arguments. Perhaps this partly explained why in those days 'she was the very incarnation of the spirit of revolt. She was determined that official brutalities must not be left unanswered. She never used extreme language, but in a soft childish voice she proclaimed the necessity of terror'.[20] She was in a turmoil of unresolved conflicts, for, as her biographer says, 'If the others went forward and changed their dogmas to suit the present, Sofya Perovskaya was too iron-willed, direct and naturally strong for her first poetry to be easily rendered into prose.' The introspective adolescent poetry of her early populism was now maturing into a more subtle sense of her political responsibilities.

Whereas the men who had committed themselves to the politics of terror could be dismissed by the government as vicious desperados, Sofya Perovskaya's personality was a total enigma to them; an article in the official *Chronicle of the Socialist Movement* refers to her 'malice, secretiveness, stubbornness, crudeness, disdain, her utter contempt for men, her heartlessness, her spite and her cruelty', an accumulation of attributes few revolutionaries could have competed with; and anyone who knew her must have laughed at this

238

descriptive overkill. For her comrades were learning to value her natural distrust of revolutionary poses. It was Vera Figner who best articulated this distrust for the man who does not falter, the awe-inspiring heroic martyr depicted so persuasively by Kravchinsky:

> The Party declared that all methods were fair, but they created a cult of dynamite and the dagger, and crowned the terrorist with a halo. Murder and the scaffold acquired a magnetic charm and attraction for the youth of our country, and the weaker their nervous system, the more oppressive the life around them, the greater their exultation at the thought of revolutionary terror. For since the effects of ideas are hardly perceptible to a revolutionary during the brief span of his lifetime, he wishes to see some concrete palpable manifestation of his will, of his own strength ... [21]

Vera Figner's life as an 'illegal' began directly after the Voronezh conference, when she returned to the capital with Kviatkovsky, who took her to Sofya Ivanova's flat, now the headquarters of the Strong Fighting Organization. All the inhabitants were 'illegals'. As Lesnoi was conveniently surrounded by forests, they could go out as if on a picnic party and hold their meetings under the pine trees, where they could see far enough in all directions to make sure they were not being observed. It was in the Lesnoi forest that a final meeting was held between the two warring factions. This ended when Plekhanov, greatly outnumbered, announced his intention of leaving Russia and abandoning active politics for theoretical Marxist study. With him went most of the anti-terrorists, including Vera Zasulich, and Chërny Peredel was effectively liquidated.

After the removal of this ideological irritant, the victorious faction met officially at Lesnoi on 26 August. The solemn and inevitable resolution was unanimously passed: the Tsar was officially sentenced to death. Vera Figner was resigned to the move.

239

Sofya Perovskaya and I, who had hesitated at Voronezh in the hope of maintaining unity, had nothing more to say when our St Petersburg friends showed us that everything was ready for action. Finally and definitely we decided on splitting up Zemlya i Volya. We divided up the printing plant and the funds – which last were in fact mostly in the form of mere promises and hopes ... And as our primary aim was to substitute the will of the people for the will of one individual, we chose the name Narodnaya Volya for the new Party.[22]

Volya is translated both as 'will' and 'freedom' but it still connoted first and foremost the more tangible *'volya'* of 1861, the emancipation of the serfs. The new party still carried with it its old populist traditions.

Anna Korba gives an interesting insight into the structure of the Party in her account of her attempts to join.[23] She had for some time been associating exclusively with party members, and was by now desperately anxious to become a member herself. Mikhailov eventually agreed to take her to Tikhomirov's to be examined as a candidate for the Executive Committee. Members, they explained to her, were of two ranks. A first-rank member knew of every decision made by the Executive Committe and was responsible for two or three second-rank members, whose knowledge of party activities was restricted to their own appointed tasks. Anna was to be a first-rank member, an honour, they told her, that she was not entitled to refuse. Nor did she have the right to refuse any task the Executive Committee might entrust to her. She was sworn to absolute secrecy and to break all ties with her family and friends. As an unmarried woman without a passport, however, she was in an ambivalent, semi-'illegal' position, known by everyone under her assumed Christian name and patronymic of Varvara Petrovna. A fictitious marriage, it seemed to her, would enable her to enter the Party with a clean passport. Pribylev was the man she set her sights on. He was a radical but had no ties with the Party,

240

and Anna was able to tell him little about it. He found the whole thing rather ludicrous, and described laconically his meeting with this young woman, who was an almost total stranger to him, and whose proposal of marriage suggested none of the idealism of the conventional 'fictitious marriage'. Anna talked to him about her need to commit herself totally to the Party, and urged him that in marrying her he would be providing the Party with a new member, finally freed of all family obligations. Pribylev was unhappy, among other things, about the prospect of appearing before Anna's parents 'like a wolf in sheep's clothing, snatching away their only daughter'. This objection seemed quite absurd to Anna: 'To think you are afraid of such a thing, and not afraid of being hanged!' Her persistence eventually won out and they were married, then separated immediately, never to see each other again.

She next moved into Marya Olovennikova's flat in the city and they both got office jobs for the railways, which kept them until the late afternoon, when they were free for party work. Here they met Gesya Helfman, one of the few women to be sentenced in the Great Trial. Anti-semitism may have operated against her, for she had been doing quite modest propaganda work in Kiev when she was arrested. She had escaped after serving two years of her exile, and had arrived in the capital in the autumn, immediately to join Narodnaya Volya. She moved into a conspiratorial flat on Grachevskaya Street with a comrade Jokel'son. Now Marya talked to them of her first teacher Zaichnevsky, arguing that work in the countryside must be discarded, the Party must be consolidated, and the organizational centre firmly established in the capital. Anna meanwhile continued, although with greater caution now, to keep in touch with her radical journalist friends.

Sofya Ivanova was engaged on a rather different kind of literary work. She and one Nikolai Bukh, equipped with passports that described them as husband and wife, had been put in charge of the press for the new party paper. The press was hidden in the back of the flat they had rented on Sapernaya Street, a respectable part of town where their presence caused no immediate suspicion. Staying with them was a young radical student, Marya Gryaznova, who acted to perfection her role of cook in this domestic ménage. But the press department was considered the most dangerous. The police had now established a special corps of listeners under windows and in corridors, and printing was a noisy business. The press was only used if they were quite sure there were no listeners around, otherwise the type would be smeared with ink, laid on paper and tapped down, a smudgy but silent process. The press itself was hidden in cupboards. They entertained their neighbours frequently and made a point of hiring a cleaning woman and consulting the porter on trivial domestic matters. However, their life was a dreary one; it was decided that the press department should be completely isolated from all party members except Kviatkovsky, who was their liaison officer with the Party. They were not allowed to leave the flat even to go to cafés or the theatre, and one young man, nicknamed 'Ptashka', who moved in with them, did not leave the flat for eighteen months on end. Kravchinsky visited the flat once and was amazed by the dedication of these workers, imprisoned in dull routine work. Sofya he described as

... a living reflection of the continuous efforts which this life cost, maintained for months and months in this terrible place, exposed to the prying of so many thousand police spies ... Are not these people, I thought, the real representatives of the Party? Is this not the living picture which typifies the whole struggle? A feeling of enthusiasm fired my heart. We are invincible, I thought, while the source is unexhausted whence springs so much anonymous heroism, the greatest of all heroism ...[24]

The Party's decision to make the assassination of the Tsar its immediate task called for another kind of heroism, the

242

heroic and agonizing determination to put aside all conflicts in the pursuit of its goal. If I have dwelt on the more candid, intimate conflicts of Sofya Perovskaya and Vera Figner, it is because I feel they represent the most fundamental conflicts of the men terrorists who did not allow themselves to reveal their thoughts in this way. A year later Sofya was able to speak for the Party when asked by her friend Ivanov of their aims:

I asked her about the seizure of power. She clapped her hands in comic amazement, since this question was raised only by those who did not belong to the organization. Her own personal view was that no programme could dictate what would happen. Not to seize control would be to concede to the enemy. But the seizure of power, though desirable, was not a fundamental point in their programme. Their opponents would claim that they were Jacobins, but 'our motto, the People's Will, is not a mere phrase, it actually expresses the essence of our ideas, since in everything we are prepared to submit to the will of the people, expressed freely and clearly. But in the name of this, another problem arises for a revolutionary party, quite apart from the present direct battle with the contemporary political structure; that is to create, after the downfall of this structure, the social conditions in which the people would have the opportunity of expressing freely their will and realizing it. Only in this sense must we understand the point about the seizure of power, only in the interests of creating such conditions. And this is written into the programme of the Party.'

The conversation then touched on political terror, and the causes that had forced it to play such an important part in Narodnaya Volya. 'Revenge is a personal issue here,' she said. 'One can justify it, and with some difficulty, as a terrorist act committed on the individual initiative of separate people, but not by an organized party. Our revolutionary history does not recognize these acts, apart from situations of self-defence. It would be impossible to organize a party around the banner of

243

revenge – or to attract any public sympathy, something that we must make use of. That first shot fired by Vera Zasulich was not revenge, but an act of retaliation against an insult to human dignity. That is how it was understood by everybody, and that is also how it was understood at her trial by the representatives of the public conscience.

The political history of nations presents eloquent evidence that everywhere where the agents of the government are not answerable to the law for their actions, people will take the law into their own hands to counteract this, and at certain periods a revolutionary administration of justice will arise. But we cannot use this formula of retaliation to justify the aims and methods of Russian revolutionary terror. By elevating it into a systematic method of struggle, the Party uses it as a powerful means of agitation, and as the most effective way of throwing the government into confusion, holding it under the sword of Damocles, and forcing it to make important concessions. All other paths are prohibited to us – prohibited by the government itself.' She then indicated that she and many of her comrades had come from populist circles, and had been driven only after lengthy hesitation and fruitless attempts at peaceful activity to force a crack in that thick wall against which all these activities had been smashed. [25]

The arbitrary brutality of Alexander II's administration of justice far exceeded that of Ivan the Terrible: 67,000 people were deported to Siberia for political crimes, three-quarters of them without trial; 2,000 or more people were sentenced to death. The Party's official decision to assassinate the Tsar opened the eighteen months of open and often bloody warfare against the State that culminated on 1 March 1881 in the assassination itself.

NOTES

1. See Glossary of Names.
2. The fictionalized account of the events preceding the trial in Dostoyevsky's *The Possessed* is probably no stranger than the truth.
3. Frolenko describes the incident in his memoirs *Zapiski*

semidesyatnika, (Notes of a Man of the Seventies), p.328.
4. 'Memoirs of Evtikhia Karpov', in Kovalensky, op. cit. vol. 3, pp.94ff.
5. Figner, V., *Work Completed,* Complete Works, vol. 1, p.99.
6. ibid., p.116.
7. Kravchinsky, S., *Underground Russia,* p.21.
8. Kravchinsky, S., *Russia under the Tsars.,* p.25.
9. Figner, V., *Work Completed,* Complete Works, vol. 1, pp.116-18.
10. Kravchinsky, S., *A Female Nihilist,* p.32.
11. Morozov, in *Stories from my Life,* describes the incident (vol. 2, p.287).
12. Korba, Anna, 'Vospominania o Narodnoi Vole' (Memoirs of the People's Will), *Golos Minuvshego,* 1916.
13. Yakimova, Anna, 'Svoboda ili Smert', (Death or Freedom), *Katorga i Ssylka,* no. 24, 1926, pp.14ff.
14. Frolenko, M. P., 'Lipetsky i voronezhske s'ezdy', (The Lipetsk and Voronezh Conferences), *Byloe,* January 1907.
15. Lyubatovich, O., 'Dalekoe i nedavnee', ('Distant and Recent Events'), *Byloe,* (see bibliography).
16. Figner, V., *Work Completed,* Complete Works, vol. 2, p.242.
17. ibid., p.172 .
18. Asheshov, op. cit. p.97.
19. Anna Korba relates this visit in her Memoirs of the People's Will, op. cit.
20. Figner, V., *Work Completed,* Complete Works, vol. 3, p.328.
21. ibid. vol. 1, p.253.
22. ibid., p.157.
23. Korba, Anna, Memoirs op. cit.
24. Kravchinsky, *Russia under the Tsars,* p.211.
25. Interview with her in *Byloe,* 1906.

CHAPTER VII
TERROR

Only a few weeks after sentence had been passed, the Tsar was to travel from the Crimea to Moscow. The Party decided to blow up the imperial train, laying mines at three major points along the line – Odessa, Alexandrovsk and Moscow. Vera Figner, Tatiana Lebedeva, Anna Yakimova and Sofya Perovskaya all played major roles in these early attempts. For both men and women, the adoption of new roles was a welcome release from their furtive illegal underground existence. If the men took on themselves the physical labour and technical expertise in these attempts, they relied on the women to play their roles unself-consciously; for they generally assumed that women, with their old populist optimism, could naturally identify themselves with the characters they represented.

Vera Figner was active in the first attempt, at Odessa. Although it was felt that her talents were better suited to literary propaganda activities, 'I could not bear the thought of the moral responsibility for actions that would expose my comrades to the risk of such terrible punishment, and so I kept demanding to be allotted an active part. At first they were angry with me for seeking my own personal satisfaction

246

instead of submitting blindly to the orders of the Committee.' But the Party was becoming more tolerant of Vera Figner's uncompromising moral standards, and 'afterwards they gave way, and sent me to Odessa with the dynamite ...' Kibalchich, whose knowledge of explosives was by now truly remarkable, had established himself there in a flat, living under the name of Ivanitsky, and Vera moved in as his 'wife'. Kolodkevich and Frolenko arrived shortly afterwards, followed by Tatiana Lebedeva. Frolenko was to get a job as a railway watchman, which would secure him a house right on the railway line. But he needed a nominal wife, a partner to give some plausibility to his role. Tatiana Lebedeva was still seriously angry with him for excluding her from the Lipetsk conference, however, and it was only with great reluctance that she agreed to become his 'wife'.

Vera Figner had discovered that she was distantly related to a high official in Odessa, Baron Ungern Sternberg, and she was tempted to use her family connections to procure the group a suitable house on the railway line. But as an 'illegal' she had irrevocably left her family behind her, and instead she went off to see him as an aristocratic lady, asking him to provide Frolenko, her 'porter', with a temporary job as a watchman since his wife had developed lung trouble and could not work as a servant. The Baron obligingly gave her a note to take to the railway manager. Vera was young and very pretty, and the Baron obviously had his own reasons for being so accommodating, since 'he did not receive me in the way a woman of good family expects to be received, and I took care that that sort of thing should not happen again'. 'When I went to see the railway manager I dressed myself up very smartly, as would anyone who had a great favour to ask. He received me with great respect, and at once granted my request.' Frolenko and Tatiana were soon installed in the house provided Tatiana's 'lung trouble' cleared up remarkably quickly. However, the group soon learnt that bad weather had forced the Tsar to travel by boat from the

247

Crimea to Odessa, which meant that the attempt would have to be abandoned. Kibalchich and Kolodkevich returned at once to the capital, while Vera remained in Odessa as resident representative of the Executive Committee.

Frolenko and Tatiana moved to Tula, where they were married. For the first few days in Odessa they had remained on formal 'vy' terms with each other, although the situation demanded that they keep up a show of marital intimacy for the benefit of their neighbours. In the week they spent together however they learnt to overcome their mutual distrust. Tatiana emerged not as a sentimental idealist but as a modest worker, with a subtle sarcastic sense of humour, a passion for poetry and remarkable powers of endurance. She was not a tender woman, but she seems to have impressed everyone with her intense loyalty and integrity. Frolenko now no longer appeared to her as a heartless manipulative terrorist. They grew passionately fond of one another, and vowed to work together whenever possible. Shortly after their marriage they returned to the capital together.

Zhelyabov was in charge of the next assassination attempt, at Alexandrovsk. He had first met Anna Yakimova in Kiev before the Great Trial. He now looked to her not simply as a nominal 'wife' in the venture, but as someone with considerable expertise in explosives. In September they had a meeting in Khar'kov with Barannikov and Presnyakov to plan the attempt. Shortly afterwards Zhelyabov entered the town of Alexandrovsk, posing as a merchant named Cheremisov and explaining that he was looking for premises in which to open a tannery. With his open, uncouth ways he soon made a number of friends and he had no difficulty in finding a house conveniently near to the railway line, to which a tunnel could be dug from the back of the house. He gave the owner six months' rent in advance and went off to collect his 'wife', his furniture and two 'employees', Tikhonov and Okladsky. Even the indomitable Kibalchich, who visited the site soon after the Odessa fiasco, considered that they had

248

taken on rather a lot. There was a deep dip between the railway line and the road where the house was, and police patrolled the area constantly. All work had to be done at night, when all four of them laboriously excavated a tunnel to the site on the railway line where the bombs were to be placed. During the day the Cheremisovs had to keep up the absurd pretence of discussing 'business' with their neighbours. They were certainly an entertaining couple, and were incessantly besieged with visitors, but it was soon observed that, for all the talk, Cheremisov's business plans were not really getting off the ground. Eventually the tunnel was built and by 18 November, when the Tsar was due to pass through, Zhelyabov was waiting by the line for Presnyakov to give the signal to derail the train; apparently the Tsar would be travelling in the fourth coach of the second train. The signal was given, but there was no explosion. Vera Figner, who tended to doubt Zhelyabov's ability, was inclined to think that he had bungled it, but it is unclear what actually happened.

After this failure, Anna Yakimova left for the capital, telling her neighbours that she had to nurse some sick relatives. Zhelyabov, who was by now sick and seriously depressed, also made preparations to leave, but he was waiting for news of the Moscow attempt before he decided what to do. The most elaborate attempt, and the most demoralizing failure, was at Moscow, and when Zhelyabov heard about it he left immediately for the capital.

Sofya Perovskaya had not yet committed herself to the new party, but when Alexandr Mikhailov was looking round for a 'wife' for Lev Hartman, who was participating in the Moscow attempt, he turned immediately to Sofya, who was delighted by his offer. She wound up her affairs in the capital, handed over all her money, her lists of contacts and her political information to the Chërny Peredel Party and then left for Moscow, where Mikhailov had made a preliminary inspection and had paid a thousand rubles for a house in the Preobrazhenskoe area, on the southern side of the city. It was a rundown house in a poor neighbourhood; the land between the house and the railway line was wasteland, with here and there a ramshackle cottage, an allotment, a rubbish tip. Most of the local inhabitants were Old Believers, mainly day labourers and gardeners. Sofya and Hartman moved in as the Sukhorukovs, Old Believers of peasant origin, and Hartman left the house every morning, ostensibly for a day-labouring job. In fact he spent his days in the city at a conspiratorial flat leased by Anna Korba, who was sending the Executive Committee detailed reports of events in Moscow. Sofya spent her days gossiping with the neighbours and doing the shopping. While she entertained her neighbours with her little antics and anecdotes, work proceeded in shifts on the tunnel to the railway line, and backbreaking work it was; Morozov soon cracked up and had to leave. The first shift of workers would arrive before daylight and dig until eight o'clock. Then the next shift would work until two. Sofya usually worked on the last shift, which finished at about ten in the evening. The work was exasperatingly slow – they reckoned on a good day to dig about one foot an hour. They had no tools, only bare hands and a cheap compass to keep the tunnel straight (which it wasn't). Shirayev was the group's technical expert, and Isayev, a worker, was the best digger, but few of the eight people involved had had any experience of manual work. Disposal of the earth was a major problem too, and it had to be dumped outside at night. It rained pretty constantly, and the tunnel slowly filled up with water. They all carried poison with them in case they were engulfed. But they were in good spirits, and spent their evenings drinking tea and inventing 'miners' songs', in which they burlesqued the vicissitudes of their work.

As the work went on, Sofya had to keep up her clownish performance to avert suspicion and to keep the neighbours from intruding. Time and again a potential crisis was averted

250

by her resourcefulness. Once it was observed that she was buying an inordinate amount of food for one couple, and she immediately launched into a series of anecdotes about her cat, which was in the habit of stealing large amounts of food. From then on, the cat was to provide material for innumerable stories as she stood chatting at the door. One day the former occupier of the house came round asking for some jam out of the storehouse, which by now was crammed with earth and explosives; Sofya told him that she had lost the key, and then went later to his house with the jam. Soon after this the storehouse caught fire, a potentially disastrous situation. The neighbours rushed up offering advice and trying to break down the door, but Sofya, like a good Old Believer, threw up her arms saying that if it was God's will the fire would go out on its own, and begging them not to interfere with His plans.

These kinds of situations taxed the already dwindling energy of the comrades. They were running out of time and had no money to buy the tools they so badly needed. It was decided to mortgage the house, and Sofya drove a hard bargain, securing them six hundred rubles with which to buy a drill. Goldenberg set off, ostensibly to retrieve the dynamite from the Odessa attempt, but he did not return (later he was discovered to have been a police informer).

Everything was ready by 19 November, when the Tsar was due to arrive. Sofya was to wait in the house, watching for the train, and then give the signal to Shirayev who was to fire the charge. A bottle of nitroglycerine was put on the windowsill, and Sofya was to fire at it with a revolver in case they were discovered. Rumours had been flying around that the nihilists were up to no good, and police patrols on the line had been intensified. In fact the Tsar had been advised to alter the order of his trains, so that when Sofya gave the signal it was the train of his cortège that was derailed. The Tsar arrived safely in Moscow, but his shaken retinue had smelt dynamite in the air.

251

Another failure. More police repression, answered on 23 November by the Party's first manifesto. Without mentioning the first two inconspicuous failures, it claimed full responsibility for the Moscow attack. 'The attempt failed,' it said. 'We do not find it necessary to go into the causes of the failure.'

On her return from Moscow to the capital, Sofya Perovskaya moved into Gesya Helfman's flat on Grokhovaya Street, where Olga Lyubatovich was also staying. Gesya Helfman had become deeply attached to Kolodkevich in Kiev, and after his return from the Odessa attempt they had become lovers. Now she was working with him on the Executive Committee. 'She did everything,' recalled Kravchinsky,[1]

> ... letter-carrier, messenger, sentinel; and often her work was so heavy that it exhausted even her strength, although she was a woman belonging to the working classes. How often had she returned home late at night, worn out and at the end of her strength, having for fourteen hours walked all over the capital, throwing letters into various holes and corners with the proclamations of the Executive Committee! But on the following day she would rise and recommence her work ... There are unknown heroines, obscure toilers, who offer up everything upon the altar of their cause, without asking anything for themselves. They assume the most ungrateful parts, sacrifice themselves for the merest trifles; for lending their names to the correspondence of others; for sheltering a man, often unknown to them; for delivering a parcel without knowing what it contains ... such precisely is the story of Gesya Helfman.

Gesya's quiet determination now helped to convince Sofya to commit herself to the Party. She talked at length with Plekhanov, who had just returned from abroad, increasingly pessimistic about the prospects of an imminent peasant uprising. She angrily rejected his advice that she go abroad until the situation became clearer, announcing that she was determined to stay with the fighters. Her mind made up, she set off to see Zhelyabov; the following evening at an Executive Committee meeting Zhelyabov announced 'with radiant joy' that Sofya had asked to be co-opted on to the Executive Committee.

The Party had suffered grave setbacks and badly needed this important new member. On 24 November Kviatkovsky had been arrested, and the Party's only link with the press department was severed; they had also lost one of their most experienced organizers. A girl student in Moscow had been arrested carrying a copy of the *Narodnaya Volya* paper which, she admitted under interrogation, she had got through Evgenia Figner, in whose flat Kviatkovsky was living. The police immediately raided the flat. Evgenia, who was still 'legal', was not at home, but Kviatkovsky was caught. Evgenia immediately changed her status. Three weeks later Shirayev was caught. There was now a strong suspicion of police informers within the Party, but the members refused to be dispirited by the loss of two of their most valuable comrades and on 3i December a rather different kind of party was organized, a New Year's Eve party. Sofya, dressed up like a schoolgirl in her party dress, presided over the samovar, and Zhelyabov was in infectiously high spirits. Spiritualism was then much in vogue, and the ghost of Nicholas I was invoked. 'By what manner will your son meet his death?' was the burning question, and everyone waited with bated breath until, after a few thumpings, the disconcerting answer came through: 'Alexander Nikolaevich will die by poison.' Poisoning had certainly never entered any of the assassins' minds, but none of them had any faith in spiritualism either, so the evening continued cheerfully.

Kviatkovsky's arrest had put Sofya Ivanova's flat, the headquarters of the party press, under suspicion, and on the night of 17 January Major Miller of the St Petersburg police arrived with a large detachment of policemen. When Sofya heard the knock on the door there was no doubt in her mind

253

that this was a police raid; visitors were rare and came only by appointment. 'Who's there?' she called, gaining time. 'A telegram,' answered a voice. 'Wake up, it's the police!' she was heard to shout. The door was hacked down and the police rushed in, to be met by a volley of shots. Sofya was in the back room, piling the stove with manuscripts, passport blanks, government seals, address books and lists of police spies. Piles of documents were set alight on the floor. Meanwhile more police had been summoned and were smashing their way in through the back windows. More shots were fired by both sides, until a man's voice was heard to shout, 'We surrender!' In the back room lay poor Ptashka, who had blown his brains out all over the floor. Sofya Ivanova, cursing her comrades for their cowardice, was led off with Bukh and Marya Gryaznova to prison, where she remained for the next fifteen years of her life.

Anna Yakimova was now living on Podyacheskaya Street, as 'landlady' of the flat where she and Kibalchich were to prepare the bombs for the next major assassination attempt, Khalturin's bid to blow up the Winter Palace. She had a special sympathy for Khalturin, whom she had known as a schoolgirl in Vyatka when he had been in exile there. In 1879 he had organized the first real trade union in Russia, the Northern Workers' Union, which actually never attracted more than about sixty members. 'In Russia, every strike is a political act,' Zhelyabov had said, but Khalturin was now determined on a more immediate form of political action. A worker himself, he was convinced that the Tsar should be killed by a representative of the labouring classes, and in late November he had moved into the Palace as a carpenter. His workmates regarded him as a clown and a simpleton and warned him against 'socialists', easily identifiable apparently for their wild eyes and provocative gestures. He worked patiently, familiarizing himself with the Tsar's every movement, and by mid-January Anna Yakimova and

254

Kibalchich had provided him with a hundred pounds of dynamite, which he hid under his bed. On 5 February he was ready to fire the charge that was to kill the Tsar in the Palace dining-room. In the event, the imperial dining plans were altered, and the blast merely damaged some empty rooms. It was hard to get any idea from him of what had actually happened, since when he arrived at the Podyacheskaya flat a little later he was raving and incoherent. He left the Party and the capital, returning only a year later. Soon after the blast the flat was raided, by which time Anna had cleared up and left for Odessa with Isaev. Kibalchich moved to another flat in the capital.

Goldenberg had been arrested in November. Under interrogation he had made some far-reaching revelations about his former comrades. After the Winter Palace attack a supreme government commission was established under which all government organs were to be subordinated. Heading this commission was Count Loris Melikov, the former governor-general of Khar'kov, whose particular brand of 'official liberalism' opened up the new and glorious era of the 'dictatorship of the heart'. Actually Loris Melikov's tentative proposals to reconcile some sort of constitution with the autocracy soon made the Tsar regret his move. Melikov had no qualms about extending his own power by cleverly playing to the liberals. He renamed the commission the Ministry of the Interior, which now incorporated the Third Division, whose very name was anathema to every citizen of the Empire. 'The dictatorship of the heart has succeeded,' said the liberals – but they were wrong. There was a period of relative calm in the capital. The Party now based its activities in Odessa, where the Tsar was to make his next visit.

Vera Figner had been the Party's representative in Odessa since the last failed attempt, and on her own initiative had conceived a plan, which she feared would not meet with party approval. She was determined to kill Totleben, the local

255

governor-general; ironically, it was his son-in-law, Ungern Sternberg, who had received her so disrespectfully when she had petitioned him for jobs for her 'servants'. Her plan was interrupted by the arrival of Sofya Perovskaya in April, who had been sent by the Party, alone and without any money, to help lay the mine on the street where the Tsar was to pass by the following month. By some miracle, Vera managed to raise the thousand rubles they needed to open a grocery shop on 47 Italyanskaya Street, and she reluctantly postponed her plans to assassinate Totleben. The two immediately began digging the tunnel from the basement of the shop to the street. Isaev arrived as Sofya's 'husband', and together they officially opened the shop. Vera had her own flat in town, and when Isaev and Anna Yakimova arrived they moved into another conspiratorial flat, where the explosives were prepared. (It is probable that at about this time Anna and Isaev, who had worked together so long, became lovers.) The digging was done entirely at night, and it was slow work; the soil was clay, and all they had was enthusiasm and a small gimlet. A local worker named Merkulov, whom Vera distrusted but who had been recommended by Zhelyabov, joined them and speeded up the work somewhat. Then one day Isaev made some technical error and a bomb went off, badly damaging his right hand. Despite all the risk and his protests Anna took him off to the hospital, where she watched over his bed to prevent him from incriminating himself in his delirium. As soon as he regained consciousness he insisted on leaving, although he was now missing three fingers of his right hand and was in great pain. All the technical work now rested on Anna.

A police raid on Vera Figner's flat seemed to be imminent. It would be hard to explain away the constant appearance of young men and women on her doorstep carrying large baskets; it was at her flat that the earth from the tunnel was dumped. After her maid had left in the evening Vera had been seen by the neighbours carrying these baskets out to deposit the earth. Then a message came through from the Executive Committee, informing them that the Tsar had decided to go to the Crimea instead and that everyone except Vera should return to the capital. On her own now, Vera was anxious that the tunnel, which was already finished, should be used to kill Totleben, and in a letter to the Executive Committee she explained that she considered this move perfectly justifiable, since the Party recognized action against pernicious governor-generals, as prominent representatives of the State. The Committee replied that all dynamite was to be reserved for the Emperor – Totleben could be 'put out of circulation by other means' (by which they meant bombs). Totleben soon left Odessa, however, and the issue was closed. The shop was closed too, and the tunnel filled up, much to Vera's anger. She was shortly afterwards summoned back to the capital, where she was reprimanded for her waywardness and told that she was to be replaced in Odessa by a rather more 'reliable' comrade.

Sofya Perovskaya returned to the capital and moved in with an old friend, Rina Epstein, who had a flat on Izmailovsky Polk. Rina had been a comrade from Zemlya i Volya days. She had not been able to accept the new terrorist line, but collaborated closely with her old comrades, helping to smuggle 'illegals' abroad. The first person Sofya went to see was Zhelyabov. They made no secret of the fact now that they were in love, and though both of them had at one time solemnly denounced any friendships within the Party as a 'violation of social justice', they now found that passion gave new meaning to their work together. They were both in constantly high spirits, working closely together on developing the workers' section of the Party. The realization that terror was only the first stage in the political struggle (even if they only lived to see this first stage) released a new flood of energy in them. That summer Rina moved out of the flat and Zhelyabov moved in inconspicuously, as Sofya's

257

'brother'. 'Sofya was for Zhelyabov his "wife" in the sense in which he understood the term,' recalls Tikhomirov.

> It meant a great deal to him. He valued her intelligence and character, and as a colleague in the cause she was incomparable. Of course one can't talk of 'happiness'. There was constant anxiety – not for themselves but for each other – continual preoccupations, an increasing flood of work which meant that they could scarcely ever be alone, the certainty that sooner or later there was bound to come a tragic ending. And yet there were times, when work was going well, when they were able to forget for a while, and then it was a joy to see them, especially her. Her feelings were so overwhelming that in any but Sofya it would have crowded out all thoughts of her work.

Their flat consisted of two rooms and a kitchen, and they had no servant. They lived extremely spartanly, and their furniture was minimal – a few straw cushions, some broken chairs and cups and a few books – including *Lost for Love* by a Miss Bradden. 'Of course you can't deny to people who are fighting for freedom the right to the happiness which marriage can bring, even if it is short lived,' Sofya said,[2] 'but for me personally that happiness is impossible, because however deeply and strongly I loved a man, every moment of pleasure would be poisoned by the persistent thought that at that moment my dear close friends were suffering under the yoke of despotism.'

By the summer of 1880 many of the Party's important members had been arrested. Olga Lyubatovich and Morozov had fled abroad some months before. There Olga had a baby. Shortly afterwards Morozov fell into the arms of the police and the baby died. Olga returned to the capital that summer distraught with grief, bent only on sharing Morozov's fate. In Zurich at the age of sixteen she had been the 'wolf-cub'; now Vera Figner recalls her as a 'veritable tigress', urging her comrades to form an ultra-terrorist faction within the Party, and then cursing them for their cowardice. Inevitably it was not long before she was arrested. Later Morozov joined her in remote exile.

By now the Party was intent on consolidating its support among the people and trying not to jeopardize the fates of those already in jail. A manifesto was issued declaring that 'to avoid anarchy no attempt must be made to undermine the authority of the Constituent Assembly'. Not that they had any faith in the State's willingness to grant a Constituent Assembly – the manifesto was meant largely to placate public opinion. The Party was by now acquiring enormous prestige, mainly among the young intellectuals, but Sofya and Zhelyabov were more interested in organizing, from scratch, a workers' detachment of the Party. It was decided that the city should be divided into six districts, with a member responsible for each district. Sofya was in charge of the central St Petersburg area, which meant smuggling copies of the party paper into the large factories, establishing contact with dissident workers, widening these contacts and holding discussions with them. Zhelyabov once said, 'My place is out there on the streets, with a crowd of workmen.' Sofya was in her element in the long daily meetings they held with workers at the flat on Izmailovsky Polk. By the end of the year, after eight months of constant effort, they had recruited two hundred and fifty members of the workers' section in St Petersburg, some twenty of whom could be relied on to recruit new members. About thirty cells were opened in Moscow too, each containing four or five members, and the example of the workers in the capital soon fired the imagination of workers in Odessa, Khar'kov and Rostov. Narodnaya Volya was now forced to admit that hitherto it had been a party of intellectuals, whose theoretical interests must be irrelevant to most workers. There was clearly a need for a new workers' newspaper.

It was decided that the press for *Rabochaya Gazeta* ('The Workers' Paper') should be under the control of Gesya Helfman, who in September moved into a flat on the Troitsky

259

Pereulok with a comrade, Tetërka. Under the name of Mr and Mrs Nikolaev, they led the same kind of featureless secluded existence as workers on the *Narodnaya Volya* paper, though now Zhelyabov was in the habit of visiting Gesya and Tetërka and their comrade Sablin, whom he helped to set up the type. Sofya too was a frequent visitor, bringing news from the comrades and helping in any way she could. It was in *Rabochaya Gazeta* that Zhelyabov, in the autumn of 1880, printed the programme of the Workers' Section of the Party. Karl Marx was gratified to receive a copy and impressed by its contents. Workers, it announced, must form secret cells and recruit members, while bearing in mind that it was the peasants who would be the decisive factor in any uprising. They must be prepared, therefore, when the Party gave the signal, to seize the factories and key institutions in the large towns.

The new paper came out irregularly and infrequently; few workers were actually prepared to write for it, and the party intellectuals continued to contribute to *Narodnaya Volya*. Vera Figner and Tikhomirov were in friendly contact with the radical journalists Mikhailovsksy and Shel'gunov, editors, respectively, of *Notes from the Fatherland* and *The Cause*. Through them they were able to write a number of articles, anonymously of course, for these journals and to persuade Mikhailovsksy to contribute, again anonymously, the odd article to *Narodnaya Volya*. But most of Vera's time was spent discussing with Zhelyabov and Kolodkevich how best to establish links with the army and navy. For the Party was concerned to extend its Executive Committee into workers' combat groups *(druzhiny)* and Strong Fighting Forces within the army and the navy.

That autumn Vera accompanied Zhelyabov and Kolodkevich to a meeting of army and navy officers at the Kronstadt Naval Institute. Zhelyabov addressed the officers quietly: 'Gentlemen,' he said, 'I should be glad to give you some details about ourselves. We, revolutionary terrorists

. . .' There was a gasp from the audience; but Zhelyabov
concluded his speech to thunderous applause, and it was
decided there and then to form a military organization.
Revolutionary officers would work to gain the sympathy of
their men, who could then be relied on to follow them in the
moment of insurrection. Large numbers of officers, many of
them being used in police work, were already sympathetic to
the cause and Vera and Kolodkevich had little difficulty in
smuggling party literature into the barracks and speaking at
officers' and soldiers' meetings. Sofya and Zhelyabov were
chief liaison officers between the Party and the Strong
Fighting Force, which by the end of that year included at
least seventy army officers.

The Party was expanding, but it was losing time and funds.
The founders of the Party, outlaws without any security or
base, pursued day and night by the police, could not expect to
instil the same kind of unquestioning discipline into their new
recruits. However, the Party continued to keep its accounts
scrupulously, and in the eighteen months of its existence it
spent some eighteen thousand rubles. Explosives, the release
of prisoners, smuggling 'illegals' out of the country, forging
equipment, even such occasional expenses as taking a cab –
all this cost the Party dear. Then there were twenty members
who were entirely dependent on Party funds. Even members
like Vera and Sofya, who could rely on their wealthy
contacts, were no less scrupulous about their accounts. Once
when Sofya was ill she asked Vera to lend her fifteen rubles
for medicines, 'since they must not be bought out of Party
funds', and she planned to repay the money by selling a shawl
she was asking her mother to send her.

In October Kviatkovsky, Presnyakov, Shirayev, Sofya
Ivanova, Tikhonov and Okladsky (the last two active in the
Alexandrovsk attempt) were all sentenced in the first trial
of members of the Party's Executive Committee. The death
penalty was invoked very reluctantly now by the authorities,
and when Kviatkovsky and Presnyakov were sentenced to

261

death the atmosphere of crisis within the Party was heightened. A general meeting was called, in which Mikhailov and Zhelyabov called for work to continue on all fronts. However, since the Voronezh conference there had been a reversal of roles and it was now two women, Sofya Perovskaya and Anna Yakimova, who opposed them, emphatically insisting that the Party must concentrate first and foremost on the assassination; only after that could it broaden its base. This view carried the day. A little later Kibalchich was heard to remark sadly: 'Have you noticed how much crueller our girls are than our men? Perovskaya has the same kind of hatred as Mikhailov, only with a different nuance, more befitting a woman. But she does not show it so clearly as he does. This feeling is noticeable in her movements, in the attention with which she follows the Tsar's movements. In Mikhailov it is strong and steady, in Perovskaya it is sharper, deeper and more vehement ...' Buried in text books and formulae, Kibalchich was not overburdened by the moral and political dilemmas of the terrorists, but he could not fail to see the similarities between Sofya Perovskaya and Mikhailov. For if Sofya embodied the Party's moral strength, Mikhailov was its most powerful theoretician. It was he, like Sofya, who constantly exhorted his comrades to guard against the 'Russian nature' – against laziness, drunkenness and indiscriminate enthusiasm. With his intelligence and circumspection he had taken on an almost personal responsibility for the security of his comrades. He was irreplaceable. On 28 November he was arrested, to spend the rest of his life in the Peter and Paul Fortress.

The Party was becoming ever more vulnerable and short of funds; resolution began to fail. When Sofya and Zhelyabov heard of the disastrous crop failure and famine in the provinces they were anxious to postpone all thoughts of the assassination and go to the Volga region in the hope of instigating peasant uprisings. But Mikhailov in his last letter to them from jail said: 'There is only one theory in Russia; to acquire freedom to own the land. There is only one way to do this: fire at the centre.' To fire at the centre they needed funds. When Zhelyabov said, 'We're using up our capital', he meant both financially and physically.

So that winter Frolenko and Tatiana Lebedeva were sent to Kherson, where they were to raid the State Treasury for funds. Frolenko was still optimistic, but Tatiana, by now seriously ill with rickets and anaemia, had little hope of their success, and was fast losing confidence in the ultimate success of the Party. She was determined to see the venture through however, and as the 'Mironenkos' they rented a house near the Treasury, where for a week they worked tirelessly on building a tunnel to the vaults. But, those days, any new arrival in town was automatically put under close police scrutiny, and the Party had already had second thoughts about the venture. They were ordered back to the capital, where all energy was now concentrated on watching the Tsar's movements and on preparing the bombs that would kill him.

A watching party had been formed, led by Sofya and helped by a young comrade called Tyrkov and Maria Olovennikova's sister Natalya, a new recruit to the Party. It was nerve-wracking work since they had to note every movement of the Tsar and then report back to the Executive Committee; the strain soon told on Natalya Olovennikova, who had a nervous breakdown and had to leave the Party. The group's findings were then noted by all party members, who were scattered in conspiratorial flats throughout the town.

Vera Figner and Isaev, as the Kokhanovsksys, had moved into an important party flat that winter. Here daily meetings of the Executive Committee were held and most of the major tactical and political decisions were made. Early in February Gesya Helfman moved out of the flat where *Rabochaya Gazeta* was printed into another important conspiratorial flat. She was to go under the name of Elena Fesenko, the 'wife' of Sablin who, with the passport of a collegiate assessor, used to leave the flat every morning, convincingly carrying his briefcase with him. It was in this flat that the bombs were being made and various experiments in explosive devices were being conducted. Kibalchich was all in favour of the use of nitroglycerine, which had just entered the revolutionaries' arsenal but which Zhelyabov for one still regarded as unreliable. He preferred the idea of hand grenades, while the majority, Sofya included, favoured mining. Eventually it was decided that the Tsar's carriage should be mined, with hand grenades at the ready as a second strategy; and if all else failed, one member should step forward and stab the Tsar with a dagger. Even the indomitable Maria Olovennikova was shocked to find on her return from Moscow that 'all they can talk about now is dynamite'. She saw the Party as bent on a suicidal rather than a tsaricidal course, and urged the establishment of a powerful second-strike force in Moscow to save the Party from being wiped out by its own devices.

Work was now far too advanced in the capital for this suggestion to be taken seriously. Sofya reported that the Tsar's normal Sunday drive took him along Malaya Sadovaya Street, which seemed a suitable place to attack. She managed to find a basement to let in the street, and in this basement Anna Yakimova and Yuri Bogdanovich were installed. Their passports proclaimed them to be the Kobozevs, Evdokii and Elena, Old Believers and cheese merchants from Voronezh, who wanted the premises to open up a cheese store. In their anxiety to secure the flat, however, they left rather too generous a deposit, and Anna, although she had not lost her rough country accent, seemed to speak rather too lucidly for a merchant. These two minor anomalies were enough in those days for the landlord immediately to notify the police, who sent the passports back to Voronezh to

264

be checked. There was such a couple, apparently, and the 'illegal' Kobozevs could only hope that the real Kobozevs would not appear too soon. More problems awaited them. Party funds could not stretch to supplying the shop with cheese and a sign outside the door. Vera Figner went in one day as a customer, and was appalled by their meagre stocks. After a quick whip-round of some of her wealthy contacts she was able to raise three hundred rubles, with which she bought some cheese. The Kobozevs made unconvincing merchants, however, and the shop became a popular subject for local gossip. One local shopkeeper, Novikov, said later at their trial: 'The Kobozevs seemed to me − well at any rate they didn't seem to be in the cheese trade. He certainly wasn't one of us. I went back to my shop and I said, "Well, there's something funny about that shop because their competition certainly isn't going to do our business any harm".'

During the day the sunny shop was festooned with icons, and Anna spent 'business hours' behind the counter where, as Vera Figner said, 'with her down-to-earth manner and provincial accent she made a perfect Mrs Kobozev.' Meanwhile work was going on day and night in the room behind the shop. Zhelyabov, Kolodkevich, Barannikov, Sukhanov, Isaev, Degaev and Merkulov were all working in shifts. Since the tunnel was being dug directly through from the front room it was extremely difficult to work quietly, and Anna had to resort to Sofya's fantasy about an obstreperous cat in order to explain away the constant thumps. One day an unbelievable stench filled the shop, and Anna had to ward off the neighbours' attempts to call in a sanitary engineer. Apparently the diggers had hit a main sewer, almost asphyxiating themselves in the process. That evening Anna joined in the digging, depositing the earth in jars, in cheese-barrels, under the sofa, anywhere she could find. When the Tsar passed on 15 February she was to wait at the window and give the signal for the charge. On the appointed

265

day the tunnel was still not ready, however, and the shop was now under the watchful eye of the police. Work continued until a new date should be set.

That winter the Tsar and his ministers had been juggling with formulae in an attempt to create some sort of constitutional placebo. But the Tsar remained adamant: the autocracy must remain intact. 'No change should be made. If popular representatives were elected they'd just be tub-thumpers.' Whether these were just the conventional euphemisms of the benevolent autocrat, or whether his decision was prompted by a knowledge of the imminent danger to his life, we do not know. Nor do we know whether he was aware of the intense discussions now going on inside the Party, desperate to make their next attempt the final and successful one.

Gesya Helfman's flat on Telezhnaya Street was now the general headquarters of the assassins, while Vera Figner's flat was used as a base for the Party's press and as an explosives workshop. It had eventually been decided to use hand grenades, made, as it subsequently turned out, with an ingenuity that unmistakably revealed the hand of Kibalchich. These were all stored in the Telezhnaya Street flat. But who was actually to throw the grenades proved to be a more difficult decision. Both Sofya and Zhelyabov were emphatic that the honour of killing the Tsar should go to his most conspicuous victims, the factory workers. Mikhailov had always insisted that important tasks should be entrusted only to the tried and true, but Sofya and Zhelyabov had no reservations about their worker comrades. Since the workers' section of the Party had been closed down, workers had become more closely involved than before in the Party organization. On 20 February there was a meeting at Telezhnaya at which four workers were selected as throwers, Grinevich, Rysakov, Timofei Mikhailov and Emilyanov, a nineteen-year-old student, all of them inexperienced but eager. Zhelyabov explained to them the mechanism of the

266

grenades while Sofya outlined what their movements would be.

By now Zhelyabov was close to collapsing with exhaustion and had stopped taking any care for his own safety; on 28 February it came as a tragic but inevitable loss to the Party when he all but fell into the arms of a police officer who had recognized him from the Great Trial. When he failed to return home that evening Sofya was not unduly worried. Even the next day, when she forced herself to recognize that he must have been captured, she still could not imagine that he would be held for long, since their flat had never provoked much police suspicion. The positive confirmation of his arrest came that evening at a meeting in Vera Figner's flat. It was decided then and there to kill the Tsar the next day, on 1 March. Sofya automatically stepped into Zhelyabov's place. 'If it had not been for Sofya,' said Vera Figner, 'the assassination would never have taken place when it did, but would have been postponed indefinitely.' Sofya now acted with an almost terrifying blindness to her own and Zhelyabov's fate. She returned immediately to her flat to clear up and move out. The porter, she realized, would by now be anxious to discover from her the movements of her 'brother'. In her agitation she cleared up hastily; a police search of the flat later discovered traces of explosives, bomb components and some cheese labels. She then went to Vera's flat, where she joined Vera, Kibalchich, Sukhanov and Grachevsky, who had all been preparing grenades since five that evening. Sofya was in such a state of agitation that they made her rest, while they continued working until two a.m. When they got up seven hours later, two grenades were ready and Sofya set out with them for Telezhnaya; Kibalchich was to follow on later with the two others.

She broke the news of Zhelyabov's arrest to the assembled throwers, and drew them a map on the back of an envelope, detailing the Tsar's movements and their positions. The Tsar, despite the pleading of his wife, who anticipated an attack, refused to give up his Sunday drive, and agreed only to change his route; instead of driving down Malaya Sadovaya he would pass along the Ekaterinsky Canal. Aware of this possible alteration, Sofya decided to station herself at the intersection between the two routes and if the Tsar turned into the Canal she would signal to the throwers by blowing her nose; then she would walk towards the Canal, where the throwers would by now be waiting, and at the sight of his arrival she would repeat the signal. Isaev had now laid the mine in Malaya Sadovaya, where Anna Yakimova was to wait and serve her customers in the shop until the very last moment. Then she would close the shop and take up her post at the window, and when she saw the carriage approaching give the signal to Frolenko, who was to detonate the charge.

Vera was to wait at home to provide shelter for the Kobozevs. Frolenko visited her flat before going on to the cheese shop, and when she saw him cheerfully sitting down to a large breakfast 'to keep up his spirits' she was ashamed of her own squeamishness. Frolenko then moved off to Malaya Sadovaya, and Vera was left to spend the next three hours alone in her flat in a torment of anxiety. Anna too was becoming impatient and anxious at her post – by now it was clear that the Tsar was taking the other route. She walked out on to the street, and there met Kibalchich in his shabby top hat, who was ambling off home, sceptical about the effectiveness of hand grenades. Anna returned to the shop to wait for news, convinced now that this was merely one more failure.

The Tsar was now approaching the Canal. Sofya gave the signal to the first thrower, Rysakov, who threw his grenade; the carriage was untoppled and the dazed Tsar stepped out. Then Grinevich threw the next grenade and the Tsar fell dead to the ground. Grinevich himself was mortally hurt in the explosion, and died a slow and painful death. Sofya was able to slip away in the confusion. Later that afternoon she met Tyrkov and another comrade in a café on the Nevsky

Prospect. Tyrkov described her face struggling to remain composed as she quietly told them what had happened.' "I think it was a success," she said "he was either killed or very badly wounded." The waiter came, and then she continued, "Nikolai [Rysakov] was killed.* I think Kotik [Grinevich] was killed too." '

Later that evening there was a meeting at Vera Figner's flat. Vera had immediately assumed that the whole venture had failed, and had begun to wander through the streets of the city to look for her comrades. Then she heard the news from the people on the street, and:

> I rushed back to my companions. I was so overwrought that I could barely summon the strength to stammer out that the Tsar had been killed. I was sobbing; the nightmare that had weighed over Russia for so many years had been lifted. This moment was the recompense for all the brutalities and atrocities inflicted on hundreds and thousands of our people. This moment was the recompense for the blood of martyrs, for everything. An overwhelming weight had fallen from our shoulders. Reaction was at an end! The dawn of the New Russia was at hand! At that solemn moment all we could think of was the happy future of our country . . .

The atmosphere at Vera's flat was one of ecstatic optimism until Sofya arrived, her face drawn, deaf to the greetings of her comrades. Now she could only repeat, over and over again, that Zhelyabov must be freed; the Party must put all its resources and energies into this operation.

Immediately after the news came through Bogdanovich had left the cheese shop for Moscow. Anna stayed in the shop until nightfall, when she lit the candles by the icons, wrote a note to the butcher asking him to feed the cat and then left the house with a small shopping basket. She caught a train for Moscow via Smolensk – the revolutionaries never travelled by direct routes. That same evening the flat was

* This was not actually the case.

269

raided and the tunnel and mine discovered. The news was telegraphed through to all the provinces, and all railway stations were alerted. It happened that Anna was sharing a compartment with people who had heard all about the notorious Kobozevs. Mrs Kobozev was said to be very beautiful, an incessant smoker who stayed out till all hours and read French novels. As this 'Mrs Kobozev' bore no similarity to the reality Anna had no fear of detection, and later at her trial was amused by the look of disappointment on the Prosecutor's face when confronted not with some exotic beauty but with an austere, self-controlled young woman.

The following day Gesya Helfman's flat was raided. Late that night there was a knock on the door, and Gesya, who had been expecting the police, left her room and took the bombs to safety in case they should explode in a shoot-up. Then the police hacked down the door and two shots were heard from inside the house. When the police charged in they discovered Gesya, dishevelled and screaming hysterically; Sablin had killed himself, his brains spilt all over the floor in the next room. Gesya was taken off to prison and a police guard put on her flat. Soon afterwards, Timofei Mikhailov walked into the trap and was arrested immediately.

The evening after the assassination the Executive Committee sent an open letter to the heir-apparent, drafted in advance, presumably by Tikhomirov and Vera Figner. It was not a work of propaganda, it simply announced its willingness now to negotiate. 'The Executive Committee', it announced in a long and detailed statement, which I shall paraphrase, 'is not justified in postponing an explanation for any reasons of natural delicacy. The inevitable alternatives are revolution or a voluntary transfer of power to the people. We turn to you as a citizen and a man of honour, and we demand: 1) amnesty for all political prisoners, 2) the summoning of a representative assembly of the whole nation.' This letter brought the Party a flood of encouraging

270

responses, including a sympathetic letter from Marx. For the statement's moderate tone had succeeded in persuading many uncommitted radicals that a new era of constitutional government was now about to be opened up. But the government was now intent on a final annihilating roundup. Rysakov, arrested immediately after the assassination, was trying to delay his own execution by talking. Sofya resolutely refused to believe in this most terrible of betrayals. 'I know Rysakov,' she insisted, 'and he will say nothing.' But her optimism was becoming increasingly out of place.

By now thousands of Cossacks had been sent into the city, roadblocks were set up, and all routes out of the city were barred. There was an indiscriminate wave of arrests; one woman, completely innocent, was arrested five times in one day, and the citizens of St Petersburg all lived in a state of constant terror. The Party was losing all its leadership and initiative.

Tyrkov now accompanied Sofya everywhere to protect her against her own blind carelessness. According to him she talked only of Zhelyabov, devising endless plans for his escape. She considered plan after plan, each of them equally unrealistic. First she considered bribing her way into the court where he was to be tried and there trying to influence the verdict. Her old friend Rina Epstein actually managed to get her a meeting with an old acquaintance, a liberal official, but her visit there was fruitless. Then she decided to set up a lookout post near the police department. 'She had become completely irresponsible. People said, ' "Sofya has lost her mind",' said Tyrkov. All her friends urged her to leave the city, but escape was impossible, and Sofya was anyway adamantly opposed to the idea of leaving. In a pathetic attempt to regain a grip on her sanity, she continued to draw up plans for Zhelyabov's escape, collecting money for his release and veering wildly between moods of manic exultation and deep depression. Although she was now barely able to walk, her expression always remained composed and gentle.

271

On 3 March, as she was walking down the street with Tyrkov, she saw a newspaper headline announcing 'fresh revelations about the crime'. Zhelyabov had claimed full responsibility for all the events of 1 March. There was little hard evidence against him when he thus signed his own death warrant, and it was this that Sofya had been relying on. A comrade had once reproached Zhelyabov with trying to take responsibility for all tasks singlehanded. 'But you can't always tell what is a trifle,' he had replied. 'It may sometimes be something important, and then it's essential to mobilize not only the whole Party but the maximum efforts of each individual within the Party. And anyhow, it's my nature to be like that. It's better that I have my own first-hand impressions of everything, and then I can take a line of my own and be sure of it.' Sofya too had shared with him this personal responsibility for every detail within the Party; his action was inevitable and characteristic. Her response, on reading the news was simply, 'it is right'.

But since 1 March an extremely forceful warrant for Sofya's own arrest had been circulated. With every moment that passed her position was becoming more precarious. She had to spend every night at a different flat, and she hated the thought of compromising her friends, especially those whose own lives were in danger. One night she turned up at Vera Figner's flat. 'May I stay the night here?' she asked. 'How can you ask?' Vera said. 'Because if they make a raid and discover me here,' she said, 'you'll be hanged.' 'I have a revolver,' Vera told her, 'and if they come I'll shoot, whether you are here or not.' This was probably the most intimate encounter between two women who had experienced so much together in the past eighteen months. Later Vera was to regret that they had so little chance to know one another. 'I saw only a part of her; in those frantic days we related too superficially to one another,' she said.

By now Sofya had lost all interest in guarding her own

272

safety, almost to the point of courting arrest. On 10 March she was stopped by a police officer Shirokov as she was walking down the Nevsky Prospect. He reported that she immediately offered him thirty rubles for her release, but this was not very likely, as she no longer placed much value on her freedom; Shirokov was probably trying to enhance his own honour in refusing, and retaining his valuable captive. She was taken at once to the Director of the Police Department, von Plehve, and interrogated. Without mentioning any of her comrades she told him as much as she could about the activities of the Party; she had personally killed the Tsar, she said. While in prison she was allowed to write to her mother, who hurried from the Crimea to petition Loris Melikov for an interview with her daughter. After being kept waiting for many hours, Melikov eventually admitted her, saying, 'I am to inform you that it is his Imperial Majesty's desire that you induce your daughter to disclose at once the names of her accomplices', to which Varvara Perovskaya retorted angrily; 'It is impossible for me to persuade my daughter to do anything against her convictions.' Sofya was allowed to see her mother twice in prison, both times attended by a police officer and a sentry. They spoke little; Sofya would lie like a child in her mother's arms.

While Sofya remained uncommunicative the roundup continued. On 14 March Tyrkov and Maria Olovennikova were arrested. Three days later Frolenko was caught, and shortly afterwards Kibalchich walked into a police trap at his house. Vera Figner's flat still served as a refuge for those on the run, but she was now in great danger herself and the flat had to be disbanded. She disposed of the dynamite, the chemical laboratory, the passport-forging equipment, the press and the illegal literature. When the police raided the flat shortly afterwards all they found was one empty suitcase and a warm samovar: Vera had just left for Kronstadt. After

273

Frolenko's arrest Tatiana Lebedeva had scraped up the money to go to Moscow where she hoped to get work in a factory.

The authorities now decided that a charge of tsaricide should be made without further delay against their most important prisoners. The Trial of the 6, Zhelyabov, Perovskaya, Kibalchich, Rysakov, Helfman and Mikhailov opened on 25 March and lasted for three days. As the Prosecutor Muraviëv read his immensely long speech, pulsating with righteous anger and grief, Sofya and Zhelyabov whispered to each other. It so happened that Muraviëv had been a childhood friend of Sofya's, and she had spent many hours as a little girl playing with the Muraviëv children on their parents' estate. But there was no recognition between the two at the trial. As Muraviëv wept and ranted, the accused whispered and giggled. 'Cast out by men, accursed of their country, may they answer for their crimes before Almighty God!' he thundered. 'But peace and calm will be restored. Russia, humbling herself before the Will of that Providence which has led her through so sore a trial, will march on, filled with a new strength, with a new and burning faith in her glorious future ... ' The defending counsels, afraid for their own professional futures, were hardly more impressive. Zhelyabov refused the offices of a lawyer, and in his own defence tried to explain some of the aims of the Party. Time and again he was interrupted by the judge, who insisted he restrict himself to his own defence; time and again he reiterated that his own interests were inseparable from the Party's. Gesya Helfman confined herself to correcting a police statement: 'I wish to point out that when I came to St Petersburg as an "illegal" in 1879, it was not to escape the police, but because I wanted to devote myself to the service of the cause I had been and have been serving.' Kibalchich was prepared at this point to agree to differ with the judge on the means necessary to bring about the revolution, but was anxious to give him some details of

274

his new flying machine – a project that had been totally occupying him during his ten days of detention.

In his speech against Sofya Perovskaya, Muraviëv had said:

> We can imagine a political conspiracy; we can imagine that this conspiracy uses the most cruel, amazing means; we can imagine that a woman should be part of this conspiracy. But that a woman should lead a conspiracy, that she should take on herself all the details of the murder, that she should with cynical coldness place the bomb-throwers, draw a plan and show them where to stand; that a woman should have become the life and soul of this conspiracy, should stand a few steps away from the place of the crime and admire the work of her own hands – any normal feelings of morality can have no understanding of such a role for women.[3]

The Imperial Prosecutor then added that the best proof of the Party's impotence was that such a matter had been entrusted to the feeble hands of a woman. In her own defence, Sofya said: 'I do not deny the charges, but I and my friends are accused of brutality, immorality and contempt for public opinion. I wish to say that anyone who knows our lives and the circumstances in which we have had to work would not accuse us of either immorality or brutality.' By this time it was midnight of the last day. The Court retired and returned three hours later. The Judge then read the long formal declaration which sentenced all the prisoners to death. Sofya, as a member of the high nobility, could appeal against sentence, which she obviously had no intention of doing. On 31 March Mikhailov and Rysakov both petitioned, unsuccessfully, and Kibalchich demanded to consult a flying expert about his flying machine.[4] On the same day Gesya Helfman announced that she was four months pregnant. She was examined by a police doctor, who confirmed this, and it was decided to commute her sentence to life imprisonment.

There were widespread rumours that the prisoners were

tortured in the days before their death. Why was there this interval between their trial and their execution? Why were the normal guards removed for several hours every day, in which period a party of unknown visitors would visit the prisoners' cells? Rysakov was going insane under interrogation. If released he would find Vera Figner, he said; this was his 'most urgent, sincere desire'. Sofya and Zhelyabov refused to talk to the police, while Kibalchich had long discussions with his interrogators about his plans for his flying machine.

At six am on 3 April the prisoners were given tea and handed their black execution clothes. 'Cheer up, Sofya!' said Mikhailov, as they were chained hand and foot to the tumbrils that were to take them to the gallows. A placard was hung round their necks with the word 'Tsaricide' on it. Then the party set off. It was headed by the police carriage, followed by Zhelyabov and Rysakov. Sofya sat with Kibalchich and Mikhailov in the third tumbril. A pale wintry sun shone as the party moved slowly through the streets, already crowded with onlookers, most of them waving and shouting encouragement. High government officials and those wealthy enough to afford the tickets were sitting near to the scaffold that had been erected on Semënovsky Square. The irreplaceable Frolov, Russia's one and only executioner, fiddled drunkenly with the nooses, and Sofya and Zhelyabov were able to say a few last words to one another. The square was surrounded by twelve thousand troops and muffled drum beats sounded. Sofya and Zhelyabov kissed for the last time, then Mikhailov and Kibalchich kissed Sofya. Kibalchich was led to the gallows and hanged. Then it was Mikhailov's turn. Frolov was by now barely able to see straight and the rope broke three times under Mikhailov's weight. Frolov was cursing by the time Sofya walked up to the scaffold. 'It's too tight,' she told him as he struggled to tie the noose. Then she died, without having to witness Zhelyabov's death. He died in agony — the noose had not been tight enough. Rysakov struggled as he was led to the block.

276

They were buried ignominiously behind the Preobraz-hensky cemetery, where their graves were soon littered with weeds and rubbish. Their execution spelt the end of this doomed movement; its remaining members were to die slower deaths.

Gesya Helfman was separated from her baby immediately after it was born. She died five days later, and her baby died soon afterwards in a foundlings' home. Anna Yakimova was also pregnant, probably by Isaev. After leaving the cheese shop for Moscow she had moved on to Kiev, where she was arrested shortly afterwards in the company of a friend. Tatiana Lebedeva, who had moved to Moscow immediately after Frolenko's arrest, soon returned to the capital to clear their flat of any incriminating evidence. Kravchinsky met her at the station, dressed as a peasant woman and carrying a basket of vegetables. When they arrived at the flat, Kravchinsky recalled: 'I was struck by the perfect order which prevailed everywhere. The furniture, the parlour, the husband's writing desk all had an inviting aspect. Nothing was wanting. It seemed a little nest of peace and joy.' [5] All incriminating papers were burnt and Tatiana insisted, to Kravchinsky's horror, on staying the night in the flat, in order to avert the porter's suspicion. The next day he bought her a ticket for Moscow and saw her off at the station, advising her not to attract attention to herself by smoking.

In Moscow there was nobody to meet her at the station, and she refused to compromise any of her friends there by accepting their hospitality. Everywhere in the city there were police photographs out for her arrest, and for the next few weeks she roamed round the streets, penniless, ill and alone. On 3 September the police eventually found her, sleeping on the floor of the railway station. She was taken to the capital and held for several months before the next great trial of the revolutionaries, the Trial of the 20, which lasted from 9 to 15 February 1882. In the courtroom she met Frolenko again, as well as Anna Yakimova, Isaev, Kletochnikov, Kolodkevich

277

and Sukhanov. At her trial Tatiana proudly accepted responsibility for every act committed by the Party, slandering herself in a desperate effort to save Frolenko and demanding to share the fate of her friends. She was charged with the assassination attempt at Odessa and the attempted raid on the Kherson Treasury, and sentenced to death, along with nine others including Anna Yakimova. Anna too was implicated in every act committed by the Party, and proudly accepted full responsibility without going into details about her activities.

Public opinion in Russia and Europe had been outraged by the execution of the six revolutionaries the previous year, and Victor Hugo among others lost no time in sending a blasting letter to the Russian government demanding a reprieve. Nine of the prisoners were subsequently reprieved, and only Sukhanov, who had been in charge of the Party's Fighting Services Section in the Army, was executed by firing squad. The others were sentenced to the slow death of permanent imprisonment.

Those sentenced in the Trial of the 20 were sent to the Trubetskoy Dungeon, one of the most horrible of Russian prisons. Few survived the ordeal; torture and rape were everyday occurrences in the dungeons, through whose soundproofed walls little information reached the outside world. It was here that Anna Yakimova had her baby, watching over him night and day to protect him from rats, trying to warm him with her breath and watching him slowly die as she ran out of milk. After a year in Trubetskoy, during which most of the prisoners had died or committed suicide, she and Tatiana Lebedeva were transferred to the Kara prison mines. The journey north, which lasted two years, was scarcely more endurable than life in the dungeons. Anna Yakimova abandoned all hope for her baby, and under such conditions it was hardly surprising that she eventually gave him over to some well-wishers who had come out to greet the prisoners with messages of support and tears of sympathy.

278

By the time they reached Kara, Tatiana was twenty-eight years old, Anna three years younger. Tatiana's experiences had turned her into a semi-blind, shaven-headed, prematurely aged cripple. Anna, despite a liver condition and boils, was composed and firm, and both were able to delight Ekaterina Breshkovskaya and the other women comrades they met there again with their laconic humour and optimism. Kara reminded Tatiana of nothing so much as the orphans' institute where she had been raised and had first developed her extraordinary powers of endurance and her passion for Russian poetry. But she had not long to live. The following year Anna Korba arrived in Kara, and as a qualified doctor was able to tend her devotedly until her death in 1887. Anna Yakimova managed to stay alive and sane for almost twenty years under the intolerable conditions of Siberian exile. During those years she saw many of her friends die, commit suicide, go insane or court death by provoking prison guards. She finally escaped in 1904, and was rearrested and then released the following year. She eventually settled in Leningrad and died during the Second World War.

The years after the assassination saw a split between those revolutionaries who still clung to their populist ideals of a Russian path to socialism and those who, like Plekhanov, had concluded that in Russia too socialism would have to be preceded by the capitalist stage. On 11 April 1881 Marx had written in London to his daughter Jenny: 'Have you been following the trial of the assassins in St Petersburg? They are sterling people through and through, *sans pose melodramatique,* simple, businesslike, heroic. Shouting and doing are irreconcilable opposites ... they try to teach Europe that their *modus operandi* is a specifically Russian and historically inevitable method about which there is no more reason to moralize – for or against – then there is about the earthquake in Chios.' A few years later, shortly before his death, Marx, after much hesitation, came down on the side of

279

the populists, agreeing with them that, thanks to the strength of the peasant Commune, Russia might be able to avoid the horrors of a capitalist society.

Vera Figner's views after the assassination were consistent with those she had expressed in the early days of the Party: 'The dilemma which had been brought to an issue appeared to us to have been solved in the public consciousness, awaiting only its embodiment in actual life.' Speaking of the Party she had said, 'The harvest was plentiful, the reapers were few.' It was now her task, as virtually the only remaining party member, to consolidate and mobilize the reapers of the future revolutionary movement. The bourgeoisie had already shown its weakness in fighting against absolutism and for a constitution. All Vera's hopes for the revolutionary vanguard now lay in the outer ring of supporters in the army and navy who were in touch with the remains of the Party Fighting Services Section. During her brief stay in Kronstadt after leaving the capital she was persuaded to go to the South, there to co-ordinate the southern revolutionary movement with the Party's Fighting Services Section. In her travels around Odessa, Kiev and Khar'kov she became known in soldiers' and workers' circles as 'Mother Commander', and the 'Mother Commander' became the most wanted woman on the police list.

After the third great trial of the revolutionaries in early 1883, the Trial of the 17, Vera was alone, deprived of virtually all her remaining comrades, including Bogdanovich and Anna Korba, who had been arrested. It was in Khar'kov, where she was organizing a group of revolutionary workers in contact with similar groups in Poltava and Rostov, that the liberal populist writer Mikhailovsky managed to pay her a visit. The future Alexander III, he told her, was still virtually immured in his palace, postponing his coronation until her arrest. Many liberals, in and out of the government, realizing that steadily mounting police terror throughout the country would do little to further their aims for a constitutional

280

government, had banded together in a 'Sacred Detachment', which was to mediate between Tsar and revolutionaries, and reconcile the latter to the idea of constitutional reforms. Mikhailovsky's visit was fruitless. Vera Figner's arguments were unanswerable.

Shortly after Mikhailovsky's visit, on 10 February 1883, it came as little surprise to her that she was arrested. Alexander III breathed a deep sigh of relief, saying, 'Thank God that terrible woman has been caught', and she was taken immediately to the capital for interrogation. The year she spent in pre-trial imprisonment in the Peter and Paul Fortress was not wasted; she wrote her memoirs of her activities up to 1881 (the first volume of *Work Completed*), she learnt English and was soon reading Macaulay in the library, where she spent as much of her time as she could. These activities were occasionally interrupted by interrogation – now threats from von Plehve, Director of the Police Department, now cajolements from the chivalrous Minister of the Interior, Tolstoy. The same Tolstoy who, some ten years before, had taken such a cavalier attitude to women's education was now anxiously asking Vera's views on classical education. After she had outlined to him in detail all her activities over the last ten years there was little Tolstoy could say but, 'What a pity there is so little time or I would have been able to convince you of the uselessness of terror.' 'I am sorry too,' she replied, equally aware that time was pressing. 'I expect I would have been able to turn you into a *narodovolnik*'[6].

Vera Figner was the outstanding personality in the last great trial of revolutionaries, the Trial of the 14 in September 1884. Vera Figner's defence counsel found her description of her activities so exhaustive that he was unable to help her. In court Vera announced that it was the feminist movement in Russia that had given her the impetus to dedicate herself to the revolutionary movement, that it was the life and death struggle for the women's courses that had put her on this road, and she was speaking as one of the first victims of

281

Tolstoy's effective suppression of the early feminist movement.

On 28 September 1884 Vera Figner was accused of all acts committed by the Party from its inception and, along with seven others, sentenced to death. The sentence was 'mercifully' commuted at the last moment to life imprisonment in the impenetrable Schlusselberg Fortress, where solitary confinement and semi-starvation in airless unheated cells was the nearest conceivable approximation of death. 'The strain under which I had been living during my years of freedom, which had before been subdued and repressed, now left me; there was no task for my will, and the human being woke within me,' Vera wrote of her early years in prison, years in which many new unexplored facets of this woman's extraordinary personality awoke. In those years she daily courted death by protesting constantly against conditions. Many prisoners who subsequently left Schlusselberg describe the enormous effect of her resilience on the morale of all those in the prison. Prisoners, she insisted in her memoirs, were not mere 'vagrant personalities', they were a firmly united collective. It was this sustained belief that enabled her to extend her own hunger strike to the entire prison, and when eventually the men prisoners threatened to commit suicide if she killed herself, she denounced their betrayal. 'Their male vanity would not permit a woman to prove herself more consistent and steadfast than they. They were ashamed and wished to bring me down to their level.'[7]

However, Vera was anxious to stress the solidarity among men and women prisoners that transcended such issues. In her brief encounters with other prisoners she met many scientists, professors who had been arrested on political charges and who were anxious to set up scientific study groups. Leaflets were passed round and soon prisoners were reading avidly in their cells about chemistry, crystallography and astronomy. Spiders and rats were welcomed into cells as specimens to be examined, and fungi, moss and mould revealed their biological secrets to this expanding group of students. Over many years the prisoners were gradually allowed to meet and discuss their studies more frequently, and a forge and a carpenter's workshop were introduced into the prison. By 1902 Vera had thoroughly integrated herself into prison life; she was deeply moved by the fate of Chekhov's *Three Sisters,* aimlessly wandering through life expecting salvation in Moscow, where their lives would inevitably be as fruitless as in the provinces. A year later, when she heard that as a result of her mother's petitioning her sentence had been commuted to twenty years, she felt only pain at having to leave her old friends and comrades.

Her prison experiences made it inevitable that Vera Figner would commit herself instinctively to the 1917 revolution, although painfully aware of the lag between her now-outmoded revolutionary consciousness and that of the Bolshevik Party. In the eighteen months between the People's Will Party's decision to kill the Tsar and the actual assassination, a period of failed attempts, innumerable arrests and growing police terror, women had become increasingly confident in their roles. And these eighteen months saw a very positive change in the men's attitude to their indomitable women comrades. Without the kind of internal democracy that existed within the People's Will Party, its members (at most five hundred of them) would not have been able to reject so thoroughly the contemporary sexual power relationships and the dominant values of the society around them.

Vera Figner spent most of the rest of her life writing, working for a short time for the People's Commissariat for Social Security under Alexandra Kollontai and joining the Writers' Union when it was formed in 1924. She died in 1942 – like Alexandra Kollontai herself, only partially assimilated into the mainstream of Soviet political life. 'You are a good woman,' Count Tolstoy had told her at her interrogation in 1884. 'Your only misfortune is that although you married you never had any children.'

NOTES

1. Kravchinsky, *Underground Russia,* p.114.
2. Perovsky, V. L., *Vospominania o sestre* (Memoirs of my Sister), p.92.
3. Asheshov, op. cit., p.127.
4. He left this to his lawyer in his will and it was filed away in police archives for forty years, at which point it was discovered by Soviet scientists to be a brilliant application of the rocket principle.
5. Kravchinsky, *Underground Russia,* p.262.
6. Figner, V., *Work Completed,* Complete Works vol. 1, p.231.
7. ibid., vol. 2, p.82.

A SELECTIVE
GLOSSARY
OF NAMES*

ÁPTEKMAN Osip Vasil'evich (1849–1926), from a poor merchant's family. Active as a young man in the Chaikovsky circle, later a member of the Land and Liberty Party, then of Narodnaya Volya. Arrested in 1880, in exile until 1886. Subsequently active in the 1905 revolution.

BAKÚNIN Mikhail Alexandrovich (1814–76), leading theoretician of spontaneous agrarian anarchism, fighting on the barricades at Dresden and Prague. Spent most of his life as a political exile.

BARÁNNIKOV Alexandr Ivanovich (1853–84), from a wealthy landowning family. An 'illegal' from 1877, he was one of the founders of the terrorist faction of Land and Liberty Party. Participated in the assassination attempt and arrested in 1882. Died in the Schlusselberg Fortress.

BARDINA Sofya Ilarionovna (1853–83), daughter of a Tambov forester. Studied medicine in Zurich in 1871, returned to Moscow in 1874 to do industrial propaganda. Arrested and tried in the Trial of the Moscow Women in

* Symbol over name indicates syllable of stress in pronunication.

1877, at which she was sentenced to nine years' exile. Commited suicide in Geneva.

BELÍNSKY Vissarion Grigorevich (1811–48), son of a poor doctor. In the 1840s he was the centre of a brilliant circle of intellectuals, and in his philosophical and literary writing he established a school of political literary criticism that profoundly affected Russia's intellectual development.

BLYÚMMER Antonina (?–?), one of the first girls to audit at St Petersburg University, and later active in the Sunday School Movement. Arrested for carrying out propaganda work, and kept under her father's supervision until 1870.

BRESHKO-BRESHKÓVSKAYA Ekaterina Konstantinovna (1843–1935), from a wealthy landowning family. Active in Kiev revolutionary circles from 1873. Arrested in 1874, in prison until 1878. Sentenced to penal servitude in Kara in the Trial of 193. Escaped 1881, rearrested; for the next forty years her life was a succession of imprisonmentso escapes. Later a member of the Socialist Revolutionary Party.

CHERNYSHEVSKY Nikolai Gavrilovich (1828–89), son of a poor priest. Leading spokesman for the radical intelligentsia in the 1850s and 1860s. In his articles he established the basis for revolutionary populism. Sentenced to nineteen years' exile, where he died.

DMITRIÉVA Elisaveta (1851–?), illegitimate daughter of Pskov landowner and his housekeeper. At seventeen decided to join the Marxist International and left Russia for Geneva; went thence to London, where she met Marx, who urged her to go to Paris to report on the situation there. Orator, organizer, fighter and Russian representative of the First International during the Paris commune days. Returned to Russia, where she married and joined her husband the Bakunist Davydov, in exile.

DOBROLYUBÓV Nikolai Alexandrovich (1836–61), priest's son. Shared Chernyshevsky's conceptions about 'civic art' and collaborated with him in journalistic work.

FÍGNER Evgenia (1858–1931) accompanied Vera to Saratov in 1879, where they did populist propaganda work for Land and Liberty Party. Joined Narodnaya Volya in 1879, arrested in 1880 and sentenced to fifteen years' penal servitude. Released in 1900.

FÍGNER Lydia (1853–?), sister of Vera with whom she went to Zurich. Returned to Moscow in 1874 to do propaganda work in factories and was sentenced in Trial of the Moscow Women in 1877, to eight years' penal servitude.

FÍGNER Vera Nikolaevna (1852–1942), from wealthy liberal Kazan' landowning family. Studied in Zurich and Paris 1872–7, and returned to Russia to join the revolutionary movement. Elected to the Executive Committee of Narodnaya Volya in 1879, and after the assassination of the Tsar tried to resuscitate the Party in South Russia. Arrested February 1883 and sentenced to twenty years in the Schlusselberg Fortress. Released during 1905 revolution, and after 1917 embarked on literary work.

FILOSÓFOVA Anna Pavolovna (1837–1912), from wealthy conservative landowning family. Joined the feminist movement in the 1860s, working mainly for advanced education for women. Continued with bourgeois feminist activities until her death.

FROLÉNKO Mikhail Fedorovich (1849–1941?), captain's son. Revolutionary activities forced him to become 'illegal' in 1874. Active in the Kiev Land and Liberty Party until 1879 when he joined Executive Committee of Narodnaya Volya. Married Tatiana Lebedeva shortly afterwards. Arrested March 1881 and sentenced in the Trial of the 20 to twenty years in Peter and Paul Prison. Released in 1905 and moved to Moscow.

HÉLFMAN Gesya Mirokhovna (1855–82), Jewish tradesman's daughter from Kiev. Joined Kiev revolutionary circles in 1874 and was arrested in Trial of the Moscow Women. Escaped from exile to become 'illegal' and join Narodnaya Volya. Ran conspiratorial flat in capital. Tried in first great trial after the assassination and sentenced to death. Sentence was commuted to life imprisonment because she was pregnant. Died shortly afterwards in prison.

HÉRZEN Alexandr Ivanovich (1812–70), illegitimate son of wealthy noble. Radical journalist, philosopher, literary critic and the greatest of the first radical intellectuals. Imprisoned 1834 for subversive writing. His philosophical and political ideas underwent many changes throughout his life, at the end of which he described himself as a 'sceptical Christian'.

ISÁEV Grigory Prokofievich (1857–84), postman's son. Joined Land and Liberty Party in 1877, and in 1879 was on Executive Committee of Narodnaya Volya. One of the Party's technical experts, involved in all the assassination attempts. Sentenced to life imprisonment in the Trial of the 20 in 1882. Died in prison.

IVÁNOVA Sofya Andreevna (1857–1927), army officer's daughter. Arrested during Land and Liberty Party's first demonstration in 1876. Escaped from exile in 1879 and joined Executive Committee of Narodnaya Volya. In charge of its printing press. Arrested January 1880 and sentenced to fifteen years' imprisonment. Died in Moscow.

JÁCLARD Victor (1840–1903), Blanquist, active in Paris commune. On the Central Committee of National Guard. Met and married Anna Krukovskaya, with whom he left for Russia in 1874. Taught at a girls' school there.

KAMÍNSKAYA Berta (185?–78), left poor Jewish South Russian family to study in Zurich. Returned to Moscow in 1874. Arrested for propaganda work in factories, but had nervous breakdown in prison and was handed over to her father. Finally collapsed and committed suicide.

KARAKÓZOV Dmitry Vladimirovich (1840–66), member of 1850s terrorist group that made abortive attempt on the life of Alexander II. Hanged in 1866.

KHALTÚRIN Stepan Nikolaevich (1857–82), peasant's son. Organized Northern Workers' Union in 1878. Responsible for first Narodnaya Volya attempt to assassinate

288

the Tsar in the Winter Palace, February 1880. Executed March 1882 for assassinating governor-general of Odessa.

KIBÁLCHICH Stepan Nikolaevich (1853–81), son of a parish priest. In mid-seventies was involved in populist propaganda in the countryside, then devoted himself to the study of explosives, to become Narodnaya Volya's technical guiding light. Arrested in March and sentenced to death in the first great trial after the assassination.

KOLÉNKINA Marya Alexandrovna (1856–1926), from small tradesman's family. Left for Kiev 1873, where she joined revolutionary circles. Exiled 1874 for populist propaganda in the countryside, but escaped and lived as 'illegal'. Joined Vera Zasulich in capital, and put up armed resistance to arrest in 1878 after Mezentsev's assassination. Sentenced to ten years' hard labour followed by exile in Irkutsk, where she ended up as a teacher.

KOLODKÉVICH Nikolai Nikolaevich (1857–84), from landowing family. Joined revolutionary movement in 1875. Attended both Lipetsk and Voronezh conferences of Land and Liberty Party's terrorist faction. Elected on to Executive Committee of Narodnaya Volya, where he worked closely with Zhelyabov. Arrested January 1881. Died in prison.

KÓNRADI Evgenia (born Bochechkarova) (1838–?), daughter of a moderately wealthy Tula landowner. Journalist and progressive feminist who presented the first petition to St Petersburg University demanding women's admission to universities in 1867.

KÓRBA Anna Pavlovna (married name Pribyleva) (1847–1930), landowner's daughter. Agitation and evacuation work in Russo-Turkish War 1877. Joined Narodnaya Volya 1879, elected on to Executive Committee 1880. Ran conspiratorial flat and did literary propaganda work. Arrested 1882 and sentenced in Trial of 17 in 1883 to twenty years' penal servitude. In Kara penal camp until 1902. Worked for the release of political prisoners until the revolution. She was

289

involved in literary work in the Soviet Union until her death.

KORNÍLOVA Alexandra Ivanovna (1853–1938), liberal merchant's daughter. Close school friend of Sofia Perovskaya. 1871 joined Chaikovsky group and smuggled leaflets into St Petersburg factories. Sentenced to exile in Trial of 193. On her release after the revolution she worked for the Museum of the Society for Political Prisoners.

KORSÍNI Natalya Yeronimovna (?–?). One of first girls to audit at St Petersburg University in 1860s. Moved in radical circles and joined her husband, the radical professor Utin, in Geneva in the 1870s, where they formed the nucleus of the Marxist Internationalist group there.

KORVIN-KRUKÓVSKAYA Anna Vasilevna (1843–87), from wealthy landowing family. Writer and friend of Dostoyevsky. Left Russia 1869 for Paris. Involved in the Commune and elected on to the Central Committee of the *Union des Femmes*. Married Victor Jaclard, with whom she returned in 1874 to Russia. Resumed her friendship with Dostoyevsky and continued writing until her death.

KOVALÉVSKAYA Sofya Vasilevna (born Korvin-Krukovskaya, sister of Anna) (1850–91). Outstanding mathematician, forced to study abroad. In 1884 became professor of mathematics at Stockholm University.

KRAVCHÍNSKY (Stepniak) Sergei Mikhailovich (1851–95), army doctor's son. A founder member of the Chaikovsky group and of the Land and Liberty Party. In August 1878 assassinated Mezentsev, head of St Petersburg 3rd Division. Lived abroad, doing literary work for the revolutionary movement.

KROPÓTKIN Pëtr Alekseevich (1842–1921), son of a rich general. Sociologist, geographer, geologist and lifelong theoretician of anarchism.

KVIATKÓVSKY Alexandr Alexandrovich (1853–84), of noble birth. Became 'illegal' after his first arrest in 1876 and joined Kiev revolutionary circles. A committed terrorist in the Land and Liberty Party and a member of the Executive

Committee of Narodnaya Volya. Arrested April 1881 and tried in the Trial of the 20. Died in Peter and Paul Fortress.

LAVRÓV Pëtr Lavrovich (1823–1900), philosopher and ideologist of populism, insisting that the intelligentsia must embark on long-term political study to prepare the working classes to revolt. Gave much support in the 1860s to the women's movement.

LÉBEDEVA Tatiana Ivanovna (1853–87), daughter of a Moscow government official. On the Executive Committee of Narodnaya Volya and worked in the Party's explosives factories. Married Frolenko. Arrested September 1881. Sentenced to life exile in the Trial of the 20. Died at Kara penal camp.

LECHERNE von GERTZFELDT Sofya (1842–98), engaged in rural populist propaganda work in the early 1870s. In the Trial of the 193 sentenced to exile from which she escaped to Kiev. Rearrested, she put up armed resistance and was sentenced to death, commuted to life exile, during which she died.

LYUBATÓVICH Olga (1855–?), of liberal aristocratic Moscow family. Studied in Zurich, returned to Moscow 1874 and sentenced in Trial of the Moscow Women to exile, from which she escaped in 1878, to become 'illegal'. Introduced to terrorist faction of Land and Liberty Party and married one of its chief spokesmen, Morozov. Various activities for Narodnaya Volya, including smuggling 'illegals' abroad. Exiled before the assassination.

MIKHÁILOV Alexandr Dmitrievich (1857–83), from the upper nobility. A founder member of Land and Liberty Party and one of the first proponents of a terrorist policy. Initiator of Lipetsk conference. Chief spokesman and theoretician of Narodnaya Volya. Arrested November 1880. Sentenced to life imprisonment in Trial of 20 in 1882. Died in prison.

MIKHÁILOVSKY Nikolai Konstantinovich (1842–1904), radical populist journalist. His political moderation enabled him to publish legally in various radical journals, although he had informal contacts with many Narodnaya Volya members.

MORÓZOV Nikolai Alexandrovich (1855–?), illegitimate son of landowner. A founder member of Land and Liberty Party and editor of its newspaper. Poet and romantic. Married Olga Lyubatovich 1878. On Executive Committee of Narodnaya Volya and co-editor of its newspaper. Spent much of his life in exile. Arrested and sentenced to twenty years in Peter and Paul and Schlusselberg Fortresses in Trial of 20 in 1882. Released in 1905, and settled in Leningrad. Still alive in 1944.

NÁTANSON Mark Andreyevich (1850–1919), son of serf. A founder member of Land and Liberty Party.

NECHAEV Sergei Gennadievich (1847–82). Active in the student movement in St Petersburg in 1868–9. Forced to leave the country to escape arrest, he joined Bakunin in Switzerland. He returned in 1869 to organize his largely fantasised 'People's Vengeance' Party, which was responsible for the murder of one of its members, a student named Ivanov, who was suspected of being a spy. He left the country once more, and in 1872 was extradited from Switzerland and sentenced to twenty years' hard labour.

OGARËV Nikolai Platonovich (1813–77), revolutionary journalist and lyric poet of 1840s and 1850s. Lived much of his life abroad with Herzen.

OSHÁNINA (revolutionary pseudonym for Olovénnikova) Marya Nikolaevna (1850–97), early Jacobin adherent of Zaichnevsky circle and member of Land and Liberty Party. Only woman present at Lipetsk and Voronezh conferences. On Executive Committee of Narodnaya Volya, served as link with Kletochnikov, Party agent within the government administration. In 1880 was party representative in Moscow. Escaped abroad 1882 and died in Paris. Married to Barannikov.

PERÓVSKAYA Sofya Lvovna (1854–81), born into upper nobility, a founder member of Chaikovsky group, later involved in populist propaganda work in provinces. On Executive Committee of Narodnaya Volya from 1879 and active in all the Party's major activities. After Zhelyabov's arrest primarily responsible for the assassination. Sentenced to death in the first great trial, and executed on 3 April 1881.

PÍSAREV Dmitry Ivanovich (1840–68), literary critic, sociologist and economist. Prominent advocate of women's emancipation in 1860s.

PLEKHÁNOV Georgi Valentinovich (1857–1918), from a noble family. Involved in the revolutionary movement from 1876 and a member of Land and Liberty Party. Split with the majority at the Voronezh conference in 1879, looking for support among rural populists. His anti-terrorist faction of the Land and Liberty Party, Chërny Peredel, was effectively liquidated when he emigrated in 1880. Outstanding theoretical Marxist, subsequently a Menshevik.

SËRNO-SOLOVÉVICH Nikolai Alexandrovich (1834–66), from aristrocratic family. Abandoned official career for revolutionary activity in 1860s, met Herzen abroad, active in Sunday School Movement and later the Land and Liberty Party. Arrested and died in exile.

SHELGÚNOV Nikolai Vasilevich (1824–91), eloquent literary critic and advocate for popular education and women's emancipation in 1860s.

SHIRÁYEV Stepan Grigorievich (1857–81), peasant, early involved in revolutionary activities. Emigrated 1876, returned to Russia to attend Lipetsk and Voronezh conferences. On Executive Committee of Narodnaya Volya. Arrested December 1879. Imprisoned with Nechaev in Peter and Paul Fortress, where he died.

STÁSOVA Nadezhda Vasilevna (1832–95), of conservative St Petersburg noble family. Pioneer feminist and advocate for women's advanced education.

SÚSLOVA Nadezhda Prokofievna (1843–1918), daughter of wealthy peasant. One of Russia's first women doctors who qualified in Zurich and returned to Russia to practice until the end of her life.

TIKHOMÍROV Lev Alexandrovich (1850–1922), from early 1870s involved in revolutionary activities. A founder member of Land and Liberty Party and on Executive Committee of Narodnaya Volya. Co-editor of party newspaper. Fled abroad in 1882 and embarked on revolutionary literary work. Turned face 1888, and on his return to Russia became extreme reactionary journalist.

TKÁCHEV Petr Nikitich (1844–85), from impoverished noble family. Radical writer, translator of Marx, advocate of women's emancipation. A profound influence on revolutionary populism, he advocated that revolution be carried out by a small body of professional revolutionaries acting in the name of the people.

TRUBNIKOVA Marya Vasilevna (1835–97), of revolutionary family. One of the most influential and progressive of the feminists of the 1860s, promoting women's collectives and campaigning for women's advanced education.

USPÉNSKY Gleb Ivanovich (1843–1902), populist writer dealing with the lives of peasants and urban slum dwellers. Informal contacts with Narodnaya Volya members.

YAKÍMOVA Anna Vasilevna (1856–1941?), daughter of a provincial parish priest. Involved in populist propaganda in the early seventies. Tried in Trial of 193 and ordered home. Escaped and joined Executive Committee of Narodnaya Volya 1879. Involved in many of the Party's activities and highly regarded for her knowledge of explosives. Tried in Trial of 20, 1882. In Kara until 1905, when rearrested. Released during 1917 revolution.

ZASÚLICH Vera Ivanovna (1852–1919), daughter of small landowner. Active in Kiev revolutionary circles in 1875. Left for capital where on 24 January 1878 she shot governor-general of St Petersburg, Trepov, for which crime she was acquitted. Left Russia to join Plekhanov in theoretical Marxist study in Geneva.

ZHELYÁBOV Andrei Ivanovich (1850–81), son of serf, arrested in Trial of 193, acquitted, became 'illegal' 1879. Recruited to terrorist faction of Narodnaya Volya, of which he rapidly became the undisputed leader. Chief organizer of Workers' and Army sections of the Party, and main strategist for final assassination. Arrested before this was realized, and tried in the Trial of the 6. Executed 3 April 1881.

SELECT
BIBLIOGRAPHY

Abramov, Yuri, *The Book for Adults,* Paris, 1872.

Abramov, Yuri, *What to Give the People to Read,* London, 1893.

Abramov, Yuri, *Sunday Schools in Russia,* London, 1897.

Antonovich, M. A., *Vospominania* (Memoirs), Moscow, 1935.

Asheshov, N., *Sofia Perovskaya; materialy dlya biografii i kharakteristiki* (Material for a Biography and Character-study), St Petersburg, 1920.

Bogdanovich, T. A., *Liubov' liudei 1860'ykh godov,* (Love of the People of the 1860s), Leningrad, 1929.

Bogucharsky, V. Ya., *Iz istorii politicheskoi bor'by v 1870'ykh i 1880'ykh godakh* (A History of the Political Struggle in the 1870s and 1880s), Moscow, 1912.

Breshko-Breshkovskaya, E., *Little Grandmother of the Revolution,* London, 1919.

Breshko-Breskovskaya, E., *Hidden Springs of the Revolution,* London, 1931.

Bulanova-Trubnikova, O. K., *Tri pokolenia* (Three Generations) Moscow/Leningrad, 1928.

Chernyshevsky, N., *What is to be Done?* New York, 1961.
                       Complete Works, 15 vols., Moscow, 1939-50.

Chukovsky, K., *'Istoria sleptsvoskoi kommuny'* (History of the Sleptsov Commune), in *Liudi i knigi* (People and Books), Moscow, 1960.

Dobrolyubov, N. A., *Collected Works,* 9 vols. Moscow/ Leningrad, 1962-4.

De Villiers, Baron Marc, *Histoire des Clubs des Femmes et des Légions d'Amazones* (History of Women's Clubs and of Amazons' Legions), Paris, 1910.

Debagori-Mokrievich, V., *Vospominania* (Memoirs), St Petersburg, 1906.

Dragomanov, L., *Le Procès des Socialistes de Moscou* (in Russian), Geneva, 1877.

Druzhinin, N. M., *Anna Vasil'evna Yakimova,* Moscow, 1930.

Dubenskaya, E., and Bulanova, O., *Tatiana Ivanovna Lebedeva,* Moscow, 1930.

Figner, Vera, *Complete Works* (7 vols.), Moscow, 1934. There is a condensed English version of her complete works, *Memoirs of a Revolutionary,* New York, 1927.

Footman, David, *Red Prelude: A Life of A. I. Zhelyabov,* London, 1968.

Florinsky, M., *Russia: A History and an Interpretation* (2 vols.), New York, 1959.

Frolenko, M. P., *Zapiski semisdesyatnika* (Notes of a Man of the Seventies), Moscow, 1927.

Karnovich, E., *O razvitii zhenskogo truda v Peterburge* (The Development of Women's Labour in St Petersburg), St Petersburg, 1868.

Knizhnik-Vetrov, I. S., *A. V. Korvin-Krukovskaya,* Moscow, 1931.

Russkie deiatel'nitsy 1-ogo Internatsionala i Parizhskogo Kommuna (Russian Women Activists of the First International and the Paris Commune), Moscow/Leningrad, 1964.

Korba Pribyleva, A., *Partia Narodnaya Volia i eë ispol'nitel'ny komitet* (The People's Will Party and its Executive Committee), Moscow, 1926.

Kovalensky, M., *Russkaya revoliutsia v sudenbnykh protsesakh i memuarakh* (The Russian Revolution in Trials and Memoirs) (4 vols.), Moscow, 1923.

Kovalevskaya, S., *Vospominania detstva; Nigilistka* (Childhood Memories and The Woman Nihilist), Moscow, 1960. *Vera Barantsova* (an English translation of The Woman Nihilist), London, 1895.

Kravchinsky, S., *A Female Nihilist,* Boston, 1885.
                Russia Under the Tsars, London, 1886.
                Underground Russia, London, 1883.

Kropotkin, P., *Zapiski revoliutsionera* (Notes of a Revolutionary) St Petersburg, 1899.

Lampert, E., *Sons against Fathers,* Oxford, 1965.
                Studies in Rebellion, London, 1967.

Lavrov, P., *Narodniki-propagandisty 1873-8* (Populists and Propagandists 1873-8), Leningrad, 1925.

Leffler, Carlotta, *Sonya Kovalevskaya,* London, 1895.

Lemke, M., *Ocherki osvoboditel'nogo dvizhenia 1860'ykh godov* (Essays on the Liberation Movement of the 1860s) St Petersburg, 1908.

Matveeva, I., *Vera Figner,* Moscow, 1961.

Meijjer, J. M., *Knowledge and Revolution 1870-73,* Amsterdam, 1970.

Morozov, N., *Provesti iz moei zhizni* (Stories from my life), (2 vols) Moscow, 1947.

Nicholas, Hans, *Russian Educational Policy 1701-1917,* London, 1913.

Pantaleev, L. F., *Iz vospominanii proshlogo* (Memories of the Past), (2 vols), Moscow/Leningrad, 1934.

Perovsky, V. L., *Vospominania o sestre* (Memories of my Sister), Moscow/Leningrad, 1927.

Polubarina-Kochina, S., *S. V. Kovalevskaya. Her Life and Work,* Moscow, 1957.

Prutskov, N. I., *Russkaya literatura 19-ogo veka i revoliutsionnaya Rossia,* (Russian Literature of the 19th Century and Revolutionary Russia), Leningrad, 1971.

298

Schepkina, E. M., *Iz istorii zhenskoi lichnosti v Rossii* (A History of Women's Personality in Russia), St Petersburg, 1914.

Seth, R, *The Russian Terrorists,* London, 1966.

Shashkov, S. S., *Ocherk istorii russkoi zhenschiny,* (Brief History of the Russian Woman), St Petersburg, 1872.

Skabichevsky, A., *Literaturnye vospominania* (Literary Memories), Moscow/Leningrad, 1928.

Sleptsov, V. A., *Complete Works* (2 vols.), Moscow, 1957.

Stasov, V. A., *N.V. Stasova: vospominania i ocherki,* (N. V. Stasova: Memories and Essays), St Petersburg, 1899.

Thomas, Edith, *Women Incendiaries,* London, 1963.

Tkachev, P., *Selected Works* (2 vols), Moscow, 1947.

Tyrkova, A. V., *A. P. Filosofova i eë vremia* (A. P. Filosofova and her Times), Petrograd, 1915.

Venturi, Franco, *Roots of Revolution,* London, 1960.

Vilensky-Sibiriakov, N. D., (ed.), *Deiateli revoliutsionnogo dvizhenia v Rossii* (Activists of the Revolutionary Movement in Russia) (7 vols), Moscow, 1934. An incomplete but invaluable biographical dictionary.

Wortman, Richard, *The Crisis in Russian Populism,* Cambridge, 1967.

'Sofya Ilarionovna Bardina' (Obituary), *La Parole Libre,* Geneva, 1883.

Reports on Education in Russia, London, 1909.

Journals

I have made wide use of three invaluable historical-revolutionry journals:

Byloe ('The Past'), London, 1903-4; St Petersburg, 1906-7; Paris, 1908-12; Petrograd, 1917-26; Paris, 1933;

Golos Minuvshego ('Voice of the Past'), Moscow, 1913-18;

Katorga i Ssylka ('Hard Labour and Exile'), Mowm 1921-35.

These contain memoirs by such revolutionaries as Figner,

Frolenko, Morozov, Yakimova and Korba, as well as extracts from the Imperial Archives. I shall refer only to the most important memoirs:

in *Byloe:*

Dzhabadari, N., 'Protses 50'i' ('The Trial of the 50'), September, 1907.

Korba, Anna, 'Vospominania' ('Memoirs'), nos 10-11, 1918.

Liubatovich, Olga, 'Dalëkoe i nedavnee' ('Distant and Recent Events'), June 1906.

Frolenko, M. P. 'Lipetsky i voronezhskys 'ezdy'. 'The Lipetsk and Voronezh Conferences'), January 1907.

in *Golos Minuvshego:*

Bervi-Flerovsky, V. V. 'Vospominania o Sofii Perovskoi'. ('Memoirs of Sofya Perovsksaya'), February 1916.

Korba, Anna, 'Vospominania o Narodnoi Vole' ('Memoirs of the People's Will Party'), September 1916.

Vodovozova, E., 'V. A. Sleptsov', no. 12, 1915.

in *Katorga i Ssylka*–

Frolenko, M. P., 'T. I. Lebedeva', 1924, pp.224ff.

Kornilova-Moroza, A., 'Perovskaya i osnovanie kruzhka Chaikovtsev' ('Perovskaya and the Establishment of the Chaikovsky Circle'), no. 22, 1926, pp.7ff.

Yakimova, Anna, 'Iz dalëkogo proshlogo' ('From the Distant Past'), no. 8, 1924, pp. ff. 'Syoboda ili Smert' ('Death or Freedom'), no. 24, 1926, pp.14ff. 'M. Kolenkina, Pamyati' ('M. Kolenkina. Memories'), 1926, pp.12ff and 1927, pp.177ff.

Yakimova, Anna, 'Pamyati' ('Memories'), 1927.

I have also used the Soviet journal *Voprosy Istorii* ('Questions of History'), which includes an article by Taubin, P. A. 'Revoliutsionnaya propaganda v voskresnykh shkolakh' ('Revolutionary Propaganda in the Sunday Schools'), 1956, pp.80ff.

INDEX

ABC of Social Sciences, 189
Abranov, Yuri, 93
Advanced Women's Courses, 94, 111-15
Al'chevskaya, Kristina, 93
Alekseeva, Marya, 96
Alexander I, 35, 179
Alexander II, 51, 61, 62, 86, 115; attempted assassinations, 227, 228, 246-8, 248-9, 250-2; successful assassination of, 264-9
Alexandrova, Varvara, 135, 138, 143, 146, 148
Allix, Jules, 169-70
Amour et Mariage, 161
Anserova, Ekaterina, 129
Anti-semitism, 112-13
Aptekman, Dora, 144
Aptekman, Osip, 225-6, 285
Arlachinsky girls' courses, 106-7, 108, 131, 179, 181, 183
Armfeldt, Natalya, 123

Bakunin, Mikhail, 45-6, 47, 116-17, 134, 135-6, 137, 140, 144, 159, 176, 178, 191-2, 200-1, 205, 285
Bakunina, Alexandra, 46-7

Bakunina, Varvara, 46
Barannikov, Alexandr, 230, 231, 248, 265, 285
Bardina, Sofya: in Zurich, 131-2, 133, 134, 135, 139, 140; in Paris, 142, 143; return to Russia, 146, 147; forms discussion group, 147, 148; arrest, 148; Trial of the 50, 150, 154; escape and suicide, 155; *see also* Glossary (pp. 285-6)
Belinsky, Vissarion, 45, 46-9, 286
Berlinerblau, Stefania, 131
Berne, women's medical studies in, 142, 144
Bervi-Flerovsky, 189
Bestuzhev-Ryumin, 111
Birzhevye Vedomosti, 85
Blanc, Louis, 85, 139, 189
'Bloody May', 163-5
Blyummer, Antonina: campaign for women's education, 64; Sunday School Movement, 89, 90, 91, 92; *see also* Glossary (p. 286)
Bogdanovich, Y. M., 215, 264, 280
Bogolyubov, Emelyanov, 210-11
Bokova, Marya (born Obrucheva), 64,

118, 120, 167

Breshko-Breshkovskaya, Ekaterina: childhood, 198; first reformist aspirations, 199; becomes committed to revolutionary movement, 200-1; and the Kiev Commune, 201; propaganda work in the countryside, 202-3; arrest, 203; trial, 205-7; sentence, 208; letters from Kibalchich, 228; *see also* Glossary (p. 286)

Brothers Karamazov, The, 167

Bukh, Nikolai, 242, 254

Burnasheva, Ekaterina, 58

Cause, The (Delo), 126, 160, 165, 167, 260

Central Committee of the National Guard, 169-71

Chaikovsksists, the, 179, 186-95, 196-7, 201, 204, 206, 233

Chaikovsky, Nikolai, 179, 186

Cherny Peredel (Black Repartition) Party, 237, 238, 239, 249

Chernyshevsky, Nikolai, 51, 52-3, 65, 72, 77, 79, 80, 97, 136, 177; *see also What is to be Done?* and Glossary (p. 286)

Chronicle of the Socialist Movement, 194

Collectives, 83, 90-1, 96

Comité des Femmes, 169-71

Communes, 79, 80-2, 196-8; *see also* Kiev Commune

Conditions of the Working Classes in Russia, 168

Condorcet, 35, 58

Contemporary, The (Sovremennik), 57, 60, 67, 83, 98, 176

'Coquettes', 71, 72

Crimean War, 56, 109

Dashkova, Princess, 24-5

d'Aurevilly, Barbey, 169

Debagori-Mokrievich, 197, 198, 201

Decembrists, the, 40-4, 85

De l'Amour, 60

De La Femme, 60

d'Héricourt, Jenny, 100-1

Desraismes, Marie, 169

Dmitriev, Pavel, 86

Dmitrieva, Elisaveta, 156-65, 168, 169, 170, 286

Dobrolyubov, Nikolai, 48, 51-2, 54, 97, 176, 177, 181, 286

Dolgorukov, Prince, 31-2, 92

Dostoyevsky, Feodor, 97, 165-7, 172, 207, 226

Domostroy, the, 14, 15, 16, 20, 39

Dzhabadari, I., 139-40, 143-4

Educational policies, 22-9, 33-8, 61-7, 140-2

Ekonomichesky Ukazatel', 59

Elagina, Princess, 45

Eliot, George, 168

Elizabeth I of England, 17

Emancipation of the serfs, 51, 69, 73, 98, 131, 198

Emancipation of women, 48-9, 57, 72-3

Engel'hardt, Alexandr, 96-7, 183, 237

Engel'hardt, Anna, 96-7

Ental'tseva, Marya, 43

Epokha, 55, 166, 167

Epstein, Rina, 257, 271

Erisman, Franz, 119, 120

Evreinova, Anna, 123, 168

Evgenii Onegin, 42

Fedorovna, Tsarina Marya, educational policies, 33-5, 109

Fictitious marriages, 70, 122, 167

Figner, Evgenia, 114, 233, 253, 287

Figner, Lydia, 114, 128, 132, 143, 146, 148, 152, 154, 219, 233, 287

Figner, Vera: childhood, 126-7; at Kazan', 127-8; at St Petersburg, 128; studies in Zurich, 128, 132-3; and Women's Club for Logical Speech, 138-9; in Berne, 149; returns to Russia, 149, 154-5; and Land and Liberty

Party, 210, 211, 212, 220-1; works as doctor in Samara, 215; revolutionary work in capital, 215-16; teacher and doctor in Saratov, 219; and Strong Fighting Organization, 232; and Voronezh Conference, 234, 235; life as an 'illegal', 239; and first Tsaricidal attempt, 246-8, 256-7; plan to kill Totleben, 255-7; and Narodnaya Volya party paper, 260; propaganda work amongst soldiers and sailors, 260-1; conspiratorial flat in capital, 263; activities during the day of the assassination, 268, 269; escape to Kronstadt, 273; rallying Party in South Russia, 280; arrest, 281; Trial of 20, 281-3; reminiscences, 283; general references to, 39, 41, 43, 114, 136, 142, 144, 146, 227, 233, 238, 240, 243; *see also* Glossary (p. 287)

Fillipov, Aleksei, 127, 128, 133

Filosofova, Anna, 86, 95, 103, 104, 106, 111, 287

Fonvizina, Natalya, 41-2

Foreign universities, Russian girls at, 109-10, 117-18, 119-20, 123, 125, 128-44

Fourier, François Marie Charles, 45, 58, 80, 81, 85, 93, 139

French educational establishments (*pensions*), 23, 24, 37, 61, 62

French Revolution, 148, 198

Frey, Professor, 135

Fritsch, Fraulein, 139

Fritschi, 139-40

Frolenko, Mikhail, 214, 230-1, 236, 247, 248, 263, 268, 273, 287

Gagarina, Princess, 44

Gan', Elena, 49-50

Garshina, Elisaveta, 88

Geneva, Russian women in, 159, 165, 169

Gershenstein, Anna, 131

Gimnazia, 36-7, 62, 94, 106, 108, 129

Gizetti, Natalya, 166

Golovachev, Appolon, 81

Golovina, Princess, 25

Goldenberg, 227, 255

Göttingen University, 117, 123

Grachevsky, 267

Granovsky, T. N., 45

Great Trial, *see* Trial of 193

Greulich, Hermann, 135

Grinevich, 266, 268, 269

Gryaznova, Marya, 242, 254

Guerrier, Professor, 108

Hard Time, A, 83

Hartman, Lev, 249, 250

Heidelburg University, 123

Heine, Heinrich, 84, 85

Helfman, Gesya: sets up sewing collective and political study group, 145; and Narodnaya Volya Party, 241, 252-3, 259-60; 'landlady' of assassins' flat, 263-4, 266; arrest, 148, 270; trial and sentence, 152, 274; birth of baby, 277; death, 277; *see also* Glossary (p. 287)

Herzen, Alexandr, 37-8, 45, 47, 85, 97, 98, 118, 134, 159, 288

Herzena, Natalya, 55

History of 1848, 189

Hugo, Victor, 85, 86

Huit Jours de Mai, 157

Industry, women in, 74-7

International Workingman's Association, *see* Marx International . . .

Isayev, Grigory, 226, 250, 256, 263, 265, 288

Ivan the Terrible, 16-17, 18

Ivanova, Sofya: employed by Myshkin, 204-5; arrest in Trial of 50, 229; escape from exile, 229-30; and Strong Fighting Organization, 232; and Narodnaya Volya party paper, 234, 242-3, 261; arrest and imprisonment, 253-4; *see also* Glossary (p. 288)

Ivashov, Petr, 85

Jaclard, Victor, 169, 171-2, 288
Journalism, women in, 58-61

Kaminskaya, Berta, 129-30, 132, 140, 143, 146, 149, 154-5, 288
Kapnist, Count, 62
Karamzin, N., 32-3
Karnovich, 76
Katherine the Great, 19, 25-9, 117
Kavelin (Petr Osipovich), 64, 65
Kessler, 105, 106
Khalturin, Stepan, 176, 254, 288-9
Khomyakov, 226
Khorzhevskaya, Alexandra: political work, 146; arrest, 148; trial and sentence, 152
Khorzhevskaya, Ekaterina, 145, 196
Kibalchich, Nikolai: knowledge of explosives, 229, 247, 255, 264, 266; opinion of Tatiana Lebedeva, 237; and planned assassination of the Tsar, 248, 254, 255, 264, 266, 267; and terrorism, 262; arrest, 273; trial, 274-5; execution, 276; see also Glossary (p. 289)
Kiev Commune, 196-8, 201-2, 213, 233
Kireevsky, 44, 226
Klements, Dmitry, 188
Klyachko, 187-8
Kolënkina, Marya: and Kiev Commune, 201; propaganda in countryside, 202-3; arrest and imprisonment, 203; revolutionary activity, 211-12, 213, 214, 216; arrest, 224; see also Glossary (p. 289)
Kolodkevich, Nikolai, 232, 247, 248, 252, 260, 261, 265, 289
Kollontai, Alexandra, 7-8, 283
Konradi, Evgenia, 97-9, 101-2, 106, 107, 289
Kopteva, Masha, 81
Korba, Anna: as medical student, 110;

becomes agitator and revolutionary, 111, 181, 226; at Lesnoi flat, 234, 237-8; and Narodnaya Volya Party, 240-2; fictitious marriage, 241; in Moscow, 250; arrest, 280; see also Glossary (p. 289)
Kornilov, Alexander, 182
Kornilov, Vasili, 183
Kornilova, Alexandra: friendship with Sofya Perovskaya at Arlachinsky Courses, 179, 181, 182, 183, 184, 185; and the Chaikovsksists, 186, 189; see also Glossary (p. 290)
Kornilova, Vera, 179, 181, 182, 184
Korsini, Natalya: woman pioneer at men's university courses, 64-5; and Sunday School Movement, 89, 90; first woman to enrol in St Petersburg University, 159; marriage to Nikolai Utin, 159; and Marx International group in Geneva, 169; see also Glossary (p. 290)
Korvin-Krukovskaya, Anna: childhood, 121; petition to Tolstoy, 122; in Paris, 123, 156, 168-71; friendship with Dostoyevsky, 165-7; writings, 166-7, 172-3; meets Tkachev, 168; marriage to Victor Jaclard, 169; joins Comité des Femmes, 169-71; death, 173; see also Glossary (p. 290)
Korvin-Krukovsky, General, 121-3, 171
Kovaleskaya, Sofya (born Korvin-Krukovskaya), 118, 120-5, 165, 167, 168, 171, 172, 290
Kovalevsky, Vladimir, 122-3, 125, 168
Kovalik, 201, 221
Kravchinsky, Stepniak, 55-6, 150-2, 188, 200, 214, 218, 224, 234, 239, 242, 252, 277, 290
Kropotkin, Petr, 71, 101, 114, 134, 187, 190-1, 199, 290
Kurochkin, Nikolai, 101, 102
Kuvshinskaya, Marya, 176-8, 189-90
Kviatkovsky, Alexandr, 226, 228, 232,

234, 239, 242, 253, 261, 290-1

La Sociale, 162
Land & Liberty Party (*Zemlya i Volya*), 175, 206, 210-12, 220-5, 227-8, 230-1, 233, 240
Lassalle, Ferdinand, 58, 85, 136, 139, 185, 226
Lavrov, Petr, 95, 96, 101, 133, 134, 137, 139, 178, 191-2, 197, 291
Lebedev, Petr and Vera, 189
Lebedev, Vasily, 188
Lebedeva, Tatiana: childhood, 188-9; breaks family ties for political studies in Moscow, 189; arrest, 195; release, 195; plans to establish cavalry detachment of revolutionary women, 211-12; joins Land and Liberty Party and works for release of major political prisoners, 223, 231; exclusion from Lipetsk Conference, 236-7; member of Narodnaya Volya Party, 246; and first Tsaricidal attempt, 246, 247-8; Kherson Treasury raid, 263; arrest, 277; trial, 278; death, 279; *see also* Glossary (p. 291)

Lecherne, Sofya, 181, 185, 224, 291
Lefrance, G., 163
Léo, André, 161, 162, 168, 169, 171, 173
Lermontova, Julia, 123
Lipetsk Party Conference, deliberate exclusion of Land and Liberty women members from, 227-8, 229, 231-3
Listok Zemli i Voli, 225
Loris-Melikov, *see* Melikov
Lyubatovich, Olga: in Zurich, 130, 134; works as typsetter, 140; return to Russia to join 'Moscow Group', 144; arrest in Trial of 50, 148-9; trial and sentence, 152; exile and escape, 154-5; attachment to revolutionary circles in capital, 224; marriage to Morozov, 225; in hiding in Geneva with Morozov, 234; return to Russia, 234; ultra-terrorist stance after Morozov's arrest, 258; her own arrest, 259; remote exile with Morozov, 259; *see also* Glossary (p. 291)
Lyubatovich, Vera: in Zurich, 130, 131; work as typsetter, 140; in Paris, 142, 143; in Kiev, 144-5, 196

Maintenon, Madame de, 22-3
Makarevich, Anna, 196
Makulova, Ekaterina, 81-2
Marinsky Institutes for Girls, 34-5, 61, 182
Markelova, Alexandra, 81
Marx, Karl, 59, 67, 73, 152, 157-8, 160, 163, 168, 176, 191, 226, 259, 279-80
Marx International Workingman's Association, 133-4, 135, 156, 157, 159, 165, 169, 177
Medical education for women, 109-10, 118-20
Melikov, Count Loris, 255, 273
Mémoires d'un Communard, 163
Mendeleev, Professor, 105, 107, 181
Mesentsev, 222, 224, 226
Michel, Louise, 161, 162, 169
Michelet, Jules, 60, 85
Midwifery, tuition in, 34, 109, 145, 202
Mikhailov, Alexandr, 54-5, 60, 66, 72, 206, 214, 224, 227, 229, 232, 234, 240, 249-50, 262, 266, 274, 275, 276, 291
Mikhailov, Timofei, 266, 270
Mikhailovsky, Nikolai, 67, 211, 260, 280, 281, 291-2
Mill, J. S., 60, 93, 103, 181, 185
Milyutins, the, 106, 107
Ministry of the Interior, 255
Mongols, the, 11-12
Montesquieu, 25
More, Thomas, 139
Morozov, Nikolai, 142, 220, 224-36 passim, 258, 259, 292
Morskoi Vestnik, 56

'Moscow Amazons', 146, 224
'Moscow Group', *see* Pan-Russian Social Revolutionary Organization
Moscow Women, 215, 224; *see also* Trial of the 50
Muravieva, Alexandra, 42-3
Myshkin, Ippolit, 204, 207-8, 221

Narodnaya Volya Party (People's Will): formation of, 232-40; decision to assassinate the Tsar, 243-4; first attempt, 246-8; second attempt, 248-9, 256-7; third attempt, 250-2; successful attempt, 264-9; setbacks experienced by, 253-4; efforts to consolidate its support among the people, 259-60; party paper, 259-60; death sentences on members of, 261-2; shortage of funds, 261, 262-3
Natanson, Mark, 179, 186, 220, 224, 292
Nechaev, Sergei, 159, 207, 212-13, 292
Nedelya, 97, 102
Nekrasov, Nikolai, 153, 202
Nicholas I, 36, 40, 45, 61, 62, 64, 95, 117
Nigilistka, 124
'Nihilists', 72-3, 81, 95, 96
Nouvelle Héloise, La, 32

Ofrosimova, Marya, 45
Oshanina, Marya (revolutionary pseudonym Olovennikova): her Jacobin convictions, 230-1; only woman at Lipetsk Conference, 231-2; and Narodnaya Volya Party, 264; arrest, 273; *see also* Glossary (pp. 292-3)
Otechestvennye Zapiski, 49
Outline for the Critique of Political Economy, 158, 168

Pan-Russian Social Revolutionary Party, 140, 143, 144-9
Pantaleeva, Vera, 128-9
Paris, Russian students in, 142, 144, 156-8, 160-5, 168-71; Council of War, 156, 157, 164, 171, 172
Passek, Tanya, 37-8
Paul I, 33, 35
Pavlov, Professor, 89, 90, 91
Pavlovna, Princess Elena, 104-5
People's Vengeance Party, 212
Perovskaya, Sofya: childhood, 179-80; studies in St Petersburg, 180; at Arlachinsky Courses, 181-4; leaves home to form study group which evolves into the Chaikovsksists, 184, 186, 187-8, 192; leaves capital to teach in countryside, 192-3; returns to capital, 194; arrest, 194; trial of the 193, 195, 206; release, 225; works in capital and Kharkov for release of prominent prisoners, 221-3; joins Land and Liberty Party, 222-3; works for party paper, 230; Frolenko's opinion of, 231; at Voronezh Conference, 233-7; and the Narodnaya Volya Party, 235-40, 243-4; and Cherny Peredel, 237-9; and the third Tsaricide attempt, 249-51; commits herself to Narodnaya Volya Party, 252-3, 259, 261; her love for Zhelyabov, 257-8; and the assassination of the Tsar, 266-9; behaviour after Zhelyabov's arrest, 271-3; her own arrest, 273; trial, 275; execution, 276; *see also* Glossary (p. 293)
Perovskaya, Varvara, 180, 181, 184, 273
Perovsky, Lev, 179-80, 181, 182-3
Perovsky, Nikolai, 181
Perovsky, Vasili, 181
Peter the Great, 18-21, 23, 71, 117
'Pilgrims', 176-8
Pirogov, Nikolai, 56-7, 89, 90, 121
Pisarev, Dmitry, 136, 169, 176, 293
Plekhanov, Georgi, 226, 228, 233-4, 237, 238, 239, 252, 293
Poggio, Alexandra, 180
Poor Liza, 32

Popular schools, 29, 35, 61
Populism, 87, 175-8, 196, 197, 213, 215
Position of the Working Classes in Russia, The, 189
Pravitel' stvennyi Vestnik, 140-1
Presnyakov, 248, 261
Pribylev, 241
Prostitution, 73-4
Proudhon, Pierre Joseph, 58, 85, 100, 139, 161
'Ptashka', 242, 254
Public lectures, 107-8
Pushkin, Aleksandr, 42, 84, 198

Rabochaya Gazeta, 259-60
Rabotnik, 147
Rassvet, 60-1
Razumovsky, Kiril, 179
Reclus, Noémie, 169, 170
Revolutionary Catechism, 159
Rodstvennaya, Lydia, 110
Rogachev, Dmitry, 188, 194, 221
Rosenstein, Anna, 136
Rousseau, Jean-Jacques, 85, 86, 198
Rudneva, Varvara, 109-10
Russkoe Slovo, 101
Russo-Turkish War, 110, 195, 217, 218, 226
Rysakov, N.: and the assassination of the Tsar, 266, 268, 269, 271; arrest, 271; trial, 274-5, 276; execution, 276

Sablin, 260, 270
St Fevronia, 13
St Olga, 9
St Petersburg Patriotic Society, 44
Saint-Simon, 45, 85
Sand, George, 48-9, 85, 101, 168
Schedrin, Saltykov, 73
Sechenov, Mikhail, 120, 167
Serno-Solovevich, Nikolai, 55, 90, 97, 293
Severnyi Vestnik, 172
Shabanova, Anna, 103
Shelgunov, Nikolai, 47, 53-5, 260, 293

Shelgunova, Lydia, 60
Shigaeva, Marya, 58-60
Shirayev, Stepan, 226, 250, 251, 261, 293-4
Shleisner, Olga, 179, 182-3, 186
Shlykova, Virginia, 131
Shpilevskaya, Natalya, 89, 90, 92
Sleptsov, Alexander, 80-3, 90, 92, 147, 219
Smirnov, Mikhail, 137
Smolny Institute for Girls, 26-8, 29, 33, 34, 35, 61
Société pour l'Egalité des Femmes, 161
Société des Citoyennes Révolutionnaires, 161, 162, 163
Society for Cheap Accommodation and other Benefits for the Citizens of St Petersburg, 87, 94-5
Society for Housing the Poor, 95
Society of Women's Care for Prisoners, 43-4
Society for Women's Labour, 95-6
Society of Women Translators, 96-7, 99-101
Solodovnikova, Anna, 106-7
Soloviev, Alexandr, 19, 215, 227, 228, 229
Sovremennik, see *Contemporary, The*
S. Peterburgskie Vedomosti, 120
Stasov, Vladimir, 77
Stasova, Nadezhda: character, 83, 84-5; and the Sunday School Movement, 88, 91, 94; and Society for Women's Labour, 95, 96; visits to underprivileged women in St Petersburg, 96; and the Society of Women Translators, 99, 100; and Advanced Women's Courses, 103-6, 11-12, 113; *see also* Glossary (p. 294)
State and Anarchy, 191
Stefanovich, Yakova, 202, 203, 214
Sternberg, Baron Ungern, 247, 256
Stockholm University, 125
Strannolyubsky, Professor, 120, 181, 183

Strong Fighting Force (for the Narodnaya Volya Party) within the Army and Navy, 260, 261
'Strong Fighting Organization', 232, 239
Stundists, the, 203
Subbotina, Evgenia, 129, 140, 143, 146
Subbotina, Marya, 129, 130, 140, 142, 144, 146, 148, 149
Subbotina, Nadezhda, 129
Subbotina, Sofya, 129
Sukhanov, 265, 267
Sukharova, Agafoklei, 43
Sunday School Movement, 87-94, 96, 123, 159, 175, 178, 181
Suslova, Nadezhda: petitions for women's university education, 64; medical studies, 109; in Zurich, 118, 119-20; qualifies as doctor, 125, 126, 294

Tarnovskaya, Marya, 87
Tartar invasion, 11-12
Tetërka, 260
Tiburtius, Franziska, 130, 135-6
Tikhomirov, Lev, 190, 220, 221, 225, 226, 232, 240, 260, 270, 294
Tkachev, Petr, 158, 167, 168, 169, 294
To the Younger Generation, 54, 66
Tochterschule, 36
Tolstoy, Leo: works of, 94, 147, 219; and public lectures, 107; and women's education, 103-4, 105-6, 107, 122; and Vera Figner, 281, 283
Tomanovskaya, Elisaveta, see Dmitrieva
Tomanovsky, Vladimir, 158
Toporkova, Anne, 129, 140, 146, 148, 152
Totleben, 255, 256, 257
Translations by the Society of Women Translators, 99-100
Trepov, 184, 211, 216-17, 218
Trial of the 6, 274-6
Trial of the 14, 281-2
Trial of the 17, 280
Trial of the 20, 277-9

Trial of the 50, 148-9, 150-6, 215, 224
Trial of the 193, 195, 203-4, 205-8, 210, 216, 217, 220, 222, 223, 229, 230, 231, 237, 241
Trubnikova, Marya, 85-6, 87, 95-6, 97, 99, 100, 101, 103, 105, 114, 294
Tsenina, Elisaveta, 81
Tumanova, Elisaveta, 145, 148, 196
Turgenev, Ivan, 97, 153
Turgeneva, Marya, 192
Tyrkov, 263, 268-9, 271-2

Union des Femmes pour la Défense de Paris, 157, 162-4, 170
University education for women, 63-7, 89, 94, 101-15
Ushinsky, Konstantin, 66
Uspensky, Gleb, 101, 102, 226, 227, 229, 294
Utin, Nikolai, 159, 169

Vakhovskaya, Varvara, 136, 205
Vestnik Voskresnykh Shkol, 90-1
Vestnik Vospitania, 58
Viazemsky, Prince, 41
Vil'berg, Anna, 181, 183, 185
Vindication of the Rights of Woman, 29
Vladimir I, 9-10
Vladimirsky Courses for Women, 107-9, 111, 124
Vodovozova, Elizaveta, 82
Voix des Femmes, La, 161
Volkhonskaya, Princess Marya, 42
Voltaire, 25, 84, 85, 198
Voronezh Conference, 227, 233-7, 262

Wage, Labour and Capital, 59
What is to be Done?, 53, 54, 78-80, 83, 120, 131
Wild Birds of America, 97
Winter Palace, attack on, 254-5
Wives of the Decembrists, The, 41
Wollstonecraft, Mary, 29
Woman Nihilist, The, 173

Women: amongst pagan and slavic tribes, 8-9; 11th to 14th century, 10-11; 14th to 18th century, 12-21; large-scale conversion to Catholicism, 21; social behaviour in the 17th century, 17-21; 18th to 19th century, 21-34; take over supervision of estates, 21-2; social life in Katherine's reign, 29-32; 19th century, *passim*, 35-6, 37-8, 69-77

Women's Club for Logical Speech, 137-9

Women's Patriotic Association, 34

Yakeshburg, Rosalia, 137

Yakimova, Anna: becomes Bakuninist at 16 and leaves home to teach in countryside, 177; enrols in pedagogical courses at Vyatka, 177; work in the Orlov area, 177, 190; arrest, 195; at Kiev Commune, 201-2; Trial of 193, 208; released, 208; propaganda in villages of Tver region, 225; to St Petersburg to study explosives, 225-6, 228; exclusion from Lipetsk conference, 229; and 'Strong Fighting Organization', 232; and Narodnaya Volya Party, 233; and second Tsaricide attempt, 248, 249; prepares exposives for Winter Palace attack, 254-5; role in successful attempt on Tsar's life, 256, 262, 264, 265, 269; escapes, 269-70; arrest, 277; trial, 278; birth of baby, 278; 20 years' exile, 279; *see also* Glossary (p. 294)

Zaichnevsky, 230, 241

Zasulich, Vera: revolutionary activity in St Petersburg, 211-12; and the Nechaev affair, 212-13; and the Kiev Commune, 213-14; to St Petersburg, joins Land and Liberty Party, 214; shoots Trepov, 216-17; escape, 217-18; returns to Russia from Switzerland, 233-4; exclusion from Lipetsk and Voronezh conferences, 234; withdrawal from active politics in Russia, 239; *see also* Glossary (p. 295)

Zavadsky, 88, 92

Zhelikovsky, 207, 216, 217

Zhelyabov, Andrei: background, 231; Lipetsk conference, 232, 235-7; confrontation with Sofya Perovskaya, 235-7; and the second Tsaricide attempt, 248, 249; and the Narodnaya Volya Party, 253, 257, 259; his love for Sofya Perovskaya, 257; meeting at Kronstadt Naval Institute, 260-1; and successful attempt on the Tsar's life, 254, 264, 265, 266-7; arrest, 267, 269; trial, 274; execution, 276; *see also* Glossary (p. 295)

Zhemstvo i Volya, see Land and Liberty Party

Zhensky Vestnik, 101

Zurich, women's medical and political studies in, 117, 139; Russian students not well received, 135; political alliance with Georgian students and formation of Pan-Russian Social Revolutionary Organization, 139-40, 143, 144-9; slanderous demands from government for Russian students' return, 140-2